The First American Frontier

The First American Frontier

Advisory Editor: Dale Van Every

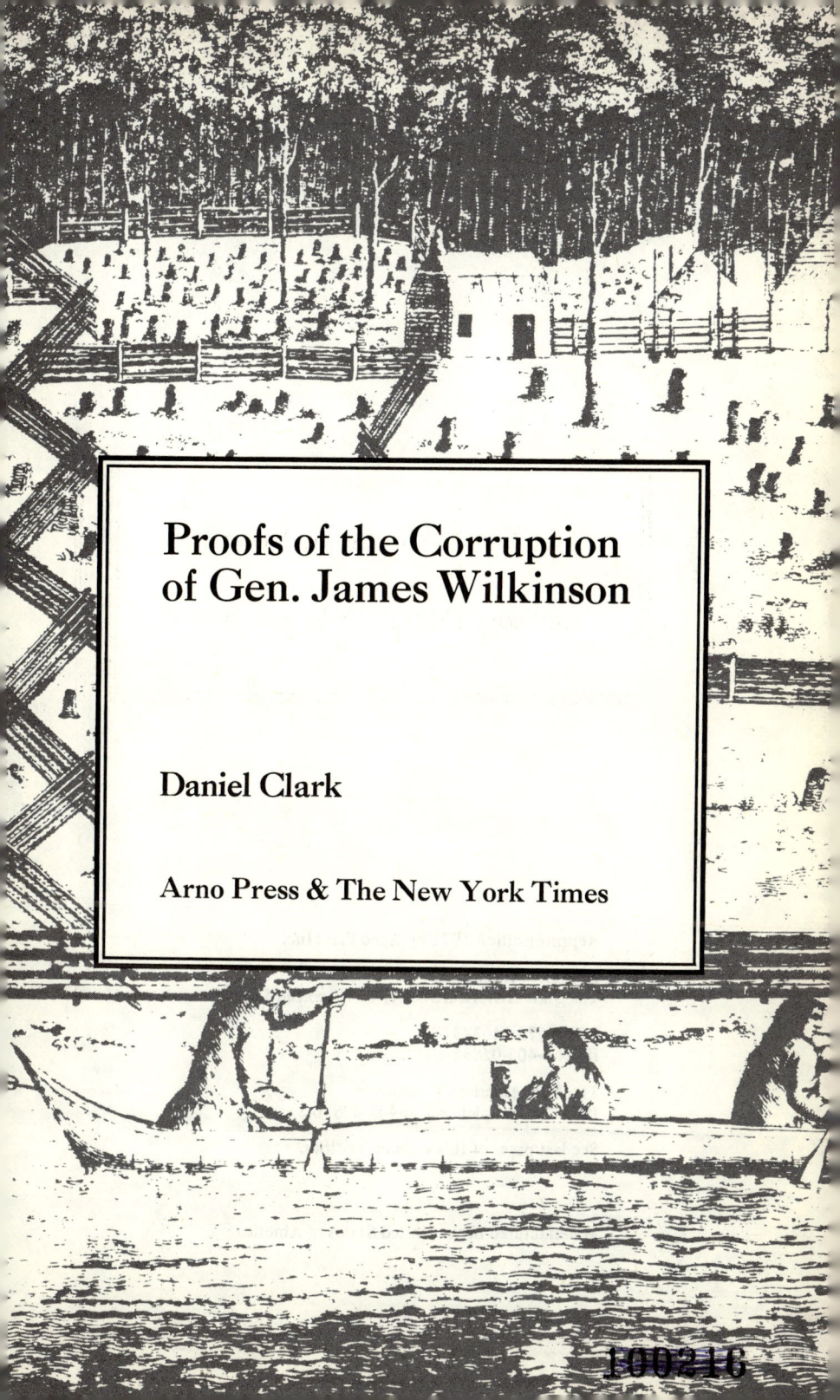

Proofs of the Corruption of Gen. James Wilkinson

Daniel Clark

Arno Press & The New York Times

Reprint Edition 1971 by Arno Press Inc.

Reprinted from a copy in
The State Historical Society of Wisconsin Library

LC # 70-146383
ISBN 0-405-02834-2

The First American Frontier
ISBN for complete set: 0-405-02820-2

See last pages of this volume for titles.

Manufactured in the United States of America

PROOFS

OF THE

CORRUPTION

OF

GEN. JAMES WILKINSON,

AND OF HIS

CONNEXION WITH AARON BURR,

WITH

A FULL REFUTATION OF HIS SLANDEROUS ALLEGATIONS IN RELATION TO THE CHARACTER OF THE PRINCIPAL WITNESS AGAINST HIM.

BY DANIEL CLARK,
OF THE CITY OF NEW ORLEANS.

Rarò antecedentem scelestum
Deseruit pede pœna claudo.
HOR.
Justice, tho' slow, is sure: vengeance
O'ertakes the swiftest villain's guilt.

WM. HALL, JUN. & GEO. W. PIERIE, PRINTERS, NO. 51, MARKET-STREET, PHILADELPHIA.

1809.

District of Pennsylvania, ss.

BE IT REMEMBERED, That on the thirteenth day of July, in the thirty-fourth year of the Independence of the United States of America, Anno Domini 1809, DANIEL W. COXE, of the said District, hath deposited, in this Office, the Title of a Book, the Right whereof he claims, as Proprietor, in the words following, to wit :———

[SEAL]

" Proofs of the Corruption of Gen. James Wilkinson,
" and of his connexion with Aaron Burr, with a full re-
" futation of his slanderous allegations in relation to the
" character of the principal witness against him. By DA-
" NIEL CLARK, of the city of New Orleans.

  " Rarò antecedentem scelestum
  " Deseruit pede pœna claudo.
       HOR.
  " Justice, tho' slow, is sure : vengeance
  " O'ertakes the swiftest villain's guilt."

In Conformity to the Act of the Congress of the United States, entitled " An Act for the Encouragement of Learn-
" ing, by securing the Copies of Maps, Charts, and Books,
" to the Authors and Proprietors of such Copies during the
" times therein mentioned."—And also to the Act, entitled
" An Act supplementary to an Act, entitled " An Act for
" the Encouragement of Learning, by securing the Copies
" of Maps, Charts, and Books, to the Authors and Proprie-
" tors of such Copies during the time therein mentioned,"
" and extending the Benefits thereof to the Arts of design-
" ing, engraving, and etching historical and other Prints."

      D. CALDWELL, Clerk of the
       District of Pennsylvania.

Advertisement.

THE originals of all the documents, cited as such in the following work, except the copies from the records of the Supreme Court in the affair of the Grand Sachem, which are of course in the office, and the papers laid before Congress, which are in the hands of the Clerk, are lodged with Mr. D. W. Coxe, in Philadelphia, who will shew them to any person desiring an inspection of them.

☞ The Reader will find the English translations immediately following the French and Spanish documents contained in the Appendix.

WHATEVER pleasure is derived from the punishment of crimes, it is always painful to become the instrument of inflicting it. It was therefore with regret that I found myself called on to lay before the house of representatives the information I possessed of general Wilkinson's treachery and corruption.

This regret was heightened by the idea that a part at least of my information had been acquired from the voluntary confession of the party accused, and a breach of confidence was so repugnant to my feelings, that although the confidence was unsought, but rather pressed upon me to prevent, I believe, a disclosure of facts I before knew, yet a strong sense of duty alone could have induced me to obey the call of the house. I complied with it; and my evidence established a direct confession of guilt. Little foresight was necessary to discover that this would expose me to every attack that could be made upon my reputation—it was verified by the event; every crime in the catalogue of human depravity was immediately imputed to me, and the basest and most contemptible arts were used to procure evidence to support them; they were used, however, with so little success, that although in a moment of warmth I had thought it necessary to promise the public a refutation of the charges, I yet, on a cooler consideration of their absurdity, had nearly determined to treat them with silent contempt. I thought that the motives of my calumniator would be plainly perceived; and that a character, which was founded in a virtuous education, and formed by a habitual attention to its precepts, could not be injured by the unsupported accusations of a wretch, weighed down still more by profligacy and crimes than by years, and sinking under a pressure of public abhorrence and contempt. I was moreover convinced, that in vindicating myself I should be obliged to undertake the disgusting task of pursuing my accuser through all the mire of speculation and vice, in which he had endeavoured to conceal his treason and corruption. My aversion to this office would have induced me to remain silent, if I had not reflected that the unaccountable favour granted to general Wilkinson by the executive might, among the partizans of the president, outweigh the strong proof of his guilt, and that every doubt on that subject must create one of my veracity.

But the important trust which has lately been committed to him forms a motive infinitely stronger than any personal consideration—knowing, as I do, that he has for years been the pensioner of a foreign power, that his hire was paid for the dismemberment and ruin of his country—and believing, as I firmly believe, that the same wages are yet paid him for the same iniquity, I cannot with indifference behold him placed in that very situation in which he can with the greatest convenience complete his treasonable purpose. I owe it to my country to call their attention to the amazing blindness, the wilful incredulity! or the co-operation in guilt, that has thus invested a detected traitor with the means of completing his treason. At the moment I write this, James Wilkinson's arrival is hourly expected; by special direction of government preparations are making to receive him with a pomp and splendour which the United States have hertofore shown only to a saviour of his country. He comes as commander in chief to the place, where but a few years since he arrived, first to sign the pact of his own dishonour, and afterwards to receive the yearly wages of infamy—where the notoriety of his guilt will make him fear a witness in every inhabitant of the country—where he may with facility renew his ancient engagements, or make others that will be more efficacious for the success of his schemes. The important province of Louisiana will in a few days be at the disposal of a man, who, by a close, long laboured system of corruption, is known to have bargained for the sale of the western states. I say at his disposal, for the civil power in this territory, as now administered, is worse than nothing in the scale; the little force it has will be immediately surrendered, and forced to operate in its own destruction; and there is no salvation for the country, but such an appeal to the people as will force conviction on the government; such demonstration of his guilt as must drive the most prejudiced to abandon his defence, and such an exposition of his treachery as will deprive him of the means, now strangely afforded him, of renewing it. A few weeks will place at the head of the executive a man, whose mind will, I trust, be open to conviction, and who will not suffer his country to be degraded by continuing a traitor in office, or her soldiers any longer to be led by the pensioner of a foreign power. This is my object in the present publication; to attain it I shall show,

1st. That general Wilkinson, from the year 1794 to 1803, certainly was, and probably is yet, a pensioner of the Spanish government.

2d. That his object was a treasonable attempt to sever the union of these states.

3d. That he knew, favoured and advised the enterprises of colonel Burr, and never resolved to be treacherous to his accomplice, until he could no longer with safety be so to his country.

It is possible that my personal knowledge of his treason and coruption induces me to suppose the other proof more conclusive than it is; but unless I greatly err, there will be no occasion to recur to my own testimony to establish his guilt. Much of the evidence now offered has already appeared before the public, but without order and at considerable intervals of time, frequently without such remarks as were necessary to make it intelligible, and never accompanied by any that would show the manner in which the different documents elucidated each other, and supported the testimony of the witnesses.

My object is now to supply this defect, to give the evidence at one view, to show how it applies to the different charges, and then let an enlightened and impartial public decide whether the testimony I was forced to give was a malicious calumny, or a simple narration of facts as they occurred—whether I am a false accusser, or he a hired betrayer of his country. I submit to this alternative, although I cannot but lament, that the strong presumptions, if not the positive proof long since in the hands of the executive power, were not deemed sufficient to have precluded the necessity of this task being performed by an individual. Let it be remembered that the man whom I accuse is commander in chief of the armies of the United States—that he is supported by the strongest marks of presidential favour—that after he was openly accused, and after my testimony and that of others was heard, he was continued in command, and that, more forcibly to express contempt for the accusation and confidence in the accused, he is sent to the very scene of his alledged corruption—is placed with the fullest powers in that very country which it is alledged he wished to sever from the union, and where the freest intercourse is afforded with his former corrupters: a private individual carries on a very unequal warfare against a man thus supported, thus invested with the power to screen himself and assail his accusers Witnesses are with difficulty persuaded to appear; documents are withheld; and in this country particularly, where the laws have been so grossly violated by this very man with impunity, the fear of military execution has, I know, prevented my obtaining much evidence which would have supported a prosecution, carried on under the sanction of government. If therefore under these disadvantages I should do no more than raise such violent presumptions of guilt as to throw the burthen on the accused, it would be enough in so serious a charge to justify the active researches of government. More has been done, and yet all is quiet; no investigation is made by the proper officers: corruption rides triumphant in the car of office—treason rears its head, adorned with the trappings of command. But the pageant is nearly past. Unaided as I have been, abandoned as I am by those whose duty it was to take the lead in the inquiry, I have fortunately for my country succeeded; and when this evidence is published, not a doubt will remain—conviction will flash on every mind. But the arrogant offender will not engross the public indignation. A strict account will be demanded of those who have thus trifled with the dignity of the nation and endangered its existence.

Previous to the year 1787, the port of New Orleans was shut against the settlers on the Ohio; their crops were more than sufficient for their own supply, but agriculture could not long flourish without a vent for its productions. The greatest discontent began to prevail, and little relief was then expected from a government then too feeble to effect it. Gen. Wilkinson had migrated, as he says, to that country some years before, being then, as we learn from the same source, in moderate if not indigent circumstances; in the year 1787 he planned and executed the project of opening a trade between the western country and New Orleans, seconded by some merchants in that city. He impressed the government with a high idea of his influence in Kentucky, and used means (which in his own language it would not be *necessary* nor *obligatory* nor *honourable* to detail) in order to procure for himself the exclusive trade between Kentucky and New Orleans. On this monopoly the gen. al does not scruple to found the assertion, " that at his own risk and expense he had procured for his fellow-citizens in the west the invaluable privileges of a free trade with New Orleans." I prove these facts by a publication called a PLAIN TALE, and signed A KENTUCKIAN, which is found in Note No. 1. This pamphlet is acknowledged to be the general's by a letter in which he enclosed it to me (Note No. 2.) But it wanted no acknowledgment, the general's style is inimitable, and sets forgery at defiance. My account of his first expedition, which is annexed to his justification, is referred to by him as a true statement, and that account expressly states the privilege he obtained to have been an exclusive one.

This transaction was in 1787. For some time previous to this period general Wilkinson had been trading in partnership with Isaac B. Dunn, in Kentucky. He continued unconnected as is believed with any other person until the 8th of August, 1788, when a partnership was formed between Wilkinson and Dunn of the one part, and Daniel Clark the elder of the other part. These articles will be found at length, (No. 3,) and they establish a community of interest between the parties in a trade to be carried on between Kentucky and New Orleans. Mr. Clark was my near relation and residing at New Orleans, and of course had the disposal of all the produce that was sent down by his partners in Kentucky. I was then his clerk, and had an intimate knowledge of the affairs of the concern—the books are now in my possession, and important extracts from them will be hereafter referred to.

This partnership was dissolved by mutual consent on the 18th of September, 1789, as appears by gen. Wilkinson's declaration of that date (Note 4.) The connexion between Wilkinson and Dunn was also dissolved about the same time by the death of the latter. Wilkinson then connected himself with Mr. Peyton Short, and their enterprises having proved unfortunate, Wilkinson in 1791 resumed his military career. Unable to brook a superior, or more probably afraid that the nature of his Spanish connexions would be discovered by his vigilance—the whole period of general Wayne's command was marked by conduct on the part of Wilkinson, which was, in the language of gen. Knox, considered as " tarnishing the military reputation of our country." (Vide extracts annexed to the *Plain Tale.*) In 1797 he attained the object of his intrigues and was placed at the head of the army. Here he has continued ever since, and in 1803 had the office of commissioner for receiving the transfer of the province added to his former trust. In this character he visited New Orleans and resided some months among his old acquaintances and friends. His subsequent appointment to the government of Upper Louisiana, his Sabine campaign, his meritorious services at New Orleans, and his later movements, are too notorious to need repetition. It was necessary, however, to give this short sketch of his commercial and military life during the last twenty years, in order to take a distinct view of the testimony as applicable to the different periods of his history.

The precise period at which gen. Wilkinson was enrolled among the pensioners of Spain I cannot designate by any positive testimony—a strong presumption, however, may be drawn from the confession contained in the pamphlet before quoted. He tells us that the monopoly of the trade was acquired by means which it would not be *honourable* to detail. The general seems to think, however, that dishonour would be attached to the disclosure, but none to the act: The world will be of a different opinion, and stamp corruption with the mark of infamy, by whatever means it may be discovered. It cannot be imagined that he meant by this phrase to say he had sold himself to obtain the monopoly; he only wishes the world to understand that the privilege was gained by bribing the governor of Louisiana, and that his delicacy was too great to betray him. The general stands much in need of this kind of indulgence, and wishes to set an example of discretion to the Spanish officers—a want of it on their part he knows would ruin him for ever. But let any one consider the circumstances of the transaction, and then ask himself what kind of bribe was offered—what equivalent was paid for this treaty of commerce and navigation?

The Spanish government at that time refused to acknowledge the slightest pretext of right in the U. S. to the navigation of the Missisippi. Our government considered their own pretensions, or their means of enforcing them, so weak, that it was proposed in their councils to abandon the exercise of the right for 25 years, in order to have it acknowledged after that period. This was a favourite point with the

B

Spanish government. Their minister was intriguing in the U. S.—their cabinet was at work in Europe, and while every engine was set at work to block up the navigation of the Missisippi, can it be supposed that a few thousand dollars paid to a governor of New Orleans would have counteracted these important projects, or that he would have dared to hazard his office and his life for any pecuniary consideration an individual had to offer? The idea is absurd; but if the governor was open to corruption, what was the bribe which Wilkinson had to offer? By his own story he came poor to Kentucky in the latter part of the year 1783, in the beginning of 1787 he went to New Orleans. Three years of the most favourable commerce on a very small capital, in a country professedly poor, and having no outlet for its produce, could not have put Mr. Wilkinson in a situation to offer an equivalent in money to a Spanish governor for the risk of his place, his fortune and his fame. But his commerce was not favourable, his " hopes" were, by his own confession, " *jeopardized, and he determined to look abroad for what he had not found at home;*" which I suppose in English means that he was a bankrupt, and that being afraid of his creditors in Kentucky, he went down the Missisippi to seek his fortune and avoid their suits.

It is clear, then, from these circumstances, that Wilkinson could not offer, nor would the Spanish officers have received money; what then were the respective considerations of this bargain, this grant of the whole trade of the Ohio to New Orleans? plainly then, that the trade of the country should be liberated at the expence of the allegiance of the inhabitants—and as Wilkinson was represented as a man of great influence, the monopoly was put in his hands; and probably the pension was then given and paid in advance as a capital to commence trade. No other explanation can reconcile the caution of the Spanish character, especially in affairs of state, with the decisive step taken by Miro, and persevered in by his successors, of yielding the object of national contention without orders and without a struggle. At this period too the cypher was formed. We have it from the general himself; and by a fatality of expression he calls this " *his first engagement.*" *(b)* It must be confessed, that whether he intended to express a connexion in contraband or treason, this was the kind of engagement with which the general was most familiar. The manner in which this cypher is spoken of shews that it was for some purpose of corruption. It was formed, says Wilkinson, at the time of " his first engagement," that is, in 1787, with a Spanish governor, and is transmitted four years afterwards, among the arcana of the office, to his successor. It is used by him, and again delivered with the archives. For what purpose was this cypher formed? " More for the security of the communications of my friend than my own," says gen. Wilkinson. But why did those communications require secrecy? If the only connexion was that which arose out of the permission to trade, it would have required no subsequent communication

(b) Kentuckian, page 9.

whatever. The permission once given, the monopoly once settled, the bribe as is insinuated once paid, the thing was at an end; no further correspondence was necessary, at least, none in cypher. It would have been a superfluous trouble for the baron de Carondelet to pore over a pocket dictionary for three hours in order to decypher the important intelligence, that on such a day a scow filled with hogs or a boat load of tobacco might be expected in town. If the object were mere friendly correspondence, there might be some reasons for the precaution, and it might not be improper to hide the delicate effusions of these congenial souls from the indiscreet eye of the public. But why then was the little dictionary handed over to the successor, when the "*general's friend left the country?*" This friendship, however, was probably an appendage to the office, and the little dictionary a talisman, that kept the general's affections always fixed upon its possessor.

The connexion thus formed, and the means of continuing it thus secured, Mr. Wilkinson returned through the Atlantic States to the Ohio. He probably laboured zealously in his new mission, for in spite of the monopoly his own affairs went to wreck, and those of his newly adopted country flourished. The seeds of disaffection were sown by a skilful hand, and men, who then stood high in the estimation of their country, are now discovered to have been the hirelings of Spain.

Hitherto my proofs have been presumptive, and such only as might be expected from the secret nature of the crime. I come now to tread on surer ground, and will clearly prove the payment of five different sums of money to gen. Wilkinson by the Spanish government, amounting to 34,563 dollars. I will prove, negatively, that no part of this was on account of the tobacco or any other commercial speculation, and then, affirmatively, that they were the wages of his *treason*.

In 1789, he visited New Orleans a second time, and returned by land, carrying with him a sum of about 6000 dollars in silver, loaded on two mules, and accompanied by Mr. Philip Nolan, and preceded, I believe, as far as Natchez, by Mr. Joseph Ballinger, both of them his *confidential agents*, as will appear by a number of documents referred to in the course of this enquiry. Before their arrival in the American settlements, the general thought it prudent no longer to accompany his treasure. It was therefore confided to Ballinger, who carried it to his own house, while the general and his faithful Nolan rode on to Frankfort. Joseph Ballinger having fallen sick, was obliged to transfer his trust to his brother John, who, after some days of anxious expectation on the part of the general, arrived at Frankfort, delivered the money to Wilkinson and took his receipt, which is still in existence, and will probably be printed in an appendix to this work. The arrival of Joseph Ballinger at his own house with the money, and the subsequent delivery of it to Wilkinson, are proved by the testimony of John Ballinger, (Note No. 5.) His being accompanied by Nolan is added, and the other circumstances corroborated, by the letter of Evan Jones, Esq. (No. 6.)

From 1789 to 1794, if any remittances were made they have eluded detection. But in that year, we have the clearest evidence that a sum of 6000 dollars was sent to be delivered to him, and though it was lost on the route, yet from a complaint in one of his letters we should judge that the shipment was on his account and risk.

Finding the means of transmitting the money difficult, or the agents unfaithful, or the suspicions of Wayne awakened, or from some other cause, the general found it necessary to dispatch a special messenger to receive the subsidy. He pitched upon Mr. Owens, a gentleman who had been driven by disappointment from society, and who was pursued by poverty in his retreat. His wants induced him to undertake the mission, and from his character Wilkinson knew that he might rely on his fidelity. He deserved a better employment and a better fate: for having received the sum of 6000 dollars, he was sent up the river in a public galley to the mouth of the Ohio, he there embarked in a perogue with six Spanish sailors, furnished by the commandant of the galley to go up the Ohio, and was a few days afterwards robbed and murdered by his crew. The whole of this transaction is circumstantially related by Mons. Francois Langlois, now an inhabitant of this territory, then the commander of the galley in which Owens was conveyed, (No. 7.) To corroborate his testimony are added extracts of two letters from the baron de Carondelet to Mr. Langlois, relative to this transaction and to the capture of the murderers. One or more of them were tried for this crime, and the trial gave publicity to the object of Owens's voyage, which, by the affidavit of Mr. Bouligny, (a planter of this province, formerly adjutant major of the Louisiana regiment, now a member of the territorial legislature,) appears to have been very publicly known, and the general's character duly appreciated.—(See No. 8.)

Grieved for the loss of his money, and alarmed lest the trial of the murderers in the United States should lead to disagreeable investigations, general Wilkinson determined to use every exertion to apprehend and deliver them to the Spanish government. One named Vexerano was taken, tried, and condemned at New Orleans. Another escaped, but was afterwards taken near the same place, and underwent the same fate. One who had not participated in the crime, immediately after it was committed, left his companions and fled to New Madrid. The other three, after wandering some time in Kentucky, were taken and confined, but were enlisted by lieutenant Smith, and as there was no evidence against them, they were suffered to join the army; but general Wayne, hearing their history, ordered them to be discharged, and reprimanded the officer for enlisting them; after this Wilkinson, by means which are not known, procured them to be transferred to Fort Washington, where he engaged Mr. Charles Smith, of Kentucky, to convey them to New Madrid. They were chained and put on board a boat for that purpose, but on his way down Smith attempted to pass Fort Massac at night, but was stopped by major Doyle, who commanded there, and who, not knowing by what authority **Wilkinson** sent men in irons to a Spanish commandant, refused to let them proceed—but sent an officer with Smith to major Portel, at New Madrid, requesting to be furnished with an interpreter to examine the prisoners, and to furnish such proofs as might be necessary to convict them on their trial in the American territory. Smith bore an order from Wilkinson on the commandant for 500 dollars, for the conveyance of the prisoners. This however was protested, but Mr. Power was sent as an interpreter to examine them. It not being the interest of the Spanish government that the affair should be investigated, no proof was sent on, and the men, after some months confinement, were discharged for want of evidence. Most of these facts subsequent to the murder of Owens are of public notoriety. The whole is detailed circumstantially in the affidavit of Mr. Powers, (No. 9,) and the names of the persons having an agency in the business being mentioned, reference may be had to them, in case the charge is more seriously investigated.

In the same year, to divide the risk, another remittance was made by sea, amounting to 6333 dollars, and entrusted to Mr. Joseph Collins, another of the general's confidential agents. On this point it must be confessed that the proof is not such as would be received in a court of justice, but it carries with it internal evidence of its truth, and may be rendered certain, whenever government shall be seriously disposed to ascertain the truth of these charges.

Mr. Collins lives at Pascagoula, in the Spanish territory. He was applied to for an affidavit stating his agency in the business, but refused, through fear of offending the officers of his government, to whom at the request of Wilkinson he had already given a declaration under oath of the whole transaction. Though taken evidently for the purpose of favouring Wilkinson, this declaration would throw light on the subject, but it will never appear; for Collins has declared that, as far as it went, it contains the truth. The gentleman who called in Collins obtained from him verbally a statement of the following facts— That he was sent by Wilkinson in the year 1794, with Owens, to New Orleans, with a sealed packet for governor Carondelet. That in consequence of the orders contained in this letter, 6000 dollars were delivered to Owens, and 6333 to him, (Collins,) with which he embarked at the Bayou St. John's, went to Charleston, and in August, 1795, delivered his charge to general Wilkinson at Cincinnati, on the Ohio. He asked for a receipt. This was refused; but he called on Mr. John Brown, of Kentucky, who happened to be there, to witness that he had settled his accounts with Collins, and that he owed him nothing. These facts are stated in a letter from general Adair to me, (No 10,) and the evidence is corroborated by a copy of the receipt which Collins gave for the money, to the *contedor* of the Spanish territory, in these words: " Received from Gilbert Leonard, 6333 dollars, for the use of general James Wilkinson, which I promise to deliver to him, the risk of the seas, &c. excepted." It may be objected that this is only hearsay testimony. It is so, but it may be rendered authentic, whenever general Wilkinson shall please to publish the affidavit taken at his request before governor Folch, or whenever our government takes measures to compel the attendance of witnesses. In the mean time, it is corroborated by the fact, that Collins was the known agent of Wilkinson; by the positive testimony which has been already detailed in that part of the story which relates to the division of the sum between him and Owens; and by the following statements: First, the deposition of Mr. Miller, a very respectable and intelligent planter on the Red river, who in his deposition (No. 11) states, that he saw Collins at the time of his embarkation from New Orleans, who had then just returned from the Ohio; that he *saw the money put on board;* that Collins mentioned the sum, and told him it was for Wilkinson, and that by a very extraordinary favour of government it was suffered to be embarked openly. Secondly, by the certificate of captain Sterrett, late of the U. S. army, who states that Collins gave him, at another period, the most minute details of the difficulties he had to encounter in the transportation of this sum. (See No. 12.) Here is then positive testimony of the delivery of this sum to an agent of general Wilkinson, and the strongest circumstantial presumptive evidence of its being for his use.

The evidence on which the next payment rests would, I confess, be weak in any other case. It is that of the general himself. In a letter dated August the 7th, 1795, to general Adair, (No. 13,) he says, "of 6590 *dollars* received for me in New Orleans, 1740 only have reached my hand, this *independent of poor Owens's loss*. The whole of this last sum is not lost, but is not within my controul, and will not be so for six or nine months."

Here then is a fourth payment from New Orleans confessed, which does not agree in amount or circumstance with either of the others. The first sum, it will be remembered, was carried up by himself six years before; the second was confided to Owens, and is expressly excepted; the third was given to Collins, was a different amount, and came safely to his hands. This, then, was a fourth and an additional payment; but how came the general so communicative? The former part of the letter gives the reason. He had just risen from " *cool Madeira,*" and the truth which is in wine had for once corrected the habitual falsity of his language.

The last item in this disgusting account between treachery and corruption is a sum of 9640 dollars, of which we have the most minute, positive and convincing proof.

The disappointments to which general Wilkinson had been subject in the former remittances seem to have engaged the attention of his employers: they feared perhaps that a long interval between their payments might give time for some lurking honest principle to rise, and bring him back to a sense of duty; or that he might be frightened into it by a fear of discovery, should such an accident again occur as had befallen Owens.

Their proselyte was then too high in command—had too near a prospect of being able to serve them with effect, for them to neglect any means of preserving his attachment. Whatever might be the cause, great care seems to have been taken to secure the safe delivery of the pension for 1796.

Some time previous to the 20th of January of that year, the baron de Carondelet shipped the sum of nine thousand six hundred and forty dollars on board a royal galley, and though ostensibly addressed to Vincent Folch, directed it to be delivered to Don Thomas Portell, the commandant at New Madrid, with the following letter:

"In the galley Victoria Bernardo Molino Patron, there has been sent to Don Vincent Folch 9640 dollars, which sum, without making the least use of it, you will hold at my disposal, to deliver it the moment that an order may be presented to you by the American general Don James Wilkinson. God preserve you many years.

THE BARON DE CARONDELET.

New Orleans, Jan. 20, 1796.

In the mean time the general, whose extravagance always anticipated the salary of his corruption, was importunate for his pay, and he requested Mr. Thomas Power, who appears to be the agent in whom both parties had the highest confidence, to go to New Orleans to receive the money. On his arrival he was informed of its being sent to New Madrid, and he immediately returned with a letter from the secretary of the governor, D. Andreas Armesto, to apprise the general that his wages were ready. He charged Power to receive them, who came to New Madrid for that purpose in June, but an unforeseen difficulty arose. Portell was by the above letter directed to deliver the money only to the general, or his order. He seems to have considered this to mean a *written order*, and as Power was unprovided with one, in order to show that he equally possessed the confidence of the Spanish government, and of Wilkinson, he was obliged to write a letter to Portell, by which he enters into details extremely edifying on the present occasion, and on which I shall particularly remark in a subsequent part of this inquiry. He details his different missions, and the address with which he executed them. He tells them of his being sent to New Orleans for this very money—of the conversations he had with the governor and secretary—of the means which he (Power) had recommended to conceal the money, by Wilkinson's special direction—of his return to Wilkinson with the secretary's letter, and of his coming now on purpose to receive the sum. He enlarges on the disappointment to the general, and the injury to the king's service that would result from any delay in making the remittance, and paints, in very strong terms, the necessity of furnishing sugar and coffee, in which to conceal the dollars. Portell seems to have yielded to the force of this reasoning, and to have acknowledged Power, by the tokens exhibited, as one of the initiated in the mysteries of the intrigue. He answers him on the different points, consents to deliver the money, and to furnish the sugar and coffee necessary to conceal it; and *gives him the copy he had requested, of the baron's official letter of the* 20*th of January.*

After having received the money and the merchandize, Power departed, and escaping the vigilance of gen. Wayne, by whose orders he was diligently watched, he arrived at Louisville, with his charge; from thence he proceeded to Cincinnati, and applied to Wilkinson to know what he should do with the money, who directed him to pay it to Nolan. He did so, and the general afterwards acknowledged that he had received it. These circumstances are proved by the letter from Carondelet to Portell, (No. 14,) the correspondence between Power and Portell, (No. 15 and 16,) and the deposition of Power, (No. 17.)

Some remarks may be necessary to shew the force of this testimony, which will be found to be irresistible: The letter of Carondelet is certified to be a true copy by Portell, who died many years ago; he was commandant of the post, and his certificate of any paper among his records bore, by the Spanish laws, the faith of an exemplification. He could at that time have had no motive for a forgery of this nature—Power could have had none to have asked him to make it, and the baron, they both knew, was a man whose signature they could not have trifled with with impunity. This certified copy was given to Power at the time, as his warrant for delivering the money to Wilkinson. Portell's letter to Power is the original draft, sworn to be exact by him, and proved so better than a thousand oaths, by its internal evidence, and by the manner in which Portell's answer tallies with it. If this evidence wanted support, it would be abundantly found in the following documents. 1st. The deposition of Mr. Derbigny, (No. 18,) a gentleman of great respectability at the bar of New Orleans, then a resident at New Madrid. He declares that he sold to Mr. Powers the coffee and sugar for the purpose of packing the dollars, and that the bags for that purpose were made in his family, and that the object both of Powers's negociation and of the payment of the money was communicated to him by a Spanish officer, and was generally known at the port. 2d. The deposition of Mr. Mercier, (No. 19,) then a clerk employed in the office of the baron de Carondelet, who unequivocally asserts the agency of Power, the correspondence in cypher with Wilkinson, and the object of it.

3d. By the following extract of a letter from Andrew Ellicott, Esq. to general Wilkinson (the whole of the letter will be referred to in another branch of this inquiry.) " About the 16th of October, 1799, captain Portell, who then commanded at Apalachy, informed me that at New Madrid, in the year 1796, he put on board a boat, under the direction of Mr. Thomas Power, 9640 dollars for your use. I questioned him frequently whether this money was not on account of some mercantile transaction—he declared it was not; he likewise mentioned several other gentlemen who received money from the Spanish government by the same conveyance, and assured me that they were considered as pensioners by the officers of his catholic majesty. I entered the sum of 9640 dollars on a piece of paper now in my possession, and handed it to captain Portell, who told me it was correct."

On Mr. Power's arrival at New Madrid, when sent down by Wilkinson for the money, he found, as was stated, a difficulty, arising from the want of an order; this produced the correspondence between him and Portell above cited. Mr. Power thought it necessary to account for the apparent indiscretion of his communications to Portell, and therefore wrote the letters to the baron de Corondelet and governor Gayoso (No. 20 and 21, dated 27th June.) On his return to New Madrid, after the delivery of the money, he again apprised both these officers of his return and the success of his mission, in two letters, (No. 22 and 23, dated 3d January, 1797;) the original drafts of those letters are now in my possession, and I beg the reader to attend to these documents, not only for the light they throw on this particular point, but for their referring to dispatches in cypher from Wilkinson, and instructions brought by Nolan, both of great importance in the subsequent part of this inquiry.

In addition to those corroborative proofs, a multitude of other depositions can be had whenever the legal inquiry is instituted; these, however, will suffice to prove, I think undeniably, the payment of the several sums I have mentioned by the *Spanish government* to an *American general*. Before we proceed to demonstrate the falsity of his excuse, that the sums he received were the prices of his tobacco, I must advert to two other circumstances, which are not supported by positive proof, but which, connected with the other facts, are extremely suspicious. The one is the 4000 dollars mentioned by me in my deposition before the house of representatives as being laden by special permission, understood to be for Wilkinson, by Mr. Le Cassagne, in the year '93 or '94; the other is the general's purchase of sugars at New Orleans in 1804. It is proved by the deposition of Mr. M'Donough, (No. 24,) that while at New Orleans, as one of the commissioners, Wilkinson purchased sugars to the amount of 9640 dollars, which were paid for in dollars contained in such bags as they are brought in from La Vera Cruz. And this affidavit, as well as the one before referred to of Mr. Peter Derbigny, prove that the circumstance was considered as an extraordinary one. Wilkinson was always known to have lived extravagantly. The savings out of his pay and emoluments could not have amounted to 10,000 dollars. And it seems to have excited not only the attention of those who were in the secret of his former connexion, but even of governor Claiborne, who, according to Mr. Bradford's declaration, appears to have entertained suspicions not very honourable to the integrity of his colleague, until he found means to remove his doubts by an assurance that the money was received from lieutenant Taylor, the military agent at New Orleans. The public, however, will not, I believe, be quite so indulgent as governor Claiborne. They will ask something more than the mere assertion of general Wilkinson. He has, by his own admission, reduced the question on this head to a single point. It would have been difficult, without the proof of his conversations with Mr. Bradford and governor Claiborne, (Note No. 25,) to have excited any thing more than suspicion; but for this he might have pointed to a variety of sources, from either of which a possibility would result of its being honestly acquired. But he has made his election—it must have been received either from lieutenant Taylor, *for the general's drafts on the treasury for extra services*, or *in direct payment of those services*—or it must have been received from some other person, for a purpose which he is ashamed to avow. Now if received from Mr. Taylor, nothing would have been more easy than to have silenced his accusers by producing the accounts.

If Taylor made the payments, he could then have been resorted to; and though he is since dead, a reference may be had to his books. If he only advanced the money on the general's drafts, a copy of these bills from the accountant's office, if drawn in Taylor's favour, and dated at the time of his residence in New Orleans, would have been strong evidence in favour of his explanation. But when it is remembered that the charge has been already publicly discussed, and that this proof so easily obtained if it really existed has never been produced, the general's silence affords the strongest reason to believe, that he cannot support the excuse which he gave to Mr. Bradford and governor Claiborne; at any rate, the officers of government may easily determine whether it be well founded. The books of the proper department will in a moment show, whether this large sum of money was actually paid during the winter or spring of 1804, when the purchase of sugars was made. If it were not, I repeat, that the proof, though otherwise light, is now conclusive. He has hung up his defence on that point, and unless he shows it to have been received from Taylor, there will be no doubt that the *Mexican* dollars in the *Mexican* bags were received from the Marquis de Casa Calvo, who then, and for a long time after, resided at New Orleans, and who, while the general staid, was on the most intimate terms of friendship with him. In the mean time I give this rather as a subject of suspicion for further inquiry, than as a positive charge; not wishing to confound it with the decisive proofs I have already adduced.

Having established the receipt of the money, let us now inquire to what account it is placed by the general and his friends. Here every one, who has at all attended to the nature of his defence, must have remarked a studied obscurity, a confusion of dates, sums and circumstances, that evidently show a design to avoid inquiry.

This charge was a serious one. It came forward in a respectable shape; it merited an answer. The general thought so too. He clamoured for inquiry, but never sought it. Instead of defending his own character, he attacked that of his accusers, and flattered himself that the public attention was withdrawn from his infamy, while it was only astonished at the boldness of his calumny. If the monies received from the Spanish government were the proceeds of a commercial speculation, how easily might his accusers have been covered with confusion. All that would have been necessary was the exhibition of an account, designating the sums he had received, and showing how they had become due. I have received, he might have said, 6000 dollars by Ballinger, 6000 by Collins, 9640 by Power; but they were the proceeds of a fair trade, and here are the accounts to support it. This is so natural a course for innocence to have pursued, that we cannot but suspect guilt when we see it departed from: a balance sheet for each year would have humbled his enemies in the dust, and his character would have been the more firmly established from the impotent attack.

Instead of this, what is done? Why the general publishes his *Plain Tale*, where, in answer to the charge of having received specific sums of money from the Spanish government, all he says is this: "his [gen. Wilkinson's] commercial engagements were exclusively with the Spanish government of Louisiana, as he never sold a cent's worth of property in the market after his first voyage; of course, the cash he received was from the government of the country, and this he received in person, on *his bills*, or by *remittance* through various channels. The last payment was made him in the year 1796, through his agent Philip Nolan, being a balance which had arisen on the recovery of some tobacco, which it had been believed was damaged and lost in the year 1789." This is the only passage of his justification in which he ever alludes to any sums received, or endeavours to give any account of the consideration for which they were paid. If he received money as he says in *person*, he can tell the amount. If he drew bills, the sums and the parties may be shown. If he received remittances, there can be no difficulty in designating them, and showing by the other side of the account the consideration for which they were paid. These vouchers would have been infinitely more satisfactory to the public than general Knox's letters, or than my *memoir* to the secretary of state, with which he has enriched his defence.

General Wilkinson *did not do this, because* HE DID NOT DARE TO EXHIBIT HIS ACCOUNT. He knew the original accounts were in my hands, that they were signed by him and his agents, and that the result of their examination would destroy him for ever. It appears, however, that before the court of inquiry he did produce some accounts which have been carefully kept from the public eye. The result, however, is stated in the sentence, and is extremely important in this investigation. The sentence (No. 26) states, 1st. That it does not appear that he received any money from *the Spanish government,* or any of its officers, since the year 1791.

2d. That it does appear by the general's statement that *his agents,* several years after '91, received and remitted to him *several sums* for tobacco, which had been stored as damaged in the year 1789. It is to be remembered that the court of inquiry did not think proper to state the amount of these *several sums,* or to designate at least the *years* in which they were paid, that we might have compared them with other payments. Not having the aid which the account exhibited to the court of inquiry would have afforded, I must use the materials I have; they will, I believe, be amply sufficient. We have it from the general's admission, as stated in the sentence, that he received no money *from the government or any of its officers*, for tobacco or other produce, since the year '91. But I have incontrovertibly shown, that the sum of 6000 dollars by Owens, of 6333 by Collins, and of 9640 by Powers, were all received from the government or its officers long after the year 1791. They were then, by his own confession, not received for tobacco. On what account then were they paid? It does not appear from whom the sum of 6590 dollars, mentioned in the letter to Adair, was received; whether from his agent Nolan, or from the officers of government. I do not therefore include it in the above calculation, but, added to those three sums, they form a total of 28,563 dollars, which were all received after '91. Now admitting them to be the produce of the damaged tobacco, and that this damaged tobacco had sold as well as that which was merchantable, there must have been at least 570 hogsheads, an extraordinary quantity to have laid forgotten for so many years. But I do not rely, though I safely might, on the evident absurdity of this poor excuse. I have promised to leave no doubt on this point, and I hasten to fulfil my engagement.

We have seen that the general came down with a small cargo in 1787, and that in August 1788 he entered into partnership with my kinsman Daniel Clark, who had been his agent for the disposal of all the property he sent down previous to the partnership. The day after that connexion was formed, the previous accounts were made out, settled and signed by both parties. (See No. 27.) This settlement presents a payment of 335 dollars to major Dunn for balance, and shews that 3000 dollars out of 10,000, the whole amount of the sales, had been advanced to Wilkinson a year before the produce came down, and that the produce was drawn for, in favour of different persons to whom he owed money. It also appears by this settlement, that Mr. Clark acknowledged to have on hand a quantity of tobacco in bulk, weight unknown, and also other parcels amounting to eight hogsheads, for which he made himself accountable when sold. None of the monies therefore, which I have shown to have been paid to general Wilkinson, arose out of any commercial transaction prior the 8th of August, 1788. On that day the partnership with Daniel Clark, senior, commenced. The accounts of that partnership from its date to the 1st May, 1789, were settled on that day, and a balance of 2681 dollars then paid to capt. Abner M. Dunn, the brother of one of the partners. The gross amount of sales, by this account, appears to be 16,441 dollars. At the foot of it is added the receipt of Mr. Dunn, for the balance. (See No. 28.)

By this account the balance appears to have been paid to capt. A. M. Dunn, and was by him taken round by sea to his brother, the partner of Wilkinson in Kentucky.

On the 5th of September, in the same year, gen. Wilkinson was at New Orleans, and there made another settlement, by which it appears that there was a balance only of $ 48 5 1-2 reals in his favour, which was paid to Nolan, his agent, by his order, (See No. 32,) and of course, that the sum of 6000 dollars, stated by Ballinger and Mr. Jones to have been taken up in this year, could not have proceeded from any of his commercial operations. An inspection of the account will show that the large payments were always made either in advance to Wilkinson himself, or to his order in favour of different persons to whom he was indebted. This account is signed by Wilkinson himself, and closes the accounts of the partnership, which, as we have stated, was dissolved on the 18th of the same month. (See No 4.) In this settlement the tobacco which is mentioned as loose, and weight unknown, in the first account settled by major Dunn, is accounted for, and appears to have amounted only to 974 dollars.

Thus all the tobacco transactions up to the 18th September, 1789, are distinctly placed before the public—they must of necessity have entered into the partnership accounts, and those accounts are annexed; and let it be remembered that it is to this year, 1789, that the general and the court of inquiry refer for the shipments which are to account for the enormous sums which he has been proved to have received. It should also be remarked that the periodical rise of the water taking place from February to June, after that period, except on extraordinary occasions, the accounts of the year close in the commerce between the Ohio and New Orleans, and therefore not much more can be expected from the accounts of this year; but there is still a portion of the time and a remnant of the transaction to be elucidated, and I will not leave a day or cent unaccounted for.

Prior to the dissolution of the partnership, Mr. Clark had sent up the river, on the joint account, a boat called the Speedwell, with a cargo amounting to about 8000 dollars. This not being included in the settlement, Wilkinson, as appears by the document before referred to, (NO. 4,) agrees that he will invest the proceeds in good tobacco, and ship it to New Orleans on their joint account in the *month of December next;* and that when he has fulfilled this and another undertaking of the same nature, with respect to a debt he was authorised to collect, *then the partnership should cease.*

It appears by a letter from Wilkinson to Mr. Clark, dated 20th May, 1790, (NO. 30,) that the shipment which was by the general's engagement to have been made in December, 1789, could not take place until the spring of the following year. And here, if our sole purpose was to refute the half-uttered hesitating excuse that has been offered, here we might stop, for confused as the defence is, thus much at least has been distinctly stated, that the sums received after the year 1791 were all for tobacco shipped in '89; but the accounts to May 1790 are closed, irrevocably closed. The general's signature to the account attests every thing to the month of September. His letter shows that nothing was sent down between that time and May. With this refutation of his only defence I might stop; but I will anticipate the answer to any amendment he might make by pretending the mistake of a year, and after showing that the sums he received did not proceed from his commercial operations in the year '89, I

E

will show as clearly that they were not produced by those of 1790, which by his own confession was the last of his commercial existence.

By the agreement for dissolving the partnership, as we have seen, it appears that the Speedwell's cargo was to have been invested in tobacco, on the account of the partnership. By the letters NO. 30 and 31, it appears that the proceeds were so invested; that purchases of tobacco to a large amount were also made on the general's own account—but that, to equalise the risk, the whole was thrown into a common account, the proceeds to be divided in proportion to the respective interests. This is explicitly stated in both letters—and in consequence of it we are furnished with proof, which we otherwise should not have had, if the Speedwell's cargo had been separately invested. As this business was nominally transacted by Nolan, his account of that investment would have given us only partial information, and it might be said that the monies we have proved to have been received were the proceeds of the residue of the shipment; but the whole being carried to one general account, Mr. Clark was entitled to an account sales of all the adventure, and he was liable for his proportion of any loss that might have happened by the damage done to any part. We accordingly find that the general in his letter is minute as to that loss, and states in the first letter that a flat with 40 hhds. had been sunk, which by the second appears to have been recovered, with a loss of about 12 or 15 hhds. In the second letter, June 20, 1790, (NO. 31,) the general expresses his mortification that the tobacco is not yet gone on, and says, " Events have justified the propriety of my making no distinction in the tobacco shipped at this time, or allotting any separate portion for the account of the Speedwell, as three of the fleet are still aground in Kentucky river, with 118 hhds. on board.

Nolan arrived with this shipment of tobacco ; it was sold to government; it was sold for the net sum of 15,850 dollars. The account, as well of the purchase as the sales, was rendered by Nolan; the former dated Kentucky, 7th May, 1790, and the latter New Orleans, 21st September, in the same year. This adventure was then finally closed. All the tobacco must have been sold, or Mr. Clark, having been charged with his proportion of the whole purchase, would have been entitled to his share of the sales of any remaining part of the tobacco. But as is evidenced by the accounts, (NO. 32,) the whole concern was closed ; Mr Clark's proportion, about 3,400 dollars, was paid him, and Nolan applied the residue to the payment of the general's debts, his creditors being at that time many and clamorous. Indeed, so much was he then pressed, that tho' an error of 473 dols. was discovered in the former accounts, and is certified by Nolan, (NO. 33,) yet he could not discharge it, but it still remains due.—In the next year Mr. Wilkinson became a general, but not before he became a bankrupt. After the death of Major Dunn, he became a partner with Mr. Peyton Short, and I am authorised, without the fear of contradiction, to state, that this gentleman felt for years the embarrassments caused by the connexion. That Wilkinson went to the army in debt to him, as well as to many other persons, who had been imprudent enough to trust him. That he availed himself of his official station to elude the payment of his debts, and when at last, by the firmness of Mr. James Hughes (to whom Mr. Short had in despair surrendered the task) he was forced to a settlement, that his accounts exhibited no outstanding debts at New Orleans, no tobacco stored there, none of those sources from whence he produced his subsequent wealth. His accounts with the estate of major Dunn will be found to be equally silent on this point, and those of his other partnership are now before the public. What device? what evasion? what excuse can now be found to hide him from this open and apparent shame? His commercial speculations afford no cover for his political corruption, and however probable it may be that he cheated his partners, this infamous excuse is insufficient, after these proofs, to clear him from the charge of having sold his country. Over any other but so arrogant, so unblushing, an offender it would be mean to triumph; but elevated by the consciousness of integrity, I look with contempt on the wretch who is grovelling beneath me, on whom punishment operates no reformation, detection no remorse—and who regrets loss of character only because it deprives him of the means of deception. Disgusted as I am with the task of exposing him, it is not yet finished. I have proved the payment of the money, and I have demonstrated that it was not the proceeds of *his commerce*. It remains to show that it was the hire of *his treason.*

I first recur to the testimony of Mr. Power, (No. 34.) I know that this gentleman, from a mistaken sense of duty to his country, a false idea of friendship, under an improper impression of pity, was induced 'to give an evasive certificate, tending to support the character of Wilkinson. But he has always supported the character of an honest man, he has always been in the most respectable society, and is highly esteemed by his friends. On this occasion, however, I use his testimony rather to justify him, by showing how strongly it is corroborated by other undeniable proof, than because I need it to support my case. His first mission was in 1795, from Gayoso, who was then at New Madrid, to general Wilkinson, at Cincinnati on the Ohio—he was the bearer of a letter, the purport of which was rather hinted at than communicated to him. On his delivering it, the general, supposing him more fully informed than he really was, communicated freely with him on the projected treason. It was to be effected by a separation of the western states from the union by the aid of Spain. The means to effect this were considered and matured in frequent conversations between the general and the emissary, who was sent by the former to Galliopolis, to sound the French inhabitants of that settlement. On his return the plan of operations was settled, and memorandums made, which have been kept by Mr. Power, and of which he now gives the copy. Employed continually in this project, he gives the detail of his different voyages and journies, and of the means by which he escaped discovery. The minuteness of his dates, and the number of persons whom he names, would certainly lead to detection, if he were guilty of the slightest inaccuracy. That he was the principal agent between the Spanish government and general Wilkinson is notorious; and the documents and other testimony to which I shall refer will, independent of his own testimony, put the object of his different missions beyond a doubt. The first of these is a letter written by Wilkinson himself to governor Gayoso, dated 22d September, 1796, after Mr. Power had made several visits to him, and had ingratiated himself by the dexterity with which he eluded the researches of Wayne, and brought to the general the reward of his treason. It is so important, that instead of throwing it among the other proofs, I insert it in the body of my work; every word is a proof—every line an argument stronger than any I can offer:

Fort Washington, Sept. 22, 1796.

Ill health and many pressing engagements must be my apology for a short letter. I must refer you to my letter to the baron for several particulars, and to a detail of my perils and abuses, I must beg leave to refer you to our friend Power, whom I find of youthful enterprise and fidelity; HE CERTAINLY DESERVES WELL OF THE COURT, and I don't doubt that he will be rewarded.

What a political crisis is the present! and how deeply interesting is its probable results, in all its tendencies, and thereby must hope it may not be carried into execution. If it is, an entire reform in the police and the military establishments of **Louisiana** will be found immediately indispensable to the Mexican provinces. I beg you to write me fully on the question in cypher by Power, whose presence in Philadelphia is necessary, as well to clear his own character, attacked by Wayne, as to support the fact of the outrage recently offered to the Spanish crown in his person, and bring me either the person or the deposition, now under your command, who has been suborned by Wayne to bear false witness against me, and afterwards, for fear he should recant, bribed him to leave Kentucky. Power will give you the perfect account of this infamous transaction, and I conjure you, by all the ties of friendship and of policy, to assist him on this occasion.

If Spain does not resent the outrage offered to Power in the face of all Kentucky. My letter to the baron will explain the motives which carry me to Philadelphia, from whence I will write again to you. Power will explain to you circumstances which justifies the belief of *the great treachery that has been practised with respect to the money lately sent me.* For the love of God and friendship, enjoin great secrecy and caution in all our concerns. *Never suffer my name to be written or spoken.* The suspicion of Washington is wide awake.

Beware of Bradford, the Fort Pitt refugee; he seeks to make peace—there are spies every where. We have a report here that you are appointed governor of Louisiana.—God grant it, as I presume the baron will be promoted. I am your affectionate friend,   W——

Copy of a letter in cypher, received from Wilkinson.—Natchez, Feb. 6th, 1797.
(Signed) MANUEL GAYOSO DE LEMOS.

In a separate paper he says what follows :

This letter will be delivered to you by Noland, whom you know is *a child of my own raising, true to his profession, and firm in his* ATTACHMENT TO SPAIN. I consider him a powerful instrument in our hands, should occasion offer, I will answer for his conduct. I am deeply interested in whatsoever concerns him, and I confidently recommend him to your warmest confidence. I am evidently your's affectionately.

WILKINSON.
A copy,
(Signed) MANUEL GAYOSO DE LEMOS.

This letter was written in cypher, which may account for the unguarded language in which it is couched. The *perils* and abuses of which he complains, were the suspicions of his countrymen and the vigilance of his commander. The crisis of which he speaks, was the prospect of a rupture between the king who corrupted him and the nation he betrayed.

With what creeping meanness does the fawning sycophant complain to a foreign officer of the injury he has received from his commander ; with what detestable malignity does he excite a foreign nation to resent an insult offered by his own ; with what abject fear does the trembling coward express his fears of discovery; and how coolly does the sanguinary traitor set the Spaniards on their guard against the attempts of one who sought to keep his country in peace.——Unexampled depravity!——Unheard of meanness!—Wickedness unparalleled in the annals of treachery!—Can this monstrous charge be true? Is it possible that a man, enjoying high command, and receiving daily marks of the confidence of his nation, should not only be tempted to betray it, but for days, and months, and years, should continue in her service—wear the honourable livery of her household—eat her bread—and yet be continually plotting her destruction, exciting her enemies to the attack, pointing out the defenceless places, and meanly receiving the wages of such depravity. How did he dare to issue a command to men, of whom the meanest had twenty thousand times his worth? How did he dare to punish crimes, when the blackest criminal might come and whiten by his side?—Did he dare to punish drunkenness, whose life was a continued scene of debauchery? Did not his hand tremble, when he signed the sentence for desertion?—or what crime in the catalogue of military offences could he punish, without thinking of his own?

Yes! he could do this without remorse; his mind is framed for treachery, and possesses a peculiar apathy, that enables him to speak of his crimes as if they were virtues, and which takes away all hope of amendment and all sense of shame. Yes! this proof of unparalleled treachery is too well authenticated to be called in doubt; it is proved better than by many witnesses, who should swear that they heard him use the expressions contained in the letter; they might be actuated by hatred or corruption, but this evidence comes in a shape that cannot be questioned: it not only carries with it the proof of its veracity, but it is invested with the forms of law, and would be received in any tribunals of the country where it was written. It is a copy, cerfied by governor Gayoso from his records; every record authenticated in this way has, under the Spanish government, the force of an exemplification in England or the United States, and an officer who should certify a fabrication of this kind would incur the same penalties that are inflicted on the highest forgery with us. This copy is altogether in the hand-writing of governor Gayoso, who has added his signature; both are extremely well known, have been proved by two witnesses, and can be by a thousand in this territory. Gayoso died in the year 1799, was the bosom friend of Wilkinson, and continued so until the day of his death, which, as is generally asserted here, was accelerated by too frequent libations to their mutual affection. He had therefore no motive to commit such a forgery for his ruin; had he any to betray his confidence by the delivery of this evidence of his guilt? None; nor did he foresee that, by the inscrutable decrees of a just and an avenging God, this paper would be the means of punishing the treachery of his friend. Mr. Power had been an active instrument in forwarding the revolution in Kentucky; he had spent much time and run great risks in the service, and he thought that his exertions merited reward. He had intended going to Madrid to solicit it, and he knew that the best evidence he could carry with him would be that of the persons whom he had brought over to the allegiance of his master. He had seen this letter from Wilkinson. The high terms in which he is mentioned in it determined him to ask this copy as his voucher. It was given him with the less reluctance, as the general had declared he could rely on his discretion, and as the letter gave him no new information, and the delivery of it could not be considered as a breach of confidence. I feel that this simple statement must be convincing to all who read it, and of course that the evidence of treachery is complete. I therefore proceed to the other proofs with reluctance; but I have imposed the task on myself, and will proceed.

We have seen in the examination of the accounts, that Mr. Philip Nolan was the agent of general Wilkinson. He acknowledges it in his publication called the *Plain Tale*. It is notorious, and can readily be proved, that he was not only a clerk and commercial agent, but a confidential friend in his more delicate nogotiations with the Spaniards. It is so stated in a paper written by the general, and annexed to the document last cited. " This will be handed to you (says the general to Gayoso) by Nolan, who you know is a child of my own raising, true in his profession, and *firm in his attachment to Spain*. I consider him as a POWERFUL INSTRUMENT in our hands should occasion offer—I will answer for his conduct. I am deeply interested in whatever concerns him, and I confidently recommend him to your warmest confidence. I am evidently yours—WILKINSON."

In the hand-writing of this powerful instrument in the general's hands—of this CHILD of so worthy a parent, who is recommended for his *firm attachment to Spain*, we have instructions evidently dictated by Wilkinson, and delivered by him to Power, (No. 35.) They begin by recommending an artful contrivance to deceive the public on the subject of his frequent visits. They enlarge much on the necessity of producing Newman, or at least procuring some affidavit from him contradictory of one he had before made, and the directions on this subject evince the hand of a master in the art of subornation. They show a great solicitude that Power should lull suspicion by ample testimonials of his character, and the first part closes with an injunction to bear no paper that carries his name. The second part, tho' shorter, is more valuable, on account of the many corroborative circumstances it contains. It begins with a direction how to employ the 640 dollars in his hands, as well as the merchandize in which his money was hid, and which he facetiously calls *la cargaison*, interlarding his treason, as he does his conversation, with scraps of French. This 640 dollars was the residue of the sum delivered by Portell, for the use of Wilkinson, to Power, and which was retained by the latter for expences. Small as this sum is, it was an object of solicitude. He requests that it may be secured to him in the settlement, and we shall find it here, after figuring in the accounts which Mr. Power renders to the baron de Carondelet of his mission, and in the allowance which the latter makes of his expences. " I have urged (says

Wilkinson in these instructions) the necessity of your presence in the metropolis." Let us refer to the letter, and we there find that the general had indeed urged it : " I beg you (he there says) to write to me in cypher by Power, *whose presence is necessary in Philadelphia*, as well to clear his own character, attacked by Wayne, as to support the fact of the outrage, &c. Again, the instructions say, " you must do the needful to expose and detect past treachery or indiscretion, and to prevent either in future. I have referred particularly on this head," and the letter shews the truth of the allegation, for it says, " Power will explain to you circumstances, which justify the belief of the *great treachery there has been practised with respect to* the money lately sent to me ; for the love of God and friendship, enjoin great secrecy and caution in all our concerns." How convincing is this proof! how irresistible the conviction of its authenticity. The letter certified by the general's best friend, long since dead, his hand-writing ready to be proved by the testimony of a whole province—the instructions copied by his confidential agent and tallying so precisely with the letter—both coinciding with the testimony of Mr. Power, corroborated by the co-existing circumstances, and throwing light as well on the preceding evidence as on that which will follow. The same note of instructions gives new weight to the reason I alledged why Power wished to obtain a copy of the letter, to wit, that he meditated a voyage to Spain—a project too, as it would seem, formed by the general himself, for he says, " if I cross the water, you are to accompany."

After having successfully fulfiled the mission on which he had been sent, having delivered his cargo of dollars, and received his returns in treasonable projects, Mr. Power came back to Natchez, from whence he rendered the account of his mission by the letter (No. 36) dated 9th May, 1797, and received an answer, of which we have the original, (No. 37,) 28th May, same year, which shows the exactness of all Mr. Power's details. The 640 dollars are not forgotten in this correspondence, and an account is rendered of the merchandise in which the dollars were concealed. In the baron's answer a new mission is spoken of, for which Power is directed to prepare. The instructions for this embassy are contained in a letter from the baron, of which the original is ready to be produced, (No. 38, May 1797.)

These instructions are written with more caution than any of the preceding papers. Wilkinson had just attained the command in chief; the governor, who knew his character, was not so certain of his co-operation, as when he was subordinate in command; he was the more doubtful, because Wilkinson had shown a disposition to disavow his former connexion, by marching a body of troops to take possession of the posts. "No person (the governor says to Power) shall be informed of your business, not even the intendant; Don Andres (the secretary) will be the only person in the secret." He then states the dispositions that the army of the United States, under the command of Wilkinson, are making to get possession of the posts, pursuant to the treaty; and instructs his agent in the pretences which he is to urge, to retard its fulfilment and stop the march of the troops. For this purpose Mr. Power is furnished with an official letter, directed to the commander of the American army. (No. 39.) This he tells us is the ostensible purport of this mission. The second object, which he warns him " no one ought to discover, and which for this reason he ought to retain in his memory, is to sound and examine the disposition of the people of the western country, the militia of which it is said had received orders to march;" in which case he is directed to give information to the commandant of New Madrid. He then gives him a kind of cypher, in which he is to communicate the most material facts on this point. After some artful instructions as to the language he is to hold to the people of Kentucky, the baron comes at once to the point, and says, " if a hundred thousand dollars distributed in Kentucky would be sufficient to raise an insurrection, I am sure the minister would sacrifice them with pleasure, and you may promise them, without much risk, to those who enjoy the confidence of the people ; with a like sum for the army in a case of necessity, and twenty pieces of cannon." On the subject of Wilkinson he says, " You will endeavour to discover, with your natural penetration, the disposition of the general. I doubt very much whether a person of his disposition can through vanity prefer the advantage of commanding the army of the Atlantic states, to that of being the founder, the deliverer—in fine, the Washington of the western country ; *his part* is as brilliant as it is easy to perform.—*All* eyes are fixed upon him—he possesses the confidence of his fellow-citizens and of the volunteers of Kentucky; on the slightest movement the people will name him general of the new republic; his reputation will form an army, and Spain as well as France will furnish him the means of paying it. *Let him seize Fort Massac*, and we will immediately send him arms and artillery, and Spain, confining itself to the possession of the forts of Natchez and the Walnut-hills, until the confederation takes place, will yield to the states of the west all the eastern shore to the Ohio, which will make an extensive and powerful republic, united by its interest and by its situation with Spain, who, in concert with it, will force the savages to make a part with it, and to mix in time with its citizens. The people are discontented with the new taxes—Spain and France are disgusted by the connexions of the United States with England.—*The army is weak, and devoted to Wilkinson.*

" The threats of congress justify me at once, and without any disguise, to succour the western states; money will not be wanting, for I will immediately send a frigate to La Vera Cruz to fetch it, as well as ammunition. One instant of firmness and resolution is all that is necessary to make the people of the west perfectly happy. If this instant is suffered to escape, *and we should be forced* to give up the posts, Kentucky and Tennessee, surrounded by the said posts, and without any communication with Louisiana, will remain for ever under the oppression of the Atlantic States. If you represent these arguments with force to *Wilkinson, Sebastian, La Cassagne*,

&c. if you spread their notions among the people by gaining the best writers, such as *Breckenridge* and others, *by promises which shall be faithfully fulfilled*, you may cause the most glorious and happy commotion, you will cover yourself with glory, and may expect the most brilliant fortune," &c. If this were our only document, it would be a most persuasive evidence of a previous intelligence between the baron and general Wilkinson. He had been his pensioner while second in command. Having attained the first rank, he was now placed in a situation, by the approaching rupture between the two nations, to elect between open rebellion and a return to duty. The Spaniard seems to have somewhat apprehended the latter, but to have calculated, from his knowledge of the general's character, that he might be brought openly to throw off his allegiance. He therefore directs Power to flatter his vanity with the prospect of being the founder of a new republic. His avarice had been successfully tried before, and now hundreds, of thousands of dollars figure in every line, money is not to be wanting, and his two ruling passions are to be excited to the utmost pitch. What can express the insolent certainty they had of the commander's treachery more fully, than that when enumerating the reasons why they counted upon success, such as that the people were discontented with their taxes, that France and Spain were disgusted with the government, and that the army was weak, the baron adds, that it *was devoted to Wilkinson?* This is the first time that the devotion of an army to its chief was placed in the list of reasons which were to ensure the success of its enemies; and the expression can only be accounted for, by supposing that the general was as much devoted to the enemy as the army were to him. Again, observe the distinction that is made between those who were already entered on the pension list, and those whom it was expedient still to tempt. " GAIN (says the baron) Breckenridge and other writers who have influence, by promises which shall be faithfully fulfilled"— " *represent* these arguments with force to Wilkinson, La Cassagne and Sebastian, and you will produce the most glorious commotion." Promises were necessary to Breckenridge, because he had not yet been bribed. Nothing but exhortation was necessary to induce Wilkinson and Sebastian—promises were not necessary to them, because they had not only been made, but recognized, and they only wanted a little encouragement to appear what they really were. Sebastian has been convicted and degraded by his country, for having been at the time this letter was written in the pay of Spain. Does not the association of Wilkinson's name with his, in this confidential letter of instructions, prove an equality of guilt?

The baron de Carondelet did not however know the character of our general. He was willing to take all the money that could be offered, he was willing to carry on any correspondence, provided it could be kept secret, and while in a subordinate station he was willing to risk a place for which he knew he could obtain an indemnity. But the scene was now changed, he was at the head of the army, his legal emoluments were great, and his rapacity foresaw the means of increasing them. His secret correspondence had been suspected. The frequent visits of Power had occasioned jealousy—and the indiscreet communications of the Spanish officers, as we learn from himself, had excited more than attention to his conduct. He was not yet prepared openly to assume the Spanish uniform, and a secret correspondence had become dangerous. Power, therefore, did not fully succeed in the object of his mission. He however undertook it, and his answer to the baron's letter, (No. 40,) which is dated at Natchez, 4th June, 1797, contains, among other matter highly useful on this occasion, the following precious extract: " I will tell W. that the difficulty and danger of carrying money by land have prevented you from sending the 640 dollars. The ambition and policy of this general are a sure pledge to me that he will support *our plans* (which have always been *his own*) with all his influence, and we may rely on Nicholas, Sebastian, Innes, Murray, Clark, &c. and all, in a word, who are attached to Wilkinson, as well as those who are to compose the army of Clark." The whole of this letter deserves the serious attention of those who wish to form a correct judgment on this point. Mr. Power sat out soon after the date of this letter, and after a variety of adventure, the detail of which would be useless on this occasion, he arrived at Detroit, the head quarters of the American general, during his absence, and was treated by col. Strong, who had the temporary command, with the rigour which the public knowledge of his former errands seemed to merit. Advice of this visit was given to general Wilkinson, while on his way to Detroit. Here let a respectable witness, whom we have before heard, speak in his own language. " On our way down to Detroit, (says capt. Sterret, in his letter No. 12) as we entered the river St. Clair, we met a command of men with dispatches for the general. The same day, after having read his letters, he invited me to go on shore with him to shoot pigeons. While on shore, he told me that Mr. Thomas Power had arrived at Detroit in his absence, that colonel Strong, the commandant, acting under an order of major general Wayne's, had him in confinement—that he was apprehensive that he would have to send Mr. Power out of the country, although he knew him to be *an honest clever fellow, a man of talents, and one that had rendered him great services;* but unfortunately that Mr. P. was suspected as a spy, and the United States suspected him, general W. and at the same time quoting the old adage, that it was more criminal in some to look over the hedge, than in others to steal a hare, asking me " how I should like to take a trip to New Madrid with Mr. Power." I answered very well; he then enjoined secrecy on me. We arrived at Detroit before the middle of September, 1797, and found Mr. P. (as the general had stated) in confinement. He was immediately set at liberty, and a few days afterwards I dined with him at the general's table. A very short time after this (perhaps a day) I was sent for by the general, who informed me that he had other duty for me than that of escorting Mr. P. that capt. Shaumbourgh was selected for that command, that I must hold myself in readiness to proceed to Kentucky, there to procure money on bills, and pay the troops at Fort Massac and Fort Knox, at Vincennes, which order I obeyed and left Mr. P. at Detroit. In the beginning of November following, I met capt. Shaumbourgh at Fort Massac, on his return from N. Madrid, where he had delivered Mr. Power. He showed me his instructions from the general relative to Mr. P. in which capt. S. was ordered not to permit Mr. P. to enter any of our ports, and denied him the use of pen, ink, pencil, or paper, &c. ; on reading those instructions I expressed some surprise at this great precaution, when I knew that Mr. Power had travelled through that country on his way, and that he had his full liberty at Detroit. Capt. Shaumbourgh, laughing, said it was a *bore*."

Before I refer to the evidence of Mr. Power himself on this occasion, let me advert to one circumstance which must be conclusive. Independent of any light thrown on the subject by Mr. Power himself, it is clear, from a document which cannot be rejected, the original instructions from Carondelet, that Mr. Power was sent for the express purpose of making proposals to W. derogatory to his dignity, and inconsistent with his allegiance as a citizen and his duty as an officer. It is clear from the testimony of Mr. Sterret, and from the general's own letters, that he was well received, that he staid some days, and that he had several conferences with him. It is impossible not to suppose that in those conferences he complied with the instructions given by his superior, and that he had made the proposition which he had undertaken to do. What would have been the conduct of an honourable man, on receiving such a proposition? would he not have treated the corrupter and his agent with indignation and contempt, knowing, as he confessed to captain Sterret, that the suspicions of the President were excited—would he not, if they were groundless, have seized that opportunity of removing them, and by the punishment of the agent and the exposure of the principal have cleansed himself from the foul suspicions under which he laboured? But he dared not to do this—he felt himself too much in their power to come to those extremities, which were necessary to the establishment of his character—there were too many witnesses of his dishonour—too many letters evincive of his guilt; he therefore, to save appearance, did no more than he meditated before he saw Power— he sent him under feigned restraint to the very place to which he wished to go ; and he wrote him a letter which he thought would impose on the world, but which is, when fully considered, the strongest proof of his duplicity and collusion. The letter acknowledges a *first* nocturnal interview, in which the return of Power was insisted on by the general ; it expresses a perseverance in that determination, because Mr. Power *approached* him, as he says, in a *public* character, and on *national* business, which required a speedy answer ; that therefore he (Power) was no free agent, so as to elect the time or route of his return, but that he stood bound by motives of political import as well to Spain as to the United

States to communicate the object of his mission with all possible promptitude," &c. Is this, I ask, the language of integrity offended by the most humiliating and degrading propositions? Whoever does not see in it the proof of an attempt to cover a co-operation in treachery by the flimsey veil of affected severity, must be insensible to the force of evidence, and will be every day the dupe of knavery. Let this letter, (No. 42,) be examined in this view, and we shall have no doubt of the positive testimony of Mr. Power; (No. 43;) his details will however convince the most incredulous, and the manner in which every part of it is supported by the other evidence leaves no doubt of its veracity; and to avoid any subterfuge to be made from the alledged frailty of memory, let it be remembered that this account was given at the time of the transaction, and is the original draft of a letter to governor Gayoso, giving the official account of Mr. Power's mission—one passage of it is characteristic : " The general received me coldly enough; in the first conference he broke out with saying to me very bitterly, ' we are ruined, sir, both you and myself, without receiving any benefit from your voyage.' Afterwards he asked me whether I had brought the 640 dollars—[eternally these 640 dollars !]—he added, that the executive had given orders to the governor of the North-Western Territory to take me and send me to Philadelphia, and that there was no other resource left for me to escape, but to suffer myself to be conducted immediately under guard to Fort Massac, and from thence to New Madrid; and having informed him of the proposition of the baron, he proceeded to tell me that it was a chimerical project, and impossible to be executed; that the inhabitants of the western states, having obtained all they wished by the treaty, would form no other political or commercial connexion, and that now they had no other motive to separate themselves from the interests of the other states, although France and Spain had made them the most advantageous propositions; that the fermentation which had existed for four years was now subsided, &c. that Spain had now nothing else to do but to give complete effect to the treaty, *which had overturned all his plans, and rendered useless the work of more than ten years.*—And inasmuch as he had, as he said, destroyed his cyphers and all his correspondence with our government, and that his duty and his honour did not permit him to continue it; that the governor need not fear that he would abuse the confidence he had placed in him; finally, that Spain having ceded to the United States the territory of the Natchez, &c. it might *happen that he would be appointed governor of it, and that then opportunities would not be wanting for him to take measures that would be more efficacious to effect his political projects.* He complained much that the secret of his connexions with our government had been divulged through want of prudence on our part," &c. Here then we have the cause of this new prudery of the general's character. The project was now dangerous, and therefore he would not embark in it. He now bethought him of his *honour* and his *duty*, which had slept for 10 years. He now for the first time recollected what he owed to his country and the station in which he was placed. But this illumination of honour was but a momentary flash; it could not support him through a single conference, and in the very breath in which he abjures the ruinous connexion, he shows that fear, not principle, induced him to make the temporary abandonment; he complains that the treaty which secured the best interest of his country had ruined his projects—adverts to the jealousy of his government, and looks forward to the happy period, when the government of the Natchez would enable him to plot with more success the dismemberment of his country. A commentary on such evidence is unnecessary; it speaks at once to the understanding, and the prejudice must be rooted indeed that can resist its force.

In a letter from the baron de Carondelet to Mr. Power, dated 23d April, 1797, (No. 44,) is the following passage: " I have just written to W. and have given my letter to Mr. Nolan, a charming young man, whom I regard very highly (garcon charmant, et dont je fais le plus grand cas.) He has told me that he had a sure opportunity to convey it to him, and it is a long time since I have written to him, for want of an opportunity, and for fear of committing him (crainte de le compromettre.)" In all the intercourse between Wilkinson and the Spaniards, we find Mr. Nolan; this " child of his own" seems to have had as versatile talents as his adoptive father, and he is alternately engaged in the dark diplomacy or the contraband commerce of his employer. If the baron de Carondelet had nothing that was improper to write, why should he so long delay his communications for a safe opportunity, and whence the anxious fear of *committing his correspondent,* if the object of their correspondence were honourable or lawful?

Here I close the exhibition of the proofs on the subject of the bribes which were given by the Spanish government, and the corruption which they produced. I close it, as will be remarked, without any reference to my personal knowledge of the general outline of Wilkinson's plan, and to his unequivocal confession, as detailed in my affidavit laid before congress. It is not for me to weigh the credit which that declaration deserves. I annex it, however, (No. 45,) that it may be scrutinised and re-examined, and that it may be compared with the other proofs; and I then leave it to my country to decide this important question between us. I ought to remark, that in stating the sum taken round by Collins, I mention eleven thousand dollars or upwards. My information of the sum came from Collins, who, I suppose, must have received the whole sum, and afterwards divided it with Owens, as the two together form a sum upwards of 11,000 dollars, as stated in my position. If I were now to make a new declaration, or if I am ever called on before a proper tribunal to testify again on this subject, I could add many circumstances, which further recollection and a perusal of documents have brought to my remembrance, but my object, as I stated, is to show that the proof, independent of my own assertion, is sufficient to have borne down my adversary, and to support my reputation for veracity. One circumstance, however, in my own justification I ought to notice. In my deposition I state, that the general's explicit confession took place in October 1798, at Loftus's Heights, where I had passed three days and nights in *his tent*. Feeling how deeply this evidence would affect him, it was necessary to throw doubts on some circumstance which I had detailed, thereby to weaken the whole. He has therefore denied that I was with him for three days—he has denied that I was at his tent, because he says he was then not encamped, but slept in his boat. (No. 46.) If I had been mistaken in these points; if it should appear that instead of three days I had been there but one; and if the confession had been made in a boat; I believe it would have been as important as if whispered in a tent. But I was not mistaken, and if I prove clearly that I was not, his denial of these circumstances will be a persuasive proof that he feels the truth of my communication, since he strives to disprove it by denying circumstances which are proved to be true, and which he must have known to be true. The fact then of my stay with Wilkinson in 1798, and of his being then encamped, though otherwise trivial circumstances, become important in this inquiry.

On this subject then I refer,

First, to a letter, dated 2d November, 1798, from my kinsman Daniel Clark, who then lived at his plantation about three miles from the camp, and who died two years after it was written, in which he says, " I presume you will not get away from *the general for a day or two to come;* indeed the weather seems unfavourable for the prosecution of your journey to Natchez. His excellency proposes a jaunt to the Desert, to see his convalescents, *as soon as you depart.*"

 Second, the affidavit of William Miller, (No. 47.)
Third, that of capt Guion   (No. 48.)
Fourth, that of David Mackey, (No. 49.)
Fifth, a letter from col. John Clay, (No. 50.)
Sixth, the affidavit of Marselis, (No. 51.)

 All of these gentlemen have a perfect recollection of my having been there, and relate particular circumstances, which induce them to remember my being with the general in his *tent.* How miserably are men blinded by the confusion of guilt. They think they must deny something—they grope about in the dark, and as they are directed by chance, not judgment, in the selection of their means, they are frequently weapons of greater annoyance to themselves than their enemies. Thus, if Wilkinson had contented himself with denying the substance of the conversation between us, I could have procured no other evidence of that particular fact, as our conferences on the subject were not held in the presence of witnesses; but finding a person whose inaccurate recollection of places and dates would, he thought, throw a doubt on my testimony, he seizes it with eagerness, he denies my visit to him, he denies the place of his residence, and he puts it in my power unquestionably to prove, by other witnesses, what would otherwise have rested on my own assertion.

 In my deposition too I state that Wilkinson desired me to propose the purchase of governor Gayoso's land, for the arrears of the pension still due to him. I have since discovered one of the general's letters which corroborates this proof; it is dated Loftus's Heights, 13th March, 1799, and contains, in reference to that subject, the following paragraph: " The *Mingo (a)* asks more than I can give for his dirty acres, therefore say not one word on that subject." This caution was wholly unnecessary, for, as I had stated in my deposition, I had refused to have any agency in his negotiation for land.

After these remarks I proceed to examine the general's means of defence against the great body of proof which has been offered. His first object was, to fortify himself by certificates of innocence—his second, to procure an inquiry by a court which he knew could not compel the attendance of witnesses— his last, and the most congenial to his disposition, to blacken the character of the witnesses against him. Let us examine separately each of these means, and see how they have succeeded. Never were attempts made with so much art as those by which the general endeavoured to support his sinking fame by the testimony of those, who had, in the service of their country, seduced him from the allegiance he owed to his own. His first address was to Mr. Power, who, then a subject and an officer of Spain, thought he would be abandoning the work at which he had so long laboured, if he suffered his proselyte to be disgraced, and deprived of that influence and

(a) This is an Indian word, meaning great chief, and is usually applied by Wilkinson to designate a governor.

command which he foresaw might be yet useful to his country. The general threw himself also on his compassion: Can you, was the substance of his address,—can *you*, Power, suffer me to be ruined on account of those very measures, into which, by your ministry, I have been led? A word from you will save me from destruction—sign a declaration of my innocence, which I may show to the president, and I shall retain his confidence, and we may yet see the success of our schemes. Moved by false pity, convinced by false reasoning, Power signed the evasive certificate that has been published with so much triumph. Short-sighted, guilty man!—you did not foresee that this success would be the cause of your ruin—that the haste with which you published a document, given to you for another purpose, would induce a disclosure of all the circumstances which it was so much your interest to conceal—a disclosure accompanied by so many irresistible proofs, that not an individual can doubt of its accuracy, and a detail of circumstances, which would otherwise have for ever been unknown—an exposition of documents, which but for this could never have been produced.

The use that was made of his certificate—the attempts to blacken his character, induced Mr. Power to come forward in support of his reputation, and his change of allegiance, and the resignation of his employment, enabled him to do it with propriety.

The next attempt was upon the compassion of governor Folch; the same arguments were probably addressed to him, that were so successfully employed with Power; and no one will require a stronger evidence of guilt, than the correspondence which is at last concluded and dressed up between them. Folch was not disposed to go further than he could with truth, though at the same time his certificate was to bear as near a resemblance to untruth (that is to say, to an assertion of the general's innocence) as could possibly be managed, without sliding into actual falsehood; for this purpose, the general asks boldly whether governor Folch knows or believes that he (W.) *is* (at the time he writes) commissioned or pensioned by Spain. Now mark the answer: First some common-place about the fraternity among those who embrace the profession of arms—then a most solemn asseveration of what nobody would be led to doubt, the period at which he arrived in the country, the intimacy in which he was with his uncle, governor Miro, and his being the most proper person to give a satisfactory answer to the general's quere. Let us now examine this answer—how satisfactory it is! Before we come to it, however, we are assured that it is barely possible that his uncle may have concealed the general's pension and commission from him; but that as neither the *one* nor the *other* is ever conferred without a patent, it is natural that he should have met, not only with the copy, but the original, as the archives have been under his care. After all this comes the important, the satisfactory answer, that is to operate, as he says, his correspondent's satisfaction, and the utter shame and confusion of his calumniators. What is it?—that he has never seen any warrant for the pension, or any record of the commission? that his uncle never told him they had been granted? that he does not believe in their existence? No: but he *asseverates* most solemnly, on his sacred *word of honour*, that no such document, nor any other paper tending to substantiate such assertions, *exists in the records in his possession*. And with this general Wilkinson is perfectly satisfied! This he thinks ought to satisfy his country. What, because governor Folch declares that the records of his guilt do not remain in his archives—when they may have been taken to the Havanna instead of Pensacola—when Folch himself may have removed them while he was writing his letter, to make it consistent with *literal* truth. Because this is asseverated upon his sacred honour, all clamour is to cease—Wilkinson is a persecuted man. There is no record of his guilt at Pensacola—he is therefore innocent. There is no commission in the archives of Baton Rouge—therefore he must be calumniated. Governor Folch asserts it on his honour—and therefore his enemies ought to be covered with confusion. There is, however, an air of irony in this letter that must have deeply mortified the general, if he could feel mortification. If this assertion, says he (to wit, that he had not then got the record) will not erase the impressions of weak minds against you, [they must have been very weak if it had,] you are to comfort yourself (with what?) with the recollection that you *are a soldier*, and with the approbation of your *unsullied conscience.*—What bitter, what cutting reproach! what a sarcastic sneer! What! to him who had betrayed his professional trust, and received the hire of infamy! the man, who, when solemnly appealed to for his exculpation, answers one inquiry by an insulting equivocation—passes the other over in silence—and has the cruelty to talk to him of an *unsullied conscience*, and to remind him of the honour of a profession, which he had tarnished by his treachery. These documents *(a)* are published by the general; let them be carefully examined, and I am persuaded that every reader will discover the evident instances of evasion which I have pointed out.

The general was not yet, however, discouraged from further attempts of this nature. His next application was to another Spanish governor, who did not take the pains that governor Folch did to save appearances. Mr. Salcedo passing through Philadelphia, to go to the government of Texas, the general thought it a good opportunity for an experiment: If Mr. Salcedo could be prevailed on to give a certificate of exculpation, it was well; if his answer was unsatisfactory, it might be suppressed. Thus reasoned the general, but he reasoned wrong; the answer was very unsatisfactory, and he could not suppress it. They were published in the Philadelphia Gazette, and the copies (No. 52) can be proved to be authentic. The queries are first pointed to Mr. Salcedo's means of information in the office of Don Andreas Armesto, in '95, '96, and '97; 2d, to the receipt of the 9640 dollars by Power, or any other money or pension to gen. W.; 3d, whether he

(a) See the papers in Note No. 1.

would not probably have known such payments had they been made? 4th, whether Power or myself had access to the archives, and what were our characters? 5th, a prayer for general information that may be useful, and, particularly, to know in what estimation W. was held by the officers of his catholic majesty.

Mark the answer.

" Governor Salcedo *cannot and ought not* to answer the foregoing queries, excepting that part which relates to the character and conduct of Mr. Daniel Clark, and hereby declares that this gentleman was universally known at all times in Louisiana as a zealous patriot of the United States, an upright man, and of the highest integrity both in his public and private affairs, always preferring the public good to his own interest."

What a dreadful rebuff is given to our inquirer by this blunt answer. Governor Salcedo cannot and ought not to answer any part of the foregoing queries, except that part which relates to Mr. Clark, and why? because he could only answer them by revealing the intrigues of his own nation, and exposing the citizens she had seduced from their allegiance. If he could have given an answer favourable to Wilkinson's views, he has shown that he could and would have done it. He has shown in my case, that when he can bear an honourable testimony in favour of innocence, he does it with pleasure. No principle stands in the way of giving exculpatory testimony. But duty prevents his answering any queries respecting Wilkinson. The conclusion is plain : he " ought not" to speak the truth, because it will expose an adherent, a pensioner of his nation, and he cannot speak any thing but the truth, if he answers at all. He is therefore silent, and this very silence is more convincing than the most energetic words.

Any other man but our hero would have been discouraged in pursuing this course of justification. He however persevered, and with the same success. The mental derangement ever attendant on guilt induces him to apply to Mr. Andrew Ellicott for some testimony in his favour. We have his answer, dated the 21st January, 1808. Let us see whether it contains a single expression, that may be construed into a presumption of innocence—this is his own testimony, and it is so important, that I lay it at once before the reader :

Lancaster, Jan. 21*st,* 1808.
Sir,

IN reply to your favour of 16th, I assure you, that during my residence in our southern country I do not recollect to have ever received a hint, that the late Mr. P. Nolan was concerned in any plans or intrigues injurious to the United States. On the contrary, in all our private and confidential conversations, he appeared strongly attached to the interest and welfare of our country.

With that candour which is due from one gentleman to another, I shall relate the whole of my agency in the business to which you allude. Mr. Eppes's resolution in some measure removes the injunction of secrecy.

Before I left Philadelphia in the year 1796, as commissioner on behalf of the U. States to carry into effect our treaty with Spain, president Washington communicated to me, in the most confidential manner possible, that *suspicions* had been signified to him of certain citizens of the U. States improperly connecting themselves with the Spanish government, among whom you were particularly noticed. He thought it a business of so much importance, both to the honour and safety of the country, as to merit a thorough, though private investigation, and directed me to pay a strict attention to that subject.

On my arrival at Cincinnati, it was hinted to me that you had had several interviews, (some of them private,) with a Spanish agent, and who it was asserted had brought a considerable sum of money into Kentucky. This information appeared to me at that time to merit so little attention, that I never communicated it to our government. Immediately on my arrival at Natchez, I heard the common reports of the time from Green, Hutchins and others;—they never had any influence on my mind. The doubts and suspicions of colonel Bruin and the late Daniel Clark made some impression, but never so much as to be the subject of a communication. About the latter end of May, or the beginning of June, in the year 1797, I was minutely informed of the mission of Mr. Power to the states of Kentucky and Tennessee—the object of the mission, with the proposition he would make to those states to induce a separation from the Union, and that he was instructed by the baron de Carondelet not to *return* without having an *interview* with *you*. His being so often detained and examined in the states above mentioned, was owing to letters which I had forwarded to some confidential friends for that purpose. Mr. Power left Natchez, to effect the object of his mission, on the 5th of June, 1797, which I believe is the date of my communication to the department of state on that subject. In October, 1797, I received (and probably) from the same source, the outlines of a plan for dismembering the United States, in which your name is mentioned as one of the principals. That the correspondence between yourself and the officers of his catholic majesty was decyphered, by the aid of a pocket dictionary. This circumstance, I think, is mentioned in my communication *(a)* to the department of state on that subject, bearing date the 14th day of November, 1797.

In the beginning of November, 1798, a confidential letter of governor Gayoso fell into my hands for a short time : in that letter you, with several others, was mentioned, as having been in the interest and pay of Spain. The interesting parts of that letter were reduced to cypher, and accompanied my dispatches of the 8th of the month above mentioned. The original is, I presume, in the hands of either D. Clark or T. Power.

About the 16th of October, 1799, capt. Portel, who then commanded at Apalachy, informed me that at New Madrid, in the year 1796, he put on board a

(a) This communication is in cypher.

boat, under the direction of Mr. T. Power, 9640 dollars for your use. I questioned him frequently whether this money was not on account of some mercantile transaction; he declared it was not. He likewise mentioned several other gentlemen, who received money from the Spanish government by the same conveyance, and assured me that they were considered as pensioners by the officers of his catholic majesty. I entered the 9640 dollars on a piece of paper, (now in my possession,) and handed it to capt. Portel, who told me it was correct.

Thus far is one side of the picture. Let us now take a view of the other. So far as your conduct in that country, while we were both employed in it, came under my observation, it was perfectly correct, and such as I should expect from a gentleman and a friend of his country, and is mentioned with eulogium in several of my communications to the department of state.

I am, Sir, &c.

(Signed)   ANDREW ELLICOTT.
Gen. JAMES WILKINSON.

This application was made to Mr. Ellicott at the time the court of inquiry was sitting at Washington. Was his answer communicated to them? I believe not. Had the witness contented himself with presenting the favourable " side of the picture," had he merely stated that the general's conduct, " as far as it came under his observation, was unexceptionable," his testimony would have been blazoned to the world. But Mr. Ellicott felt too deeply the duty of a conscientious witness. In telling the truth, he felt himself bound to tell the whole. The rank of the applicant, his favour with the government, could not induce him to pass over in silence those circumstances which in his opinion marked the general's conduct with suspicion, and had excited those of his government—he has detailed them, and in every point they corroborate the testimony of Mr. Power, and coincide with the other public facts I have laid before the public. The " SUSPICIONS OF WASHINGTON ARE WIDE AWAKE," says Wilkinson, in his cypher letter to Gayoso. " President Washington communicated to me," says Mr. Ellicott, " that SUSPICIONS had been signified to him of certain citizens of the United States improperly connecting themselves with the Spanish government, AMONG WHOM YOU [Wilkinson] WERE PARTICULARLY NOTICED." Again, compare the hints which Mr. Ellicott says he received at the time of Mr. Power's *frequent and private interviews with the general*, the *minute information* he received in May or June, 1797, of his mission to Kentucky and Tennessee, his orders from the baron not to return without an interview with Wilkinson, the impediments he met with, occasioned by the active patriotism of Mr. Ellicott, the confidential letter he perused from Gayoso, the *pocket dictionary* cypher, and the communication of Mr. Portel—compare these with the testimony of Mr. Power, remark the coincidence of dates and other circumstances—reflect that this proof could not have been obtained but by the agency of Wilkinson himself—and then adore that Providence, which thus leads guilt to produce evidence for its own conviction.

All these attempts at exculpation proving abortive, the accusation appearing in a most respectable form, something was necessary to satisfy the public mind—an investigation of some sort must be had; and one of that species was resorted to, which offered the greatest facilities to his acquittal: a military court of inquiry must be composed of men intimately connected with the general, and in some degree under his controul, while the want of a compulsory process to procure the attendance of witnesses, it was foreseen, would deprive the prosecution of the most material evidence in its support.

The result of this inquiry, without intending any reflection on the gentlemen who composed the court, was such as might have been expected. Their sentence expressly states that they had no evidence of the receipt of any money from the Spanish government, but the copy of an account current presented by him, (W.) together with several letters from Nolan. The court therefore could give no other sentence than the one they have signed, that there was no evidence (meaning, I suppose, that none had been laid before them) of the general's having received a pension or money for corrupt purposes from the Spanish government. It is extraordinary, however, that none of the documents presented to the court, particularly this all-important account current, have ever been laid before the public. They are expressly referred to in the sentence, and as they were essential to the general's justification, as well as to that of the gentlemen, who acquitted him of all suspicion. Had he desired it, doubtless those vouchers would have been published. He has not desired it; and he has important reasons for the omission. Precision is dreadful to guilt; dates and sums are troublesome articles to get rid of; and it is much more convenient to say I have presented a satisfactory account, than to give the items of which it is composed. Though I have not had it in my power to examine the papers presented by general Wilkinson to the court, yet the administration may compare them with the evidence I now produce. If this be done, as I trust it will, without prejudice or partiality, I have not the slightest doubt that evidence may be drawn from them, which will confirm the truth of the charges I have made.

On the subject of this enquiry I need not enlarge; it has deceived nobody; it has not removed a single imputation of guilt; and its result was clearly foreseen from the moment of its institution.

It gave, however, to general Wilkinson, an opportunity of making and ushering into the world charges on my reputation of the most serious import, which it is one part of my present design to evince were false and malicious.

Let me remark, however, before I commence this investigation, on the singularity of the court's permitting witnesses to be examined to discredit a man, who did not appear as a witness before them, and to contradict testimony which they refused to admit, for I take it for granted that my evidence, as laid before the House of Representatives, and the documents I then produced, were not considered as being before the court, or they could never, with any decent regard to their reputation, have declared in their sentence that there was NO EVIDENCE of the general's having received money for corrupt purposes.

I am endeavoured to be discredited—

1st. By an attempt to shew that I continued an intimacy with Wilkinson, inconsistent with a knowledge of his guilt.

2d. That my evidence had been contradicted by other testimony.

3d. That I have before profaned the sanctity of an oath.

4th. That I was concerned in the conspiracy of Burr.

Under some one of these heads I believe all the public calumnies resorted to by general Wilkinson may be arranged. I shall examine and refute them in their order.

It is said, first—That my continuing on terms of intimacy with general Wilkinson, long after the period at which I pretend his guilt was known to me, is an evidence that I had no such knowledge. This argument, however, if it proves any thing, proves the homage which the general undesignedly pays to my character. It shews that he thinks it such as to make my associating with a man I knew to be guilty so improbable, as to outweigh the other strong positive testimony (I do not now speak of my own) against him. If my character were not unblemished, where is the improbability of my continuing on good terms with him after I knew of his corruption? He appeals, therefore, for his justification, to the purity of that character, which he tacitly acknowledges was unsullied, but which he now says has suddenly been forfeited, by a malicious attempt to injure his. *Nemo repente fuit turpissimus*, is an adage established by long experience; and I should present a singular exception to its truth, if, after passing through poverty and riches, and all the vicissitudes of life, with a reputation, to the excellence of which my most deadly enemy bears his reluctant testimony, I should at once have plunged into the depth of crime, where he wished to persuade the world I am sunk.

That my countrymen may fully appreciate both the charge and defence on this head, it will be necessary to state, that although I always had the sincerest attachment to the United States, and frequently pursued their interest to the utter disregard of my own, I could never claim the privileges of a citizen until the year 1798, when the establishment of the American government in the Missisippi Territory below Natches, and an oath of allegiance I then took, gave me a title I had endeavoured by previous services to merit, and which no subsequent conduct has tended to disgrace. Previous to this period, though I had an intimate knowledge of general Wilkinson's treasonable designs, I was under no particular obligation to reveal them. I resided in a Spanish territory, and, though not a subject of Spain, I was employed and trusted by the Spanish government, and I might have been excusable, if, under those circumstances, I should have regarded Wilkinson's project rather in the light of a revolution, favourable to the government under whose protection I lived, that as a rebellion against his own. Becoming an American citizen, however, I thought it my duty to discover whether this disgraceful connexion continued, and I then had the conversation with general Wilkinson at Loftus's Heights, which is detailed in my affidavit. *(a)* The result of this

(a) Since writing the part of this address which relates to the proof of the fact denied by the general, of his being *encamped* at Loftus's Heights, and of my stay with him there, I have discovered the following evidence among my uncle's papers, which establish that fact beyond the possibility of doubt. 1st. A letter from general Wilkinson to my uncle, dated " Head Quarters, Loftus's Heights *Camp*, October 23d, 1798," in which he says, " I am obliged by your favour of the morning, and congratulate you on the *arrival of your nephew*, to whom be pleased to present me in terms of affection. I shall look for the pleasure of taking you both by the hand *to-morrow*." Now then the general confesses he was *in camp* on the 23d of October, that I was in the neighbourhood, and that he expected me daily. 2d. A letter dated *Loftus's Heights*, Wednesday, 1st November, in which he says—" When Mr. Clark gets tired of us, I will call and treat you with a ride to the desert." Here then he confesses I was with him on the 1st of November. And on the 5th of November, by a letter, also dated *Camp* Loftus's Heights, he says—" Well, my dear sir, Mr. Clark is off with my courier." Now then we have my stay of several days at his camp fully proved, under the hand of the very man, who has procured an affidavit to prove that I only remained a day with him, and that he then had no camp. In addition to this, I find a letter of my own to my uncle, dated the 3d November, in which I announce my intention of leaving camp on

was, as I have stated, an acknowledgment of the guilt which he knew I was before acquainted with; but an assurance that the disgraceful connexion should be broken off, an assurance to which I gave credit, and for several years from that period considered him as totally disengaged from the treasonable engagements into which he had entered. Perhaps it was wrong to yield this ready credence to the professions of a man, whose conduct ought to have convinced me that he wanted principle; but when the general's insinuating manners and my comparative youth are considered, it will not I believe be imputed to me as a crime sufficient to destroy my credit, that I should continue with him on terms of civility, for really all the letters which he has adduced amount to no more. At any rate, I feel it as a fault, and I am sure it has been one of the greatest misfortunes of my life, ever to have been numbered among his friends, or even acquainted; but if society in error or misfortune could console me, I should find comfort in the number and the rank of those, who will soon have as much reason as I have had to regret the countenance and support they have afforded him.

It is next said, that my evidence has been contradicted by other testimony. I have anticipated the answer to one point, which I understand has been much relied on by the general and his friends, viz. the encampment, and my stay at Loftus's Heights.

the next day. All these original documents are lodged, with those contained in the Appendix, in the hands of the person mentioned in the advertisement prefixed to this work.

My conversation relative to the 10,000 dollars laid out for sugar at New Orleans is also adduced as conclusive proof, that my deposition was not founded in fact. But how futile is this objection! Because I told Mr. Smith and Mr. Alston that I was then convinced gen. Wilkinson had not received this particular sum of money in the year 1804, is it conclusive evidence that I am not to be believed, when I say on oath that he had received other sums in 1796? Let it be remembered, that I had not charged general W. with the corrupt receipt of this 10,000 dollars; and even now, tho' I firmly believe the fact, yet I have, as I before stated, no legal evidence on which to ground the charge. The truth is, that in the spring or summer of 1804, after general Wilkinson's departure from New Orleans, on my return from a visit to the country, I was informed by Dr. Watkins, who was then in the confidence of Gov. Claiborne, that general Wilkinson had purchased a cargo of sugar for 10,000 dollars; that it was suspected this money had been received from the Spaniards; and that Gov. Claiborne was desirous of investigating the business, that he might communicate it to the government of the United States. Relying on Wilkinson's assurances to me that the Spanish connection was dropped, and supposing that I should have heard something of it from the officers of that nation then in New Orleans (if the fact had existed) I expressed my disbelief of the report. But Dr. Watkins having resumed the subject to me, I offered to investigate it, on condition, that if the report were found to be groundless, I should be at liberty to communicate the information to general Wilkinson. I then went to the Intendant's, where I made enquiries, the result of which convinced me that no such sum had been paid. I reported this to Dr. Watkins and to Mr. Evan Jones, requesting Mr. Jones to communicate the circumstance to general Wilkinson.

At Washington, in the winter of 1806-7, some conversation took place between Mr. Alston and myself on this subject, occasioned by a letter which had been received from colonel Claiborne, of the Missisippi territory, removing the suspicions on this subject. I then freely expressed my opinion that the report was unfounded. Mr. Alston, however, having mentioned that he understood that this money had been received for tobacco, and that this way of accounting for it had come from gen. Smith, my suspicions were again excited; for I knew that all the tobacco accounts had been long before settled. I therefore called on general Smith, to know whether the receipt of the money was admitted by Wilkinson. He having denied any knowledge of the business, I concluded the report mentioned by Mr. Alston to be groundless, and repeated to general Smith what I have above stated respecting my enquiries at the Spanish treasury, and authorised him to mention it. This he construed into an assurance that Wilkinson had at no time received money from the Spaniards, and published something to that effect.

In May 1807 I learned, from a person in whom

I place implicit credit, that the Marquis de Cassa Calvo had informed him that 12,000, not 10,000, dollars had been paid by him (the Marquis) to general Wilkinson, at New Orleans, in the year 1804, while W. was commissioner for receiving the transfer of the province.

Being at Baltimore, on my way to Philadelphia, in October 1807, gen. Smith met me at the Coffee-house, and requested that I would give him a certificate of the conversation between us. I then particularly explained the error into which he had fallen, and refused the certificate. Hearing afterwards that the business had been represented in a manner I did not think correct, I called on general Smith, in company with Mr. White, of the Senate, to whose statement, (No. 53,) I refer, for the elucidation of this branch of the enquiry.

As the proceedings before the court of enquiry have never been fully published, I know not whether any other attempts were made to disprove any part of my testimony. These only have come to my knowledge. I hope they are properly repelled; and I shall meet, in like manner, any future disclosure of this nature that may be made.

My account of this transaction is moreover fully confirmed by the examinations of Mr. Harper and Mr. D. W. Coxe; the first taken at the request of the Judge Advocate, the other by the desire of Wilkinson himself. Both show the most perfect consistency in my declaration on this subject. Both these gentlemen being on terms of intimacy with me, and the latter my partner and most confidential friend, they were the most proper persons to resort to for testimony of my most unguarded conversation. It is now before the public, (NO. 54 and 55) and shews that my solemn official declaration is in perfect conformity to those made in the confidence of friendship. I call the attention of the reader particularly to the evidence of Mr. Coxe, as showing the progress of my opinion with respect to Wilkinson, and the nature of that intimacy with which I have been reproached. At any rate, if I could have been so lost to truth, as to assert the general innocence of Wilkinson, though it might weaken my evidence, it would not have destroyed the force of that proof which I now produce.

The boldest and most unprincipled attack upon my reputation is a charge, that in the year 1795 I had given a deposition, which the general now undertakes to assert was false. The proof, however, on which he relies to support this assertion so completely contradicts it, that I did not think it necessary to make any thing more than a denial of the charge, hoping that no one would give credit to so foul an aspersion, without weighing the proofs produced in its support, and knowing that such an examination must result in the conviction of my innocence. Further reflection, however, has taught me to believe that some more serious investigation on this point might be expected. I therefore intreat the attention of my fellow-citizens to the following statement, which will enable them to judge correctly on this point, so important to my reputation.

By the letter of the Spanish commercial laws, all trade is prohibited to her colonies, except it be carried on by natives, or naturalized residents. The extreme rigour of this rule defeated its execution, and the very existence of several of its colonies depended on its relaxation. This accordingly took place at New Orleans, particularly during the administration of the Baron de Carondelet. The first indulgence was granted, by extending the privilege to residents, altho' not naturalized. The second, by the officers of government contenting themselves with the simple declaration of any individual, commonly the consignee, that he was the owner of the vessel. This declaration was not made under oath, nor was it in most cases supported by any documents. Sometimes it was even accepted from a person, who, though not actually resident, had declared his intention of making a settlement in the country, or who had obtained a licence to introduce goods. It deceived nobody, but it furnished the officers of government with a very flimsy pretext for registering the vessel on their books as Spanish property, and thus preserving an apparent compliance with the law; but so little attention was paid to this formality, that the Governor and Intendant gave certificates that the vessel was American property, even while she stood on their Custom-house books as being owned by a resident. This is proved beyond contradiction by the certificates, (NO. 56, 57, and 58;)

the first granted in the very case now in question; the two last in that of the brig Charleston.

This being the state of things, a Mr. Wooster, an American, alledging that he intended to settle in New Orleans, obtained a permission to introduce a cargo of merchandize. This licence he transferred to John Blagge, John Jackson, and Leffert Lefferts, of New-York, in consideration, among other things, that he should have a passage for himself and family in the vessel that was to carry out the cargo. These gentlemen accordingly sent out the brig Grand Sachem, belonging to them, with a cargo, which arrived at New Orleans early in the year 1792, with Mr. Wooster and his family on board. The permit being in his name, the vessel and cargo were of course introduced as his; but the real owners had their supercargo, Mr. Matthias Nichols, on board, who had the sole charge of the adventure, Mr. Wooster having no manner of interest whatever, or having ever received any transfer, either real or covered, for the same.

Soon after his arrival Mr. Nichols became suspicious of the conduct of Wooster, apprehending that he might use the circumstance of the vessel's being reported at the Custom-house as his to some fraudulent purpose. In order to avoid this, Wooster was with some difficulty induced to pass a nominal sale to a resident merchant, which was accordingly effected to me. I knew that he had no title. I never paid any consideration, or received any interest; my only object in lending my name to the transaction being to defeat any fraudulent attempt that Wooster might, by the pressure of his circumstances, have been induced to make. The whole of this transaction was communicated to the Baron de Carondelet, and received his sanction. The vessel then returned to New-York, where she was purchased from Mes. Blagge, Jackson & Lefferts, by Mr. Jonathan Arnold. While she was his property, she made several voyages between New-York and New Orleans, and in 1794 sailed for the Havanna, with the Governor's lady and his suite on board, he prefering an *American vessel* (Spain being then at war with France) to a Spanish armed brig of 20 guns, then lying at his orders. On her return from the Havanna, the Grand Sachem sailed for Philadelphia, but was captured by a French privateer, called the Mountain, owned in part by a Monseur Lavergne, residing in Charleston. She was ordered to Charleston, but off the bar was re-captured by a British frigate. Arnold came to Charleston, and commenced a suit against the owners of the privateer, who pretended that the Grand Sachem was not the property of Arnold, but of some Spanish subject residing at New Orleans. While this suit was pending, I accidentally arrived at Charleston, and was called on as a witness. I then gave the testimony which has been made the foundation of this odious charge. It fortunately was reduced to writing, so that every word may be compared with the facts. The following is an exact copy :—

Daniel Clark sworn and examined in this cause.

I, Daniel Clark, do hereby solemnly swear that I was not ever, at any period, interested, either in whole nor in part, in the brig Grand Sachem, neither had I, nor any other person whatsoever, to the best of my knowledge, any title deed or transfer of her from Jonathan Arnold, or the former proprietors of said vessel; that I was only agent for her while in the port of New Orleans, where I received a commission for transacting her business from said Jonathan Arnold, whose sole property I know her to be; and I further swear that said Arnold had contracted to deliver in New Orleans in four months, to commence from the fifth day of July, 1794, the quantity of three thousand barrels of flour, at the rate of thirteen dollars one and an half rials per barrel, or twelve dollars free of duty, and if he exceeded the space of four months, he was to receive but eleven dollars and an half rial per barrel, or ten dollars free of duty, at which price captain Gideon Guyer, of Wilmington, in the state of Deleware, did in my presence propose to said Arnold to deliver to him, in New Orleans, the whole, or any part of the same, within the period of four months, which said Arnold would not agree to, from the persuasion, as he informed me, that he could himself import it cheaper; and the said Arnold is, to my particular knowledge, liable to be prosecuted for not complying with his contract.

Charleston, 24th January, 1795.

DANIEL CLARK.

Sworn 24th January, 1795, before me,

THOMAS HALL, Clerk, &c.

Daniel Clark's answers to interrogatories, administered to him by Mr. Peace in this cause.

Answer.—She never was represented as belonging to Spaniards, or naturalized subjects of Spain.

2d Answer.—Nor did Jonathan Arnold or any other person make any sale or transfer of the said brig Grand Sachem to me, or to any other person, to my knowledge and belief, since she was the property of the said Arnold; and I do not believe it was necessary for her to have been made over to any person, for the purpose of obtaining permission to trade to New Orleans as he did. Captain Baldwin cleared her, and entered her, and to my certain knowledge it was known to the governor and officers of government that she was American property, having myself carried and left with him, the governor, for examination, the register and president's sea letter, in order to induce him to let his lady go passenger in her as a neutral vessel.

3d Answer.—I do not remember any receipt was shewn to me, in which she is mentioned as my property. If any such receipt should exist, it must have been through mistake.

4th Answer.—With respect to colours, I never knew her to have any other than American; that when she went down the river Missisippi, with the governor and his lady on board, she wore American colours; she had a small Spanish jack on board, which might be for the purpose of making signals for pilots, as they are not obliged by Spanish laws to go on board of Spanish vessels without a Spanish signal, in token of amity. If she had not her name in her stern, and place she belonged to, I cannot account for what reason, as she ought to have had them, and I suppose she must have had them, as well as any other American vessel that frequents New Orleans.

DANIEL CLARK.

Sworn before me, 24th January, 1795.
THOMAS HALL, Clerk.

Now let this testimony be compared with the facts in the case, as proved by the annexed documents. Let it be scrupulously weighed, and all suspicion of the foul crime, which I blush even in my justification to see coupled with my name, all idea even of the slightest impropriety, will vanish, while the abortive attempt to discredit me will shew the desperate nature of that cause, which can only be supported by calumnies like these. Without any statement of the facts I have exhibited, it would naturally be asked, what motive could have induced a man in my situation to volunteer the commission of so detestable a crime? For even supposing that I had received an interest in 1792, it is clear, even without the proof I offer, that I had none when the vessel was lost. What motive then could induce a man of good character and respectable station in life wantonly to prostitute the one, and forfeit all title to the other. This reflexion would naturally lead to a close examination of the charge, and that must end in the persuasion of my innocence. But as unfortunately there are many, who, too indolent to examine for themselves, take up their opinions from the biassed representations of others, I have thought it my duty to draw their attention to the points of accusation, and show those on which I rely for defence.

1st. It is stated, that when I alledge in my affidavit that " neither I, nor any other person what-
" ever, to the best of my knowledge, had any ti-
" tle deed or transfer of the vessel *from Jonathan*
" *Arnold, or the former proprietor of the said ves-*
" *sel,*" I must have misstated the fact, because Wooster had before conveyed her to me. But by the testimony of Mr. Blagge, (NO. 59,) it appears that Mr. Wooster, the only person from whom it is pretended I had ever received a conveyance, never was a *proprietor* at all. Consequently, my testimony in this respect is perfectly correct, and I could have made no other, without violating the truth.

2d. That in my answer to the second interrogatory, I declare that " the (Grand Sachem) ne-
" ver was represented as belonging to Spaniards,
" or naturalized subjects of Spain," and that this is disproved by the production of the transfer to me. But I was neither a *Spaniard*, nor a *naturalized subject* of Spain. For the proof of this fact, I refer to the certificate of Don Andres Armesto, (NO. 60.) This gentleman was Secretary of the province, who must have known my relation to the government; and he states explicitly that I would never take the oath of allegiance, altho' it was frequently proposed to me. That the vessel never

was represented as Spanish appears too from the certificate, (NO. 56,) above referred to.

3d. That my answer to the second interrogatory denies that any sale was made by Arnold, or any *other person*, to me, *since* the brig was the property of Arnold. This is exactly according to the fact; for it appears, by the declaration of Mr. Blagge, that the vessel was not conveyed to Arnold until *long after* the date of Wooster's conveyance to me; which also appears by the register of the brig, given when the property was changed, and which bears date the 10th of January, 1793, (NO. 61.)

The other circumstance stated in my deposition, relative to the knowledge of the government, is proved by the certificate above referred to, (NO. 56,) and the testimony of Mr. Porter, (NO. 62;) and the assertion, that a transfer was not necessary to obtain the permission to trade, is evident, from her being permitted in the first instance to enter, without any nominal sale to Wooster. What, then, appears, from the whole of this transaction? Testimony given according to the exact and literal statement of facts. But if the *letter* of the fact has been adhered to, the spirit of the truth has been equally preserved; for I should think as contemptibly of the man who should shelter himself under the literal meaning of his words, while it was evidently his intention to convey an idea different from their strict import, as I would of the bold abandoned perjurer. To constitute this species of guilt, there must be deception. Upon whom could any have been intended? Not the government; they were fully apprized of the true character of the vessel. The owners? It was done with the consent of their agent, and for their benefit. The enemies of Spain? As little; no Spaniard having any interest, they could not complain either of my conduct or my declaration. Let it be remembered, that the whole value of this vessel was about three thousand dollars, and then determine what sum Mr. Arnold could have given, to induce me to come from New Orleans to Charleston, to perjure myself for his benefit.

The very transfer to me, upon which general Wilkinson relies, was before the court; and yet they determined in favour of Arnold, and the decision was affirmed by the Supreme Court of the United States. The case is reported by Mr. Dallas; and it is very extraordinary that a crime of this heinous nature should have escaped the attention of these tribunals, and should be discovered, after a period of thirteen years, from the very evidence which was then before both those Courts. Is it not evident, from the affirmance of the judgment in favour of Arnold, that there was no contradiction between my testimony and Wooster's deed; for I again repeat that this deed was produced on the trial, forms now a part of the record, and is not a hidden proof, now first starting up to convict me of falsehood.

The remaining charge is, that I was an associate of colonel Burr's in the treasonable or other illegal designs he had formed. This has assumed all the shapes which the ingenuity of its author could give. Editorial paragraphs, extracts of letters, communications from correspondents, have all been resorted to, in order to deceive the world into an opinion that there was a single person who could believe, and more than one that could assert, the charge. And if I should be content to sit down under the charge, what then? If it should be proved that I had been fool enough, to expose a large fortune and a respectable standing to certain destruction on an impracticable scheme, would that exonerate general Wilkinson from the charge of a treason totally unconnected with this plan? It might, indeed, gratify his vengeance, by reducing me to his own level in guilt, but it would by no means wipe off a single suspicion that must attach to his character. This was an imprudent as well as a groundless charge. Knowing my innocence, and his own guilt, the general should have reflected, that the demonstration of the one would naturally lead to the exposure of the other; and he ought to have trembled, lest the knowledge of his double treason should cap the climax of infamy, rendered more glaring from the AVOWED PERJURY by which he has attempted to conceal it. Such will be the result, and it will be made out to the satisfaction of the most incredulous.

As the accusation against me is totally unsupported by proof, I have the difficult task imposed on me of proving a negative; for if there be any, the slightest, proof of my being connected with col. Burr in his schemes, or even being acquainted with them, such proof has totally escaped me. I shall presently adduce, as an evidence in my favour, certain documents, which were published, I suppose, with the intention to injure me on this point.

My first acquaintance with col. Burr dates only as far back as June 1805, and that acquaintance was formed by a letter of introduction which he brought to me at New Orleans from general Wilkinson. He staid ten days or a fortnight at that place, and, as well to do honour to the recommendation he brought, as because I was pleased with his society, I shewed him the civilities usual on such occasions. In this I was not singular. He dined, I believe, with governor Claiborne, and I know received the greatest attentions from several of the principal inhabitants, and, on his departure, I lent him my horses to go as far as Natchez, with a servant to bring them back. About the end of June, in the same year, I concluded a contract with Mr. B. Bosch, for the delivery of a large cargo of goods, at my risk and expence, at La Vera Cruz. For this purpose I purchased a ship, called the Caroline, and prepared her for the voyage. On the 11th of September following I embarked in her, with a cargo amounting to 105,000 dollars, and sailed for La Vera Cruz. I remained there about two months, and then returned to New Orleans, leaving behind me about 56,000. In February, 1806, I made a second voyage to La Vera Cruz, with the double view of bringing back the funds before left there, and of disposing of the cargo of the ship Patty, which was to follow me in a few days with a cargo amounting to 55,000. I effected both these objects, but returned, leaving at La Vera Cruz about 40,000 dollars, which I did not receive until the next year. In these mercantile transactions, alone, I think may be found a full refutation of the charge of being concerned in any hostile designs against Mexico. A man conscious of such designs, and knowing that they were *suspected*, and perhaps *known* to the Spanish government, and that his name had been mentioned as connected in the scheme, would never, without a madness that has not been imputed to me, have placed so large a property, still less his life, within the power of the nation he was about to attack. To prove that I was apprised of this design being suspected by the Spaniards, I cite the letter written by me to general Wilkinson, and relied on by him as a proof of my understanding with Burr. I must remark of this, and the other letters addressed to W. that I kept no copy, and therefore must trust to the fidelity of those he has furnished or published. In the month of August, 1805, a short time previous to my first embarkation for La Vera Cruz, Mr. Thomas Power informed me that the Spanish government were much alarmed by the rumour of a projected invasion of their provinces, under col. Burr, and that I was mentioned as connected with him and gen. W. in the scheme. Knowing the falsity of this report, as respected myself, I hoped that it was equally unfounded as to the other persons mentioned. It did not therefore deter me from prosecut-

ing my voyage; but before I went, I thought it necessary to write to gen. Wilkinson, apprizing him of the report; which I did in the letter, (NO. 63.) Let this letter be examined, and if any inference of guilt can be drawn from it, I am ignorant of the force of language. It treats indeed too ludicrously the idea of general Wilkinson's being concerned in the project—but surely contains not the slightest indication of my being so myself. Besides, with whom does the general say I was connected? Not with himself surely. Yet the letter speaks in the same jocular style of the general's concern in the business as in that of Burr. The truth is, that the reports, though I could not credit them fully, had made some impression on me. I could not, without offending the gentlemen whose names had been mentioned, demand a serious explanation, and I then adopted the light familiar manner of treating the subject, that will be remarked in the letter. The manner in which the general treats this letter in his answer, (NO. 64,) where all he says on this subject is, " Not knowing whe-
" ther you have returned from Mexico or not, I
" have forborne to address you since the receipt
" of your land claims, and the *tale of a tub of*
" *Burr*, &c. &c." If I swell my publication with the whole of this and several other letters, though short passages only bear upon the case, it is to avoid the suspicion of any concealment, and to let the public judge, from the correspondence, the whole nature of my connexion with general Wilkinson.

The slight manner in which my information is mentioned by general Wilkinson, in his answer, is a complete refutation to any charge, of which he now endeavours to make the proof. If my letter is any evidence of guilt, why is the whole treated so lightly? The answer is plain; the general saw in it complete evidence that I was not engaged in HIS and Burr's plans, and he treats it thus lightly, that I might no longer pursue the enquiry, and perhaps develope his participation therein.

Soon after my return from my second voyage to La Vera Cruz, I found the rumours of col. Burr's project much more prevalent and alarming. A variety of circumstances induced me to give credit to them, and col. Bellechasse, then commanding the militia of the territory, had informed me of his having been solicited to join an association to undertake some enterprize against Mexico. I was then a Delegate to represent the territory in Congress. I was the owner of a very large real estate, and connected, very extensively, in commerce. A great proportion of my capital was, as I have shewn, and for a long time had been, in the Spanish dominions. Is there the slightest reason to believe that a man thus circumstanced would have risked an acknowledged fortune, an extensive commerce, have sacrificed friends, character and office, for a scheme, of which we can scarcely comprehend the madness and absurdity. Fortunately, however, I am not left to probabilities for support. My conduct was open, was known to numbers, and is proved by the depositions, (NO. 65, 66, 67,

68, and 69.) I was then about to depart the territory. I had reason to fear that several of my friends would suffer their ill opinion of the governor, and the idea we had all formed of his want of capacity, to prevent their giving that support to the government which the times might demand. I therefore assembled several of the most influential among them—the commandant of the militia, several members of the legislature, the clerk of the legislative council, and the captain of the port.—I entreated them to forget their prejudices, and sacrifice their personal feelings towards the governor, and to render government every support in their power for its defence. All these gentlemen have attested these facts, with others of a like nature, and I beg the reader to refer to their depositions.

It seems to have been a part of col. Burr's policy, now universally acknowledged, to mention or insinuate that persons, who were supposed to have influence, were concerned in his plans, for the purpose of impressing his hearers with an high idea of his resources. With this view, it appears that he spoke in Kentucky of drawing upon me for large sums of money. My credit there, he knew, stood high, and that nothing would impress the public with a better idea of his fiscal operations, than a persuasion that I was his banker. This report reached the ears of Mr. Graham, who was employed to collect all the information on this subject, and transmit it to the executive, and he faithfully detailed it, with the suspicions it excited. Finding, however, that they were without the least foundation, he readily, and without the slightest intimation on my part, voluntarily retracted them, and endeavoured to counteract the effect his former communication was calculated to produce. This appears by the following letter, addressed to me, when Mr. Graham was about to leave the territoy.

New Orleans, 13th May, 1807.

DEAR SIR,

I REGRET exceedingly that I have not had an opportunity of explaining to you in person what I am now about to put on paper. You will no doubt have heard that I was directed by government to transmit them from the western country any information I might be able to collect there, relative to the plans, resources, &c. of col. Burr. When in Lexington I was told by Mr. Alexander Parker and others of that place, that col. Burr had stated that he was authorised to draw to the amount of $200,000. In consequence I wrote to Mr. Madison, from Lexington, as follows:—" It is stated,
" with what truth I know not, that col. Burr was
" authorised to draw on Mr. Daniel Clark, of New
" Orleans, for $200,000. I believe it is certain
" that he proposed to draw on that gentleman, and
" finding that bills on Orleans could not be nego-
" ciated, said he would order his funds round to
" New York, and wrote accordingly to the house
" of Chew & Relf, who are the agents and partners
" of Mr. Clark." I took the earliest occasion after my arrival here to mention this subject to Mr.

Relf, and in consequence of the conversation I had with him, I wrote to Mr. Madison as follows:—
" Since my arrival here Mr. Relf (my friend Mr.
" Chew being absent) gives me the most positive
" and satisfactory assurances, that they never had
" any funds in their hands liable to the order of
" col. Burr. He urged me to look at Mr. Clark's
" account on their books, which I did, and I now
" take the earliest occasion to say that I saw no
" item in that account, which induced me to be-
" lieve that Mr. Clark has advanced any money to
" col. Burr. Mr. Alexander Parker, of Lexing-
" ton, told me that Burr had offered to draw on
" Mr. Clark; and col. Lynch mentioned, as I was
" told by Mr. Jordan and Mr. Hunt, that he had
" forwarded the letter to Chew & Relf from col.
" Burr, ordering his funds round to New York.
" The probability I think is, that this supposed
" letter was nothing more than a cover for Burr's
" communications for Bollman, which were direct-
" ed to the house of Chew & Relf, and delivered by
" them to gen. Wilkinson." I trust you will see, sir, from these extracts of my letters to Mr. Madison, that I have endeavoured faithfully to perform my duty, both to the government and to yourself. Should you consider any farther explanation necessary or desirable, a letter addressed to me, at the city of Washington, to the care of Daniel Brent, will probably reach me. I shall probably have the pleasure of seeing you next winter at the city; if not, I know not when we shall

meet, for I leave this country without the expectation of returning.

> With sentiments of great regard,
> I have the honour to be,
> Your most obedient servant,
> (Signed) JOHN GRAHAM.

The Hon. DANIEL CLARK.

It is extraordinary that the affidavit of the writer of this letter, relative to facts before its date, should be resorted to as evidence to confirm suspicions which he there so explicitly disavows. This affidavit has been relied on, and I therefore break the thread of my narrative to insert it, that it may be compared with the letter, and that the reader may perceive on what correct inferences the suspicions against me are endeavoured to be hung.

MR. GRAHAM'S EVIDENCE.

[*Interrogated by general Wilkinson.*]

Quest. DID Daniel Clark, of New Orleans, ever acknowledge, as a communication from himself, the paper now produced by you from the Department of State, endorsed " History of the " trade of Louisiana," an extract of which was published in the President's Message of the — day of January, 1808 ?

Answ. Mr. Clark once asked for that paper ; he had it in his hands, and spoke of it as one transmitted by himself; he mentioned that it was in the hand-writing of Mr. Chew, his clerk.

Quest. What conversation have you ever had with the said Daniel Clark concerning a Mexican expedition, or Burr's conspiracy?

Answ. There have some communications passed between Mr. Clark and myself, which I would not wish, without an indispensable necessity, to make public, on account of their bearing upon some delicate points in relation to a foreign nation. I will, however, relate the substance of what passed, and leave it to the discretion of the Court and the Judge-Advocate to decide, whether it would necessarily advance the purpose of justice to use it as evidence, and under what reserves and restrictions as to the publicity to be given to it.

In the winter of 1805-6, while I was acting as the Secretary of the Orleans Territory, a gentleman of New Orleans informed me that Mr. Daniel Clark, of that city, had some important information, which he wished to communicate to the government, but which he did not choose to communicate through governor Claiborne. This produced an acquaintance between Mr. Clark and myself. He gave me some papers, extracts of which I copied, and sent to the Secretary of State. These papers related to the affairs of Mexico, and gave rise to a conversation about that country.

Quest. Of what did those papers principally consist?

Answ. That is a part of the subject, which, I confess, I could have wished in particular not to speak of, as it might be disagreeable to Mr. Clark to have it known to the Spanish government he had been engaged in making such observations, while passing through their territory, as these papers seemed to indicate. I will, however, not hesitate to submit it to the discretion of the Court, upon the principles before mentioned.

Among these papers were estimates of the military force of the country, both the regulars and the militia, particularly of the garrison towns between Vera Cruz and Mexico; also of the naval force at Vera Cruz. Mr. Clark, at the same time, showed me the Baron Humbold's statistical tables, in the Spanish language.

Quest. Had Mr. Clark then lately returned from a journey through the Spanish provinces?

Answ. I understood he had lately returned from Vera Cruz. I was induced, by the apparent probability of a war with Spain, and by belief that Mr. Clark's acquaintance with the situation of the country would enable him to give important information on the subject, to make several enquiries of Mr. Clark concerning Mexico. He was of opinion that it might be invaded, with every prospect of success. I asked him, whether, if the United States should undertake the invasion, he would bear a part? He evinced an unwillingness to have any thing to do with an expedition carried on by government, but expressed himself willing to join in such an enterprize, undertaken and carried on by individuals. He said, all they would want would be the permission, not the aid, of government; that they would cut off all communication with the country they left, and establish a new empire of their own. He mentioned, hypothetically, addressing himself to me—Now suppose such a person as yourself should join in the expedition, you might be made a duke? I answered, that my republican notions would not allow me to aspire to any such situation, and that I would have nothing to do with any expedition not conducted by the government. Here the conversation on the subject ended. He asked several questions, what Burr was doing?—Col. Burr had been in New Orleans the summer preceding. I have endeavoured to give a faithful statement rather of the substance and effect of what passed, without pretending to a minute detail of every circumstance as it occurred, or of the precise language used. It did not strike me, at the time, as evidencing the real existence of any such design, but as being the wild talk of an eccentric restless man. Afterwards, however, when I was informed at Lexington (Kentucky) that Burr had drawn bills to a large amount on Mr. Clark at New Orleans, this circumstance combined itself in my mind with the preceding conversation, and appeared so suspicious, that I wrote to the Secretary of State the intelligence I received of the drawing of these bills. When I arrived at New Orleans, and found that no such bills had been taken up by Chew and Relf, I became uneasy at the apprehension of being instrumental in raising unjust suspicions against Mr. Clark, by my former communication to the Secretary of State, and I wrote a letter to Mr. Clark, at ——, informing him of the suspicious intelligence I had received at Lexington, of my proceeding thereupon, and assuring him of the satisfaction with which I had received, at New Orleans, information doing away those grounds of suspicion.

In May, 1807, Mr. Clark arrived at New Orleans. He took me one side, and said I would recollect he had formerly told me of the existence of the Mexican Society, and of Doctor Watkins being a member. I denied his ever telling me so, and expressed my utter astonishment at being charged with being a member. He insisted he had given me the information, but I was confident, and still am, that he never did. I recollect the surprize with which I first heard of the existence of the Mexican Society, which was subsequent to my former conversation with Mr. Clark. Blennerhasset was the first who told me of it. I proposed giving information of the charge made against him,—to which Mr. Clark seemed unwilling. I, however, did inform Doctor Watkins, who had some correspondence with Mr. Clark about it, but I do not know precisely how it ended. Mr. Clark at the same time remarked, that he would himself have nothing to do with the Association, from which I understood that he had been applied to.

Quest. Did not Aaron Burr visit New Orleans some time in the month of June, and leave there some time in the month of July, 1805? and was not Daniel Clark there at the same time?

Answ. Yes.

The first part of this deposition relates to a paper published in general Wilkinson's plain tale. (See Note NO. 1.) It is an extract from a memoir sent by me to Mr. Secretary Pickering, in the year 1798, on the trade of New Orleans with the country on the Ohio; and because in this paper I do not speak of the general's treason, he infers that I knew nothing of it. But I have a word or two of explanation to give on this point, which I believe will take away every argument to be drawn from it.

Shortly previous to this time I had been extremely active in protecting the Americans against the rapacity of the French privateers, and had used my influence with the Spanish government with so much effect in their favour, that though I was not then an American citizen, capt. Guion, the commander of the troops in the Missisippi territory, and Mr. Ellicott, the commissioner for establishing the boundary, wrote to governor Gayoso, requesting that I might be allowed to exercise the functions of Consul until one should be appointed by the President. This was granted. I prosecuted the owners of French privateers, put an end to their depredations in that quarter, and succeeded in obtaining from the Spanish government the reduction of duties on imports, in American vessels, from 21 per cent. on dry goods, and 26 per cent. on liquors, to 6 per cent. I thought it my duty not only to act, but to give information to the government which employed me; and I therefore wrote the memoir in question. Major (now col.) Freeman, of the American army, was then my guest, and was to be the bearer of this memoir.

My new official order induced me, at first, (I confess) to entertain the idea of inserting all I knew of the general's Spanish connexion. *I hinted this to col. Freeman; who told me, that he would deem it improper to take charge of any paper containing reflections on his commanding officer.* This, and the reflection that I was writing a mere history of the commerce of the Missisippi, and not an account of political crimes, induced me to be silent on the subject at that time; and the general's subsequent assurances, as detailed in my affidavit, which took place very soon after, prevented my mentioning the subject afterwards, until I had reason to believe that he continued the connexion which he then promised to break, and until I was called on by my country to make the disclosure.

The affidavit then states, that on my return from my first voyage to La Vera Cruz, in the winter of 1806, I communicated to Mr. Graham, then secretary of the territory, important information as to the military and naval force in Mexico; and also Baron Humbold's statistical views; and that the interview, in which this information was communicated, was sought by myself. Astonishing!— the country was supposed to be on the eve of a war with Spain, and I, with the most traiterous intentions, sent for the second officer in the territory (not being able to communicate with the first) and then and there wickedly gave him information, that might be of the greatest use to my country in the approaching contest. And this is the evidence that is to convict me of being engaged in an attempt to overturn the constitution. As to the cock and the bull story of the conquest of Mexico, and Mr. Graham's being made a duke, I am persuaded it will make as little impression on the public, as Mr. Graham confesses it did on him, and though the story of the bills made him revert to this circumstance, yet, when satisfied on this point, he tells us in his affidavit, that " he became uneasy at the " apprehension of being instrumental in raising " *unjust suspicions* against me, and that he had " written the letter above quoted, assuring me of " the satisfaction with which he had received at " New Orleans information *doing away those sus-* " *picions.*" As to the latter part of the deposition, all I can say is, that I have a most perfect recollection of having giving Mr. Graham the information therein referred to. Since he does not re-recollect it, it must have escaped his memory. But it is in no sort material, whether I gave the information to him or not. It is proved that I induced col. Bellechasse to give it; and that, so far from being engaged in the plan, I used all the influence I possessed to counteract and defeat it, as soon as it came to my knowledge. The last query is, whether Burr did not visit New Orleans in 1805, and whether I was not then there? If the affimative answer to this question is to imply guilt,

every part of the continent which he so rapidly visited in that year would be involved in it, and my immaculate accuser himself would scarcely escape suspicion; for I might in my turn ask,—Did not colonel Burr, in the year 1805, visit St. Louis, and was not general Wilkinson governor there?—Was he not received with distinction, and sent down with a military barge to New Orleans? Did not general Wilkinson correspond with colonel Burr, and was not that correspondence in cypher? But I anticipate another branch of my enquiry. I am now on the defensive, and will proceed to shew, that not only the general's witnesses, but the general himself, has attested my innocence of the charge he now makes, and that long after he must have known every thing he now pretends to know. On the 10th of December, 1806, he writes to me, from New Orleans, as follows:—
" I refer you to the bearer, Mr. Donaldson, for
" the interesting scenes which agitate our darling
" city and poor devoted Louisiana. I am here to
" defend her against revolution and pillage from
" a hand I have loved. Suspicion is afloat! and
" numbers are implicated. *Thank God, your advice*
" *to Bellechasse, if your character was not a suffi-*
" *cient guarantee, would vindicate you against any*
" *imputation.* At the time this letter was written general Wilkinson had received all those letters, on which he has since founded his charge—he had had the post office at his command—he had exercised an inquisitorial power in procuring evi-

dence—and yet he was so far from finding any against me, that he cites that of Mr. Bellechasse as being sufficient to vindicate me against any foul imputations. (See Note NO. 70.)

On the 8th day of January, 1807, as appears by the post-mark, he wrote a letter, without date or signature, directed, on the out side, to my partner, D. W. Coxe, at Philadelphia, but designed evidently for me, and directed, within, to D. C. Esq. This letter is in the hand-writing of Wilkinson, and is highly characteristic of the man. He wished to create an obligation towards him for supporting my character, which he falsely insinuates was implicated, knowing the facts I possessed against him, fearful that I might discover that he had broken the engagement, entered into at Loftus's Heights, of quitting his Spanish connexion, and that I might then feel myself at liberty to expose his guilt; and he therefore, while he acknowledges my innocence, wishes to make believe that he has been at some pains to support it.

" It is a fact," he says, " that our FOOL has
" written to his CONTEMPTIBLE FABRICATOR,
" that you had declared, if you had children,
" that you would teach them to curse the United
" States as soon as they were able to lisp, and
" he gives the Mayor and Gurley for authors.
" Cet Bete is at present up to the chin in folly
" and vanity. He cannot be supported much
" longer; for, Burr or no Burr, we shall have

" a revolt, if he is not removed speedily. The
" moment Bonaparte compromises with Great-
" Britain will be the signal for a general rising
" of the French and Spaniards; and if the Ame-
" ricans do not join, they will not oppose. Take
" care! Suspicion is abroad; but you have *a*
" *friend worth having.*" (See Note N0. 71.)

Let us stop here, to contemplate the finished perfidy of this character. At this moment he was cajoling Claiborne, and flattering Mr. Jefferson, by the most fulsome adulation; yet he calls one a *fool*, and the other *his contemptible fabricator*,—he was assuring the people of Orleans of his highest confidence and regard for the old inhabitants, yet he anonymously denounces them at the seat of government as malcontents, ready for insurrection. The truth is, he wanted Claiborne's place, and thought that, by exposing his imbecility, and raising a fear of war, he would secure it. I communicated this letter, as soon as it was received, to Mr. Madison, who appeared astonished at the duplicity and perfidy of the writer.

The next assurance which I received from him was dated the 20th of March, and also unsigned, tho' in his hand-writing. It is headed *(Confidential.)* and will be found in the Appendix, (N0. 72.) He there says,— " It has been
" hinted, that much pains have been employed
" to induce you to believe that general Wilkin-
" son is hostile to you, and even reported you.

" This is a stale device to augment the num-
" bers of a desperate party; for the *suggestion*
" *is without the shadow of foundation.*"
On the 24th May, in another letter, (NO. 73,) he declares, " that it shall be his peculiar duty, " pending the highly important developements " which are at issue, to watch over and defend " your fame."

Finally, in a letter dated 10th July, 1807, from Richmond, he says:——

Extract from a letter of James Wilkinson's, dated Washington, 10*th July*, 1807.

DEAR SIR,

THE papers will expose to you the proceedings had in the case of Burr, and the artifices of the little scoundrel to excuse himself by criminating me,—as if my sins would lessen his guilt.

It would seem that he has made very free with your name, as it appears, from sundry depositions, that he offered bills on you and Ogden, indifferently, declaring that you were one of his bankers. I, however, have the satisfaction to assure you, that I did not understand your name was mentioned to or by the Grand Jury, and where it has been uttered elsewhere, in my presence, I have put every injurious idea to ridicule.

The Hon. D. CLARK.

Hearing, however, that I had been subpœnaed

by colonel Burr, he became alarmed, and he wrote the letter, (NO. 74,) dated the 10th of October, 1807, from Richmond, of which he sent a duplicate in the note, (No. 75,) by lieutenant Murray, whom he directed to wait my arrival. In this communication it will be perceived how greatly the style is changed. Instead of testimonials of innocence, here are inuendoes of charges, of blind accusations, with which he endeavours to deter me from giving my testimony. My memoir to Mr. Pickering is resorted to as a certificate of his innocence; my *tale of a tub* letter, as he once called it, is now proof of my guilt.

After perusing this correspondence, it will be naturally asked, when did general Wilkinson become suspicious of Mr. Clark's Burrism? when was he convinced of his guilt? The answers may be taken from his own record. He had not a doubt of my innocence, until he believed I was about to testify against him, and he became fully persuaded of my guilt, the moment my duty obliged me to appear as his accuser.

I had forgotten, in this enquiry, to notice two letters which the general has thought fit to publish, as proof, I suppose, of my connexion with Mr. Burr. I have not been able to discover, after the closest attention, that they have the slightest bearing on the subject. I annex them, however, (NO. 76 and 77,) that the reader may exercise his ingenuity in the same way. The passages in the first, printed in italics, and capitals, are noticed in that way by the general. Why I know not—unless perhaps he would have it understood, that by the *thorny path* I had entered, and the *trouble I expected,* that I meant a confession of my being entered into the path of treason, and that I expected to be hanged. But what then means my request of his *advice to direct me?* If, indeed, I had intended to enter that path, I could not have applied to a better guide. But of what use would be " *the letters to members of Congress disposed to favour Louisiana,*" in such a journey? All comments on this are ridiculous. I was just setting out for Congress, to be the sole representative of an immense country in a high deliberative assembly, and I ask his advice and letters of recommendation. If this can be tortured into proof of treason, no one is innocent.

Here ends the proof against the several charges that have been made to invalidate my testimony, at least such as have come to my knowledge. As I live at a distance, others may be in circulation, which have never been communicated to me. This publication will produce enquiry. It will then become the interest of general Wilkinson to substantiate any charge he can make. Without seeking for celebrity, I may say that I court enquiry into my character, my morals, and every action of my life. I am conscious of none that will render me unworthy the friendship of good men; and with bad ones, I desire no further communication than that I have unfortunately had.

I come now to perform that part of my promise, which relates to gen. Wilkinson's connexion with col. Burr. Enough has already appeared before the public to convince every one, who will take the trouble of reflecting, that if the plan did not originate with Wilkinson, he was at least one of the chief conspirators. This plain, palpable evidence has been looked on with an indifference that has astonished me. That he betrayed his associates is but an equivocal merit, when we recollect the period at which his disclosure was made; and the forlorn situation of Burr's affairs will show us that it was the impracticability, not the wickedness of the scheme, that induced Wilkinson to abandon it. At any rate, though his disclosure might excuse him from punishment, it ought scarcely to have entitled him to confidence. The *King's evidence*, by hanging his accomplice, sometimes slips his own neck out of the halter, but I never yet heard that it gave him a claim to any office of profit or trust. Nor would it, I think, be deemed wise to put the city watch under the command of a robber, because he had quarrelled with and impeached the rest of the gang: A little attention to the subject will show this to be literally the predicament of the COMMANDER IN CHIEF of the American army.

We have seen, from a question put by general W. to Mr. Graham, that he thinks my being in New Orleans at the time Mr. Burr made a visit of ten days there is a cause of suspicion. What then shall we say to the closest intimacy for a series of years, to the warmest professions of confidence, and to the highest degree of friendship, if indeed such a sentiment can exist with such men? What shall we say to a confidential correspondence kept up in cypher? To visits paid at the distance of many thousand miles, and conferences procured by traversing a pathless wilderness? What shall we say to these? that they prove guilt? No; we will not be so unjust. The intimacy *might have* have existed without a communication of illegal designs,—the friendship *might* have had a purer basis, might itself account for the extraordinary interviews,—and the correspondence *might* have been on innocent subjects. Thus would a candid man reason, if these circumstances alone were urged as proofs of the charge. But when others are disclosed,—when this intimate friend speaks of the other as his associate in treason,—when part of the correspondence is discovered,—when it is confessed to be of a treasonable nature,—when the party prevaricates as to the subject of the frequent conferences, and denies a knowledge of designs which it can be proved were communicated to him,—then these circumstances, which it would have been unjust to urge before, become presumptions of the deepest guilt, presumptions sufficient in themselves to convict, unless destroyed by the fullest exculpation, but which, unhappily for the honour of our nation, are turned, by other incontrovertible evidence, into damning proofs.

The very long and very close intimacy between

general Wilkinson and Burr is not only proved, but admitted. We have seen that the former had engaged in a scheme for the separation of the western country from the United States, and I think the evidence I have adduced incontestibly proves, that he received the wages of a foreign power for his co-operation in *that* treason. At an interval of about ten years we find col. Burr engaged in a plan, of which the same dismemberment forms a principal feature. During the whole of this interval, the closest, the most mysterious intimacy subsists between the leaders of the two attempts. During the period in which it is acknowledged that the latter plan was in agitation, they correspond in cypher, they have secret interviews, and the intercourse is broken off precisely at the period when it was demonstrated that the scheme must fail. Then, and not till then, the general accuses his accomplice, and, by a kind of political pantomime, the wand of executive favour changes the conspirator into a saviour of his country. Are not these circumstances of strong presumption? Do they not require the fullest disclosure of the nature of the correspondence, of the basis of the intimacy, of the subject of the conferences? Yet what satisfaction on these interesting points has been given? Why, truly, the intimacy was the effect of pure friendship—the correspondence cannot be declared, without a breach of delicacy ; *(a)*—and the journies to Massac and to St.

(a) See the evidence of general W. as communicated to Congress, page 311, where he says :—" Between the period

Louis were undertaken by Burr, merely to assure general W. that he had a great project, which the general did not think proper to interrogate him about, though he says he afterwards wrote several letters, to draw from him the nature of his scheme.

The winter of 1804 was the last period of Mr. Burr's term of office as Vice-President. Wilkinson passed that winter with him at Washington, and in the spring the latter was named to the *first*, and the brother-in-law of the former to the *second*, office in the territory of Louisiana; and Burr himself was to proceed to the western country, furnished with letters of recommendation from gen. Wilkinson. [See gen. W.'s evidence, Pres. Mess. p. 309.]

On the 26th March, the 30th April, and the 19th of May, Burr writes three letters to Wilkinson (letters which would no doubt throw great light on this subject, but which the general's delicacy forbids him to produce) and having spent six weeks in the western country, on the 8th of June had an interview with general Wilkinson at fort Massac, on the Ohio. Here is the first period at

" of Mr. Burr's leaving St. Lewis [August, 1805] and May,
" 1806, I received six letters from him. I have said that
" those letters blended matters political with matters person-
" al. I have considered those letters *confidential ;* they were
" so received, and I will not expose them but in the last ex-
" tremity, without col. Burr's permission; but if I have that
" permission, I will do it now. I have asked it, and do again
" ask it. Those letters were of an ambiguous aspect, speak-
" ing of some enterprize, without designating any, and were
" calculated *to inculpate me,* should they be exposed."

which I have *positive* proof of the general's participation in Burr's plans. " Col. Burr," the general says in his evidence, " the *next day prose-* " *cuted his voyage to New Orleans.*" How long he staid I know not; but while there, the general furnished him with a letter of introduction to me, in the following words :

Massac, June 9th, 1805,

MY DEAR SIR,

THIS will be delivered to you by colonel Burr, whose worth you know well how to estimate. If the persecutions of a great and honourable man can give title to generous attentions, he has claims to all your civilities and all your services. You cannot oblige me more than by such conduct, and I pledge my life to you it will not be misapplied. To him I refer you for many things improper to letter, and which he will not say to any other.— I shall be at St. Lewis in two weeks, and if you were there we could open a mine, a commercial one at least. Let me hear from you—Farewell, do well, and believe me always your friend.

JA. WILKINSON.

DANIEL CLARK, ESQ.

What were *these things improper to letter,* for which I was *referred to col. Burr, and which he would not say to any other,* I can only tell from the public exposition that afterwards took place ; for col. Burr, during our short acquaintance, hazarded no proposition of an illegal or improper nature to me. Neither the tenor of my conversation, nor my circumstances, nor standing, could invite any confidence of this sort, and col. Burr has never been charged with dulness of perception on such points. The things, however, which it was improper to *letter*, to me are pretty plainly expressed in a communication made about the same time to general Adair. The letter is dated Rapids of Ohio, May 28th, 1805, 11 o'clock, and contains these expressions:—" I was to have introduced my friend " Burr to you, but in this I failed by accident. He " understands your merits, and *reckons* on you. " Prepare to meet me, and I will tell you *all*. We " must have *a peep* at the unknown world beyond " me."—(See Note N0. 78.) The letter to me I think fully proves that some secret plan of Burr's was known to Wilkinson in May, 1805. That to general Adair leaves no doubt on the subject. Immediately after this he went to St. Louis, where his very first act, before he had broken bread in the territory, was an endeavour to bring major Bruff into his plans. He tells him that he had a " *grand scheme*," that would " make the fortunes " of all concerned;" and though major Bruff's manner of receiving this overture put a stop to any further disclosure, yet we may judge of its nature, for it was introduced by a philippic against democracy, and the ingratitude of republican governments. [See President's Message to Congress, communicating the evidence in Burr's trial, page 81, & seq.] In the same year the general wrote another letter to colonel M'Kee, enquiring whether he " could not raise a corps of cavalry, " *to* " *follow his fortunes to Mexico.*" [Vide President's Message, page 22.] Now contrast this with the general's declaration, on oath, before the Grand Jury at Richmond, when he declared—" That he had an interview with Burr, at St. Louis, in which he [B.] stated that he had some great project in contemplation; but whether it was authorised by the government or not B. did not explain, nor did W. enquire; *that this was all the information he was possessed of, at that time, of B's designs;* that he was satisfied B. had had some *great project* in view, *but had not expressed what that project was*. [See Mr. Tazewell's evidence, President's Message, page 5.] Is this of itself probable, if it stood alone? that Burr should travel to St. Louis, to have a confidential conversation with W. and should only tell him that he had a grand project; that he should stop here; and that Wilkinson, the most intimate friend he had, should enquire no further; all this is almost incredible. But the general does not leave us to doubt on this subject. By the letter to me it appears, that on the 8th of June, near three months before B's visit to St. Louis, Wilkinson knew that he had a scheme, and knew enough of it, to know that it was *improper to letter*. In the same month of June he knew so much, as to assure general Adair that Burr " *reckoned*" on him—so much, as to promise him that he would tell him *all*—and so much, as even then to let out a part, which was a visit to the world *beyond* him. Yet he pretends [see Mr. Tazewell's Evidence] that he wrote several letters, to endeavour to discover his plans. He, however, defeats himself, for he acknowledges that he told Burr in one of them, " Miranda has taken the bread out of your mouth;" and " I shall be ready before you." How does the first of these expressions quadrate with an utter ignorance of the plan, or the second with his innocence of any participation in it? The truth is, that this letter had been seen by Mr. Swartwout; he had repeated these sentences to the Grand Jury; and the general was obliged to tax his ingenuity to account for them. As to the affected delicacy about producing the six letters written to him by Burr, it imposes on no one, any more than the offer to do it, if Burr would give him leave, or would set him the example, by producing the letter of 13th May. The pretence is too ridiculous. He knew that Burr could not consent to their production, without convicting himself of treason, and the same reason restrained Wilkinson; for he tells us, in the passage I have before quoted, that " *the* " *letters were calculated to inculpate him,* [W.] " *should they be exposed.*" What more do we want than this plain, this unequivocal confession. Can any one read this, and doubt his participation in all the projects, whatever they were, that were entertained by Burr? Could the magistrate, who communicated this testimony to Congress, have perused it, before he sent it in? If he had, would our gallant troops be still disgraced by ————.

What he writes to me in June, that Burr had

things to communicate, which it would be improper to commit to paper, he details in the same month a part, and promises to disclose the whole of those schemes to Adair. He solicits his cooperation, and assures him that Burr relies upon his assistance. He declares, upon oath, that he had received a number of letters which he will not produce, and which he confesses will inculpate him, if they are exposed.

And yet he dares, under the solemn sanction of an oath, to date his first suspicion of any plan from the time of col. Burr's visit at St. Louis in August, and has the hardihood to swear that, even then, all he knew of it was, that it was a *great project*, and that *this was all the information he was possessed of, at that time, of B.'s designs*. From the time of the visits to the general, in his government at St. Louis, the correspondence was briskly kept up. Six letters are acknowledged to have been received from Burr; and two, exclusive of that of the 13th May, to have been written to him; all in cypher, all of a nature *to inculpate the general*, if they were produced. Burr, during all this time, was busily employed in making his enlistments, and preparing for the execution of his plan, and yet the world are to believe that there was no connection between the two. But let us hasten to the developement, which the general, with " *the honour of a soldier and the fidelity of a* " *good citizen*," thought proper at length to make. If we before wanted conviction, it awaits us here. The nature of the communication he then received, the time at which he disclosed it, the manner of doing it, and the gross perjury and contradiction by which he has endeavoured to conceal his connexion, incontestibly prove it.

Let us first examine the nature of this communication. The following is Burr's letter, as decyphered by a member of the grand jury, at Richmond:

REAL.

YOUR letter, post-marked 13 *May, is received.* I have *at length* obtained funds, and have actually commenced; the *eastern (a)* detachments, from different points, and under different pretences, will rendezvous on Ohio on 1st November. Every thing internal and external favours *our* view—naval protection of England is secured. Truxtun is going to Jamaica, to arrange with the Admiral there, and will meet *us* at Missisippi;— England—a navy of the United States ready to join, and final orders are given to my friends and followers. It will be an host of choice spirits. Wilkinson shall be second to Burr only, and Wilkinson shall dictate the rank and promotion of his officers. Burr will proceed westward 1st August,

(a) In the copy *sworn to be true,* and afterwards *sworn to be false,* by gen. W. the word eastern is changed into *expedition;* and the stop taken from the word commenced, and placed after the word *expedition,* so as to read—" *have actu-*" *ally commenced the expedition; detachments,*" *&c.* And in the general's sworn copies, for he has made *two* at a considerable distance of time, all the passages and words marked in this in italics were purposely omitted by the general, to avoid, as he says, giving a handle to his enemies.

never to return; with him go his daughter and *grandson.* The husband will follow in October, with a corps of worthies. Send forthwith an intelligent and confidential friend, with whom Burr may confer; he shall return immediately, with further interesting details; this is essential to concert and harmony of movement. Send a list of all persons known to Wilkinson, westward of the mountains, who could be useful, with a note delineating their character. By your messenger send me four or five of the commissions of your officers, which you can borrow under any pretence you please; they shall be returned faithfully. Already *(a)* an order to the contractor to forward six months provisions to points you may name; this shall not be used until the last moment, and then under proper injunctions. *Our project,(b) my dear friend,* is brought to the point so long desired. I guarantee the result with my life and honour, with the lives, the honour and the fortunes of hun-

(a) " Already *an* order to the contractor," &c.—this is changed in the *sworn copy* to—" already *are* orders to the con- " tractor *given*"—this is somewhat obscure. If they were already given, how could he say in the same sentence— " *this shall not be used, until the last moment.*" It appears to me that *already* is, by some mistake in the cypher, used instead of *have ready.* The omission of the word *given,* in the original, and the substitution of *are* for *an,* which W. has adroitly supplied in the *sworn copy,* favours this conjecture. It is, however, only given as one. But it would then read—" have ready an order to the contractor," &c. which appears a more probable reading.

(b) " *Our project, my dear friend,* is, in the copy, reduced to " *the project.*"

dreds, the best blood of our country. Burr's plan of operation is, to move down rapidly from the Falls on the 15th November, with the first 500 or 1000 men in light boats, now constructing for that purpose, to be at Natchez between the 5th and 15th December; there to meet you; there to determine whether it will be expedient in the first instance to seize or pass by Baton Rouge. On receipt of this, send me an answer; draw on me for all expence. The people of the country which we are going to are prepared to receive us; their agents now with me say, that if we will protect their religion, and will not subject them to a foreign power, that in three weeks all will be settled. The gods invite *us* to glory and fortune; it remains to be seen whether we deserve the boon. The bearer of this goes express to you, he will hand a formal letter of introduction from me. He is a man of inviolable honour and perfect discretion, formed to execute rather than to project, yet capable of relating facts with fidelity, and incapable of relating them otherwise. He is thoroughly informed of the plans and intentions of ——, and will disclose to you as far as you enquire, and no further. He has imbibed a reverence for your character, and may be embarrassed in your presence; put him at ease, and he will satisfy you.

22d *July.*

Doctor Bollman, equally confidential, better informed on the subject, and more enlightened, will hand this duplicate.

29th *July.*

Can any man read this letter, and say that he thinks the person to whom it was addressed had no previous knowledge of the plan? Without such previous knowledge, the letter itself must have been unintelligible. Nor can it be considered as a proposal to seduce the general from his allegiance, because the disclosure which it makes is not of the plan, but of the means to effect it. Every thing relative to the project is spoken of as resting already in the knowledge of his correspondent; and it mentions only such details as were necessary still to be arranged, in order to ensure its success. Examine it more in detail. It begins with acknowledging the receipt of a letter, post-marked 13th May, and then immediately enters on the business—" I have at length obtained " funds, and have actually commenced." *Funds* for what? What is commenced? These would be the natural exclamations of a person who had been, as the general pretends he was, totally in the dark as to his correspondent's plans. From the wording of this letter is it not plain, that the want of funds had been the subject of former communication, and that the operations which were commenced related to an undertaking formerly agreed between them. *The Eastern* detachments are to rendezvous on the Ohio the 1st of November, to move down rapidly on the 15th, and to be at Natchez between the 5th and 15th December, to meet Wilkinson there, and then to determine—what? whether Wilkinson will join? whether he will, after he knows the plan, approve of it ? whether he will a second time turn traitor to his country, and apply those arms to her destruction, which were intrusted to him for her defence ? No ; all this is previously arranged. The only point to determine, after the junction, is whether it will be better to take Baton Rouge, or to pass it by. The *eastern detachment* is to proceed under Burr. Where is the *western* ? Under Wilkinson, under the very man who dares now to claim our admiration and gratitude for defeating this very scheme which he himself had planned. Again—" *Our project, my dear friend,* is brought " to the point long desired."—But I waste my time in comments on this document. Those who are not convinced, by a bare perusal, that this is the language of one accomplice to another, will never yield to any reasoning. Add to them the two letters received at the same time from Mr. Dayton, (See Notes 79, 80) and no doubt will remain that the commander in chief of the American army, if not the father of the project, was at least as deeply engaged in it as any of the others. Yet I admit that a letter written *to* another is not in itself complete evidence of guilt in the person to whom it is addressed. A contrary doctrine would put any innocent man in the power of the first villain, who chose to write to him in the style of an associate. To judge of the weight of such evidence, we must examine the previous connexion of the parties, the motives that might have actuated the writer, and, above all, the conduct of the party on receiving the communication. If we should in the prior correspondence discover no mystery, no evidence of a previous knowledge of the plan—if the writer could be supposed to have an interest in endeavouring to implicate his correspondent—and if the party receiving the proposition made a *full* and *immediate* disclosure, was guilty of no evasion or prevarication in his account of it—I confess that I should think it unjust on such evidence to condemn. Let us then fairly test the conduct of general Wilkinson by these rules.

1st. His previous knowledge of the plan. This may be fairly inferred from his engagement in a similar scheme under the Spanish government, and is fully proved by the mysterious correspondence, which is even now refused to be produced, by his acknowledgment, under oath, that it was calculated to implicate him, by his confession that he had written to Burr that he would be " *ready before* " *him.*" Ready for what?—Why for a plan, of which, according to general Wilkinson, he knew nothing. And, finally, by his own letters to me, to general Adair, and to colonel M'Kee.

2dly. What motive could Mr. Burr have had in writing such a letter, if the general were ignorant of his plans, and if he had not sanctioned them? Would a conspirator, who is generally supposed to have been a man not deficient in understanding, have made this disclosure to the commander of the army that was to oppose him, unless he had reason to count upon his assistance. I search in vain for some motive, that would have influenced either colonel Burr or Mr. Dayton to write those letters. I find none which can be made, consistent with the idea of innocence in their correspondent. I have heard of such stratagems, in order to render officers suspected by their commanders; but in those cases it was always contrived, that the paper should fall into the hands of the person whose suspicions it was intended to excite. Here, the letters were sent by a confidential messenger directly to the person to whom they were addressed. They were written, too, some time previous to that fixed for the commencement of the expedition. This discloses the time and place of rendezvous, the order of march, and the number of the forces; so that, unless they were assured of the general's co-operation, they put it completely in his power to destroy their scheme, and ruin its authors. The idea of this being a contrivance to implicate Wilkinson is therefore absurd.

Let us apply, however, our third and surest test. How was this proposition received? when was it disclosed? and has that disclosure been fully made, without any concealment or prevarication? It was received, he tells us, with the caution necessary to procure from the messenger a developement of the plan. [See the general's deposition, Note 81.] But, after obtaining this developement, *he writes to colonel Burr a letter, which he dispatched, but afterwards recalled.* This is an important feature in the transaction, and I therefore submit the evidence on which I assert it. In the report of Burr's trial communicated to Congress, page 209, there is the following passage:—

"*Mr. Wickham*" (to general Wilkinson.) " I think you said that you wrote to colonel Burr from Natchitoches." *General Wilkinson*—" You guess well; but if I am not mistaken, you got that information from Swartwout. *Q.* Did you write? *A.* I did. *Q.* What did you do with the letter? *A.* Destroyed it. *Q.* Did it go out of your hands? *A.* It did; it was sent to Natchez, to which place I *followed, recovered, and destroyed it.* I will give you my reasons for so doing. After writing, I received the letter from Mr. Donaldson, dated 30th of October, and conveying the information received from Myers Michael, which removed my doubts as to the extent of Mr. Burr's designs, and their sinister nature. *Mr. Wickham*, then I understand you to say that Mr. Donaldson gave you the first correct information. *A.* It excited very strong apprehensions in my mind, that some general and deep-rooted conspiracy had taken place above." This evidence is important, not only as it shews a continued correspondence with Burr, even after the general acknowledges that he had obtained a knowledge of his plans from the cyphered letter, and from Mr. Swartwout, but for a reason as important to the general, because it convicts him of direct perjury; for in his affidavit, (No. 81,) he directly asserts that Mr. Swartwout informed him he was to meet Burr the 20th of November, and requested him (W.) to write him, which (says the general) *I declined.*

What were the contents of this letter to colonel Burr, or by whom it was sent, we know not; but it is enough to convict him, that he carried on a correspondence after he had full conviction of his guilt; that he destroyed it after he had determined to turn state's evidence; and that he has tried, by perjury, to conceal it. This letter is a strong proof, too, that the interval between the 8th, when he received the communication from Burr, and the 21st, when he dispatched lieut. Smith, was spent in deliberating whether it would be most advantageous to betray his country or his accomplice. We shall presently see what inducements turned the scale in favour of duty.

He says, indeed, that he disclosed the plan to col. Cushing. I have no doubt of the fact; but what does this prove? he enjoined secrecy, *(a)* and he prevented his acting or making any discovery, until the general himself was determined. If that determination had been one of adhering to his treason with Burr, col. Cushing's knowledge of it could have been of no consequence, the mask must have been taken off, and all the world would have known as much as col. Cushing. Whereas, if he should find his associate's affairs desperate, and determine to betray him, then col. Cushing's testimony would, he thought, be useful, in order to prove that he had made the communication in time. It is observable here, too, that the general declares in his deposition, (Note NO. 81,) that *the*

(a) See colonel Cushing's deposition, page 233, President's Message.

moment *he decyphered the letter he put it into the hands of major Cushing*, and that by the general's examination before the court, as well as by col. Cushing's deposition, it appears that the letter was not fully decyphered at Natchitoches, and that he only told him of the contents, but did not put it in his hands at all. The delay of a whole fortnight, between the receipt of Mr. Burr's letter and general Wilkinson's first communication to the President, is a material circumstance in this enquiry. Burr had written that he was to rendezvous at the falls of the Ohio on the *first of November*, with a large force—Mr. Swartwout informs him that this force was to be employed in seizing on New Orleans as soon as it could descend. General Wilkinson receives this intelligence on the 8th of October, time enough to have put the governors of the states and territories on their guard, to have collected a force sufficient to disperse the rebels, or at least to impede their descent. Yet this immaculate saviour of his country eases his conscience by a secret confession to col. Cushing, and gives no kind of notice either to the governors of the states or territories, or to the President of the United States, until the 21st. Why this delay? plainly, to see whether Burr could execute his promise of collecting a force; plainly, to deliberate whether he should betray his associate or his country. Not indeed to determine which was the best, but which was the safest course, that he might have time to weigh accurately the legal profits of a return to duty against the illicit gains of treason. He did

weigh these, but neither honour, nor integrity, nor duty, nor any manly virtue of the soul, at all contributed to form his determination. The balance was nearly suspended until dastardly fear fell in, and made his treason kick the beam. Mr. Burr's movement about this time became extremely suspicious. Wilkinson knew that he was watched; he knew that the western states did not favour his views; he found that Burr overrated the strength of the *eastern detachments;* and therefore he thought it most prudent not to join him immediately with the *western*. Still, however, he had a hankering after the treason, and he acted in such a manner as to enable him to return to it, if Burr should succeed in obtaining an efficient force; for he does not, *even on the 21st of October, send to the President a copy of the cyphered letter*. Why did he withhold this? I have always thought that it was done to prevent his committing himself too much with Burr, whom circumstances might induce him afterwards to join; while the partial disclosure he had made would always be an evidence of his patriotism, if, as was then most probable, the enterprize should fail. I have never seen this letter of the 21st, but it was produced on the trial of Burr, and the following is an extract from it, contained in a question, put by Mr. Wickham to general W. [page 204 of the Pres. Mess. before quoted]—
" You say," in your letter to the President, " that
" you were not only *uninformed of the prime mover*
" *and ultimate objects of the daring enterprize, but*
" *you are ignorant of the foundation on which it*

" *rests, of the means by which it is to be supported,* " *and whether any immediate or collateral protec-* " *tion, internal or external, is expected.*"

Now, is it possible rationally to account for this communication otherwise than my supposing that so much was intended to be told, as would secure to himself the credit of an informer, and that every thing was concealed, that would materially injure his accomplice. A fortnight had intervened between the writing of this letter and the receipt of Burr's letter, accompanied by the explanations of Swartwout; a fortnight had elapsed since he had told Mr. Cushing,—" Yes, my friend, a " great number of individuals, possessing wealth, " popularity and talents, are at this moment asso-" ciated, for purposes inimical to the government " of the U. S. *Col. Burr is at their head.*"—" I " have discovered that the *object is treasonable,*" &c.—Yet he tells the President that he cannot discover either the prime mover or the ultimate objects of the daring enterprize ; that he is ignorant of the means by which it is to be supported, or whether any protection is *expected* from without or within. My distance from the records prevents my procuring a copy of this letter at large, but this extract, the only part of it I have seen, is an incontestible proof that his communication meant no more than to secure the pardon granted to an informer, in case the enterprize did not succeed, but not to place any impediment in the way of Burr's expedition. Why else did he pretend ignorance of the prime mover, of the internal and external resources, or of the objects of the enterprize, all which had been fully detailed both by the cypher letter and by Mr. Swartwout. Why did he not send a copy of that letter? Why was a paper, containing intelligence on which the fate of the Union depended, forwarded by only one conveyance? Why was it thirty-five days in reaching its destination, at the most favourable season of the year, when the usual course of the post from New Orleans, which is about the same distance, is only twenty-one days? Why was no notice given to any of the governors of the states and territories through which Burr must necessarily pass? and why was no other communication made to the President until three weeks afterwards (12th November)? Why was not a copy of Burr's letter sent *even then*? And why was this last dispatch confided to an old gentleman, who was, as it might have been foreseen, nearly two months on his journey? On an affair of this importance, surely the general might have been justified in adding the expence of half a dozen expresses to the millions which he squandered in his military movements and other preparations.

At length, on the 14th day of December, more than two months after the letter in cypher had been received, a copy was for the *first time* sent on to the President. Then it was reduced to a certainty that Burr must fail. He had collected no force, the country was alarmed, the western states and territories evinced their attachment to the Union. Burr, instead of opposing the military force of his country, was exercising his ingenuity in escaping the researches of the public prosecutors. Before this period every measure of the commander in chief was calculated to insure Burr's success, if he had come down in force, and to have executed that plan of *sham defence* which was *obliqued* to him by Bollman. He alarmed us with daily reports of the expected invasion from *above*, and yet he drew down all his force from the upper country, which is strong by nature, and where the most effectual opposition could have been made, to concentrate it in a town, situated in a plain, and totally without defence. He constructed a fort in the centre of that town, so situated, that it is impossible to fire a single gun without destroying an house. And he endeavours still more to weaken the upper country, by a requisition of all the militia to be sent to him at New Orleans. The firmness of Mr. Meade defeated him in this part of the project; but governor Claiborne, with more politeness, invested him with full power over the whole effective force of the territory, which he employed in the degrading drudgery of his illegal arrests. Burr, he said, would descend with two or three gun-boats; Wilkinson had four; and lest Burr should have too much trouble in taking them, they were distributed, at the distance of several leagues from each other, up the rivers. But the master stroke still remained. He had heard from Swartwout, as he tells us, that the intent was, to provide funds by the plunder of New Orleans, and transports, by the seizure of the shipping; he therefore persuaded Claiborne to agree to an embargo, and lest any of the ships, so necessary to this expedition, should sail, and carry away the money or merchandize which was to support it, no vessel of any description was suffered to depart. Here then every thing was prepared, if Burr could realize the hopes he so strongly expressed. If he could have descended with a competent force, he would have found not the least impediment to his progress. The upper country was deserted, Fort Adams dismantled, the gun-boats so stationed as to have been successively taken, and the farcical fortifications at New Orleans calculated only to awe the town, in case its citizens should have been inclined to resist the invader. He would have found the stores filled with merchandize, the money untouched in the vaults of the Bank, and a fine fleet of merchantmen waiting to convey him to his final destination. Wilkinson could soon have convinced him that all these dispositions were the effect of his fidelity to his engagements, and might have found much better excuses for the partial disclosures made to government, than he can now give to his country for these worse than equivocal arrangements. But Burr did not come down at the head of a military force; he became a wanderer, almost an outlaw and a convict; and his worthy associate, fearful of the same fate, became a *patriot*, a *faithful citizen*, an *honourable soldier*. Great God, what a profanation of the most sacred names!—We must hereafter invent some new terms to express our admiration of public worth—

these have been indelibly disgraced by their application. At this period, then, the copy of this letter was for the *first time* sent on to the seat of government. A copy did I say? No; it was not yet time—the general's patriotism had not yet attained so strong a growth, as to bear the shock it would receive from a full disclosure of the contents of that letter. He accordingly cut it, and scraped it, and distorted it, to his and his counsellor's fancy, and by suppressing a sentence here, altering a word there, and inserting one wherever he found it necessary, he thought it at last fitted to his purpose. He then copied it fair, and swore, by the HONOUR OF A SOLDIER and the HOLY EVANGELISTS OF ALMIGHTY GOD, that it " *substantially was as fair an inter-* " *pretation*" as he had been able to make. Is this true?—do you not slander him?—can this monstrous accusation be supported by proof?—if known to you, why did you not sooner disclose it to the government?—why have you suffered the President to disgrace himself and the nation, to dishonour the army, and endanger the safety of the people, by continuing in command a man capable of this conduct?

Alas! it is not to me alone that the confidence was made of the commission of this crime; it was stated to the government, it was recorded in the tribunals, it was proclaimed to the world! The evidence is not that of witnesses who might be prejudiced—of writings which might be forged—but it is contained in the open, unequivocal, unblushing confession of the party, and the testimony of the gentleman who advised the act. (See Notes NO. 82 and 83.) The words printed in italics in the letter are those, which were omitted by Wilkinson in the copies which he *twice* (once on the 14th January, before Mr. Carrick, and afterwards on the 26th of the same month, before Mr. Pollock) deliberately swore were *substantially as true interpretations as he could make.* The copy I have inserted above is taken from that laid before Congress by the foreman of the grand jury, who decyphered it. By comparing it with the one sworn to by Wilkinson, in his affidavit, (Note No. 81,) another material variation will be seen. In the beginning of the letter he says,—" I have obtained " funds, and have actually commenced. *The* " *eastern detachments,* from different points, will " rendezvous on Ohio." This mention of the *eastern detachments* would naturally lead to an enquiry, where the *western* detachments were. It was therefore necessary to employ the scraper and the pen, as well as the blotter ; this was ingeniously done ; the word *eastern* was changed into *expedition;* the place of the period was changed, and the sentence was made to read—" *I have actually com-* " *menced the expedition.* Detachments from dif- " *ferent points will rendezvous on Ohio,*" &c.

But it was not my object to convict Wilkinson of either perjury or forgery. It was to shew that his manner of making a disclosure of this letter, when at last he resolved to do it, was such as evinced a consciousness of guilt ; and the perjury, and the forgery, and the prevarication, are only the means which he employed to effect concealment.

I have now completed my design, which was, principally, to show that the testimony I gave could be supported by the strongest evidence, independent of my own—and to answer the calumnies which have been used to destroy my reputation. I dare hope that I have done this satisfactorily. I believe, that after reading these observations, and the proof that supports them, no one can entertain a doubt, either of the treasonable and corrupt connexion of Wilkinson with the Spaniards, or with the unprincipled, if not traiterous, designs of Burr. Let it be remembered, that the evidence I now produce is brought forward only by individual exertion. Let the high station, the actual means of oppression, and the great favour shewn to the accused, be considered, and it will, I believe, be acknowledged that many witnesses have been deterred by fear, or biassed by interest, to conceal their knowledge of facts important in this enquiry. As soon as one shall be instituted by the executive, these causes will cease to operate, and the fullest evidence may be obtained to corroborate that which I have given.

Before I conclude this address, I cannot but complain that I have been rather hardly dealt with by the President; first in the message to Congress of the 20th January, 1808, (Note No. 84.) In this he says, " A paper on the commerce of " Louisiana, bearing date the 18th of April, 1798, " is found in the office, supposed to have been

" communicated by Mr. Daniel Clark, of New
" Orleans, *then a subject of Spain,*" &c. The
paper alluded to in this message is the same that
is published by Wilkinson, in his " Plain Tale,"
(Note No. 1,) and was sent to Congress by the
President, for the same reason, I suppose, that it
was published by the general. I have shewn how
little this purpose is answered. But in making
this communication, I think justice, as well as
duty, would have required that all the evidence,
as well to corroborate, as that which it was supposed would impeach my testimony, should have
been sent, and, above all, that nothing should be
asserted as fact, which was not incontrovertibly
proved. A slight recurrence to the message will
shew how little attention has been paid to either of
these requisites. It is asserted that I was, at the
time I wrote that memoir on the trade of the Ohio,
a subject of Spain. I have shewn that this was
not the fact; but as it is important to me to leave
no doubt on this subject, I join the proofs (Notes
No. 85 and 86.) It remains to shew that my
situation, in that respect, was *not unknown to
Mr. Jefferson.* In 1802, when my nomination as
consul of the United States at New Orleans was
confirmed by the Senate, a commission was made
out, in which I was styled a subject of Spain.
On the receipt of it I waited on the President,
and explained to him my situation there. I had
never been a Spanish subject, but had been naturalized, as an American citizen, in the latter part
of the year 1798, at Natchez. In consequence

of this explanation, the commission was changed, and I received one, in which I was described as a citizen of the U. S. resident at New Orleans. A reference to the document (Note No. 87) will prove this fact. Again, the President says, " that " about a twelvemonth after he (Mr. J.) had come " to the administration of the government, I gave " some verbal information, and the letter of go- " vernor Gayoso, *addressed to myself.*" Now the letter from Gayoso was not addressed to me, but to my uncle.

The President too says, that I " forwarded to " the secretary of state other papers, *with* a re- " quest that, after perusal, they might be burnt." A reference to documents will prove how incorrect this statement is. The papers were communicated to Mr. Madison by letter, dated 8th March, 1803, an extract of which was sent to Congress on the 4th February, 1808. By this it appears that the package had been left with Mr. Morton, of New-York, on my departure for Europe, and that on my return I sent an order to Mr. Madison to receive them. In the letter inclosing this order, (Note No. 88,) it will be seen that I refer to a former conversation with the President, in which I had informed him, that in 1795, or 1796, negociations had been carried on with Spain by the inhabitants of the western country—that I put the government in a track to discover it—and that I offer to come on myself, if necessary, to elucidate them. I have kept no copy of this letter, but I have to complain, that the part of it has been suppressed, which stated my reasons for referring to the old Spanish conspiracy. These reasons were, that as the French were about to take possession of the country, I was extremely apprehensive they might find the clue of the old conspiracy, employ the same agents, revive the same intrigues, and, by their superior management, succeed better than the Spaniards had done. If this had been communicated, I think, instead of an officious interference to revive suspicions, which the President thinks ought to be forgotten, my letter would have appeared at least worthy of some notice. The French were then hourly expected—their genius for intrigue was known—and they had fixed their eyes on the *mountains*, as the natural boundary between the two countries, (See Note N0. 89) and openly spoke of the impossibility of remaining at peace with the U. S. Under these circumstances, I thought it necessary, by my letter before referred to, (Note N0. 88,) to put the government on its guard against the renewal of the old intrigues. This letter, however, has been only partially communicated. The part containing those cogent reasons was suppressed, and no other notice was taken of it than by the note, (N0. 90,) dated near a year after, and written on another occasion, this subject being only mentioned in a cursory manner, and closing with an enquiry, what was to be done with the papers. It was then, that in my answer, (Note N0. 91,) in which I apologize for having pressed a subject, which it was not thought proper to investigate, and which subsequent events had rendered of less importance; and *then* request that the whole may be burned, *in order that they might be no further trouble to the government.* There may be discovered in this request some little resentment for what I thought a neglect, but surely no desire to conceal any thing I had before communicated; and this statement of facts gives a very different idea from that conveyed by the message, that I had communicated these papers, " *with a request that* " *they might be burned, after perusal.*"

The President also says, that " no other infor-
" mation, within the purview of the request of the
" house, is known to have been received by any
" department of the government, from the esta-
" blishment of the present federal government.
" That which has been recently communicated to
" the house of representatives, and by them to me,
" is the *first direct testimony ever made known to*
" *me, charging general Wilkinson with a corrupt*
" *receipt of money.*" With Mr. Jefferson's motives for asserting to the house of representatives that mine was the first accusation, I have, personally, nothing to do. That account must be settled between him and the nation.—But it is due to my own character, to shew that the information given by me was not unsupported by prior accusation, and that, contrary to the language of the message, mine was not the first direct testimony made known to Mr. Jefferson, charging general Wilkinson with the corrupt receipt of money. The proof shall not be light.

On the 10th day of January, 1806, better than

two years before the date of the message, Joseph H. Daveiss, district attorney of the United States for Kentucky, wrote an official letter to the President, which deserves serious attention. It is contained in (Note No. 92.) It puts the President on his guard against a renewal of the old Spanish plot, and contains the following passage: " I am " told that Mr. Ellicott, in his journal, commu- " nicated to the officers of state the names of the " Americans concerned. If this be true, you " are long since guarded ; but I suspect either " that it is not, or that it has escaped you, or you " consider the business as *dead*—BECAUSE YOU " HAVE APPOINTED GENERAL WILKINSON AS " GOVERNOR OF ST. LOUIS, WHO, I AM CON- " VINCED, HAS BEEN FOR YEARS, AND NOW " IS, A PENSIONER OF SPAIN. Should you ask " me to prove it, I must resort to an extensive " chain of circumstances, which, separately, seem " small and inconclusive, &c." Here, I think, is a *direct charge*, and made in pretty explicit terms, and offered to be substantiated, and by a man in office, whose duty it was to prefer the accusation—and this direct charge did not miscarry, it came safely to the President's hands ; for on the 15th of Feb. 1806, he wrote to Mr. Daveiss a letter, acknowledging its receipt, (Note No. 93.) In this letter he requests the names of parties and witnesses, and Mr. Daveiss, on the 28th March, the 29th March, and the 21st April, replied, giving the names of the persons concerned, and the witnesses to prove the several charges. *Among*

these, the payments by Owens and Collins are particularly noticed. (See the extracts of these letters, Notes N0. 94, 95, 96 and 97.) And these letters are acknowledged by Mr. Jefferson to have been received on the 12th September, 1806, (Note N0. 98.) This correspondence is taken from a publication made by Mr. Daveiss, which is extremely interesting, and of which I regret that I cannot give more copious extracts. But this is not all. From the President's message itself it appears, that there was a letter and a reference from Mr. Ellicott, that was not sent to Congress, because Mr. Ellicott had desired that it might be kept secret. Now, if in this letter, and in a verbal communication, Mr. Ellicott had expressly charged gen. W. with the corrupt receipt of money, how will it agree with the assertion before quoted, that my testimony was the first direct charge, and the one preceding it, that one letter only (and that *anonymous*) specified any particular fact? yet such is the case. In the testimony of Mr. Coxe, (Note N0. 55,) we find the following passage—" Jan. 30.
" Andrew Ellicott informed me this evening, that
" in the month of June 1801, as well as I recol-
" lect, *he communicated personally to Mr. Jeffer-*
" *son the exact sum of money that had been sent by*
" *Don Thomas Portel to gen. Wilkinson; that this*
" *sum was not on account of any mercantile trans-*
" *actions, but of the pension allowed the general by*
" *the Spanish government; that general W. was*
" *not a man to be trusted; and, if continued in em-*
" *ploy, would one day or other disgrace and involve*
" *the government in his schemes.*" In the letters

of Mr. Ellicott to the general himself, *(ant.* page 69,) he expressly states that the copy of Gayoso's letter, in which the general and others were mentioned as being in the interest and pay of Spain, were, as well as the information received from captain Portell of the 9640 dollars, reduced to cypher, and communicated to the President. Now even if it be allowed that Mr. Ellicott's desire should excuse the President from communicating his letters, yet surely no desire of any individual could impose on the President the necessity of asserting that no such communication had been made. On the 14th of January, 1808, Mr. Ellicott wrote me, as follows:—

Lancaster, January 14*th,* 1808.
DEAR SIR,

THE letter mentioned in the 183d page of my journal, from governor Gayoso to a confidential Spanish officer, is, I presume, in the hands of Mr. Thomas Power. A copy of the interesting part will be found in the office of the Secretary of State. This letter places the improper conduct of general Wilkinson, and some others of our citizens, in a point of view not to be mistaken. If corruption is criminal, this letter establishes the criminality. Whenever I think of our army, and the state of our country, the following lines from Anacharsis never fail presenting themselves to my mind:—

" Les peuples de la Grece sont affoiblis & corrompus. Plus de lois, plus de citoyens, nulle idee de la gloire, nul attachement au bien public. Partout, de vils mercenaires pour soldats, et des brigands pour generaux."—

To my knowledge, the present administration has been minutely informed of the conduct of general Wilkinson, and why he has been supported, and patronized, after this information, is to me an inexplicable paradox.

All the information that I was able to obtain on the subject of those intrigues was faithfully detailed both to the former and present administrations; and beyond those documents (which are deposited in the office of the Secretary of State) I have no knowledge of those transactions. I now begin to wish that I had kept copies of those papers—but I have none. I am, with great esteem,

Your sincere friend, and
humble servant,

(Signed)   ANDREW ELLICOTT.
Hon. DANIEL CLARK, Esq.

It is true that the President, in the Message, suggests that the testimony of Mr. Ellicott might be procured from himself, and that for that purpose he had directed him to be summoned before the court of enquiry. But he refused to attend—there was no force to compel him—and I think, that, after his refusal to attend was known, I, as well as the country, have some reason to complain that evidence so important to support my declarations—so essential to the conviction of guilt—should have been withheld from the court *(a)*

(a) Mr. Ellicott refused to attend the court of enquiry—Mr. Jefferson was in possession of his letter, containing the intercepted dispatch from Gayoso, of which Mr. Ellicott, in his impressive language, says, " *if corruption be criminal,*

and from the public. Nay more, that by the language of the communication to Congress it should have been asserted, that no such evidence had been given to the executive.

I have now completed a work which was forced upon me, in justification of my own character. I regret deeply, that the nature of this justification has obliged me to appear as an accuser; and that a task, which I cannot help repeating was the duty of a public officer, has thus devolved upon an individual. My regret on this occasion is not produced from any apprehension that my proofs are deficient, or my defence incomplete. My own understanding is satisfied with their force, and my conscience has always been at rest. Of the effect this address may have on my countrymen I cannot doubt. In common with the great mass of them, I anticipate much good from the approaching change in the administration;—and if I shall have furnished the new Cabinet with the means of throwing off this dishonour from the nation, I shall not regret the trouble of my research.

New Orleans, March 1st, 1809.

" *this letter establishes the criminality*"—and yet this letter was not submitted either to Congress, or the court, or the public. In what manner is this to be accounted for? Mr. Ellicott's request of secrecy seems to have been more rigidly attended to, than the express promise given to Bollman. In his letter to W. Mr. E. declares, that he thinks the reasons for secrecy no longer exist, and would have declared the same thing to the President, *had he been* applied to.— (See his letter, Note No. 99,) addressed to me—and mark his astonishment that only the nugatory parts of his correspondence were communicated.

NOTES.

No. I.

A Plain Tale, supported by authentic Documents, justifying the character of General Wilkinson.—By a Kentuckian.

ADVERTISEMENT.

The following Plain Tale is republished in this form, without even the knowledge of General Wilkinson, by a man, who is no otherwise his friend than the dictates of truth and honour require; for if the slanders that have been published against him could be substantiated by adequate proof, he would be among the first to abandon him.

Previously to the perusal, the reader is requested to ask himself a few questions.

Has not General Wilkinson, by his prompt, energetic and decisive conduct, saved our country from a civil as well as a foreign war?

Has he not crushed treason in the bud, and prevented a dissolution of our Union?

Are not his accusers those, and those only, whose daring and wicked hopes he has frustrated?

Has any proof been offered in support of any one charge against him, unless indeed assertions could be raised to the dignity of testimony?

After a candid answer to these questions, from the breast of a conscientious reader, the publisher has no doubt but the following statement and documents will have their weight. If any man, to whose hands this small pamphlet shall come, should decline reading it for want of time or inclination, let him throw it aside, but as a man of honour he should throw aside his prejudices with it; for he who first refuses to listen to a justification, and then repeats or supports the charges, becomes himself a principal in the calumny.

The publisher assures himself, that few if any such characters will be found among those whose applause is honour, whose esteem is a desirable acquisition.

FROM THE INQUIRER.

Richmond, October 27th, 1807.

SHALL General Wilkinson respond to the slanders of a host of enemies, whetted by disappointment and stimulated by revenge? Shall he enter the lists of controversy with the partizans of the very rebellion he has himself crushed, or descend to controvert the slanderous assertions of a band of calumnious discontents, who, without the spirit to emulate a meritorious deed, possess the low ambition to envy it? We hope not—we hope his attentions will be carried to very different objects, in the present crisis of public affairs, standing, as we do, on the threshold of a war, which may require the exertion of the skill, conduct, and courage of the whole nation.

Pending the trial of Aaron Burr, we have beheld the most extraordinary scenes ever presented before a tribunal of justice; to impugn the character of general Wilkinson, as much solicitude has been manifested, as to vindicate the conduct of the traitor himself! and it has been with astonishment we have beheld volumes of testimony let in, totally irrelevant to the cause, and calculated to blacken the character of a public officer, who (taken by surprize) found himself without other defence than that which accident provided him.

We have seen witnesses of almost every country and denomination, the avowed enemies of General Wilkinson, hunted up from the remotest extremes of the Union, to violate the seal of confidence, and rip up the private transactions of his life!

We have been apprized, that the notorious accomplice of Burr was the bearer of blank subpœnas to Edward Livingston, who ran over Louisiana to fabricate exparte depositions, shaped for the occasion, and to collect testimonies against the General; and, by artifices the most foul, to aid the cause of his suffering friend.

Wherefore is the General thus persecuted and abused? Wherefore are transactions of twenty years standing—transactions purely commercial, now distorted, misrepresented, and brought forward, to defame him? Is it because he has been guilty of any act of infidelity to the government? Is it because he has failed to do justice to the high and honourable trust successively reposed in him by Washington, Adams, and Jefferson? Is it because he has neglected a duty to be performed, or has failed in one solitary instance to promote the national weal, with that zeal and ardour which characterise the man? No! his enemies may continue to howl, but it will be impossible for them ever to substantiate against him political defection, or a dereliction of personal honour.

In what then has he offended, thus to draw down upon him the rancorous malice and ruthless vengeance of a motley tribe of adversaries? It is a crime with the invidious that he should have passed, with repute, through three successive administrations, and rendered satisfaction where he was responsible; and the sweets of office could not be permitted him, without that alloy of detraction which we find inseparable from public station in free governments. But, he has sinned beyond forgiveness—because he refused to violate his oath, abandon his allegiance, turn his arms against the country he had sworn to defend, and dishonour his sword by becoming a military traitor. Herein we perceive " the very beard and front of his offendings." He has baffled the sinister aspirations of ambition—has destroyed the golden prospects of the sordid—and blasted the full-blown hopes of those deluded citizens, whom mortification and disappointment may have inclined to barter the union and independence of these happy states for the humiliation of their political opponents. Reverse the scene; and what would have been the merits of this officer, if he had swallowed the gilded bait, and attached the seal of infamy to his name! What the effects would have been is manifest, but surely those who now condemn him for exposing a traitor, would have then applauded his conduct, and in place of a cross would have assigned him a crown.—Perjury in that case would have been meritorious; the enormity of the offence would have been lost in the blaze of military glory, and a successful career might have sanctified the deed!

After various feints of attack and changes of position, from the " Port Folio" down to the " post-marked letter 13th May," the main assault is carried under the tattered banners of the Spanish conspiracy; and here too the assailants will be baffled, and those political rooks, who have hovered around the walls of the Capitol, with the fond hope of rioting on the spoils of the General's reputation, must retire with empty craws.

However unpleasant the occasion, the arts, frauds and falsehoods of his enemies seem to render it necessary that the private dealings and transactions of General Wilkinson, of twenty years standing, should be obtruded on the public attention, and that the motives, by which his personal speculations were produced and regulated at that remote day, should be exposed.

It will be remembered, and by the citizens of Virginia particularly, that the situation of the settlements of Kentucky, pending the years 1785 and 1786, was not only humiliating, but perilous.—

It is not forgotten that the torrent of emigration to the west was considered a pernicious drain from the population of the east, that the progressive improvements of our western wilds were viewed with jealous eyes by many; and men of distinction had been heard to implore Heaven, that the Pacific Ocean should wash the western foot of the Apalachian mountains. On the eve of a separation from the parent state, those sympathies and obligations which had heretofore cherished and protected the district of Kentucky were about to be dissolved. The inhabitants of that, then sequestered, region, without protection from the general government, saw their frontier settlements every where exposed to the tomahawk and scalping knife; and without the navigation of the Missisippi, the products of their labour were left to perish on their hands. What, let us enquire, was the government at that period? A mere rope of sand. Nerveless, without resource, and subsisting on diurnal expedients. What was the policy of the Administration in those days? Narrow, local, exclusive, and invidious. State interests and state distinctions were then predominant, and the national family had not yet sat down to a single repast. An objection from the smallest state was sufficient to mar the most salutary proposition, and the most precious interests of the confederation were subject to the caprice of a single member. It was in the year 1786 that a proposal was offered to Congress for the concession of the exclusive navigation of the Missisippi to Spain for twenty-five years, under the pretext of an exchange for certain commercial privileges to the Atlantic States, and in order to acquire the rights of estopal. The proposition terrified the western people, and suggested the necessity of their looking to their own rights and interests. The alarm and abhorrence produced by this measure were universal; the children of the woods began to think and to speak for themselves: and but for the seasonable production and adoption of the glorious fabric, which cements United America, a separation long before this period would have ensued as a necessary consequence. Gen. W. had migrated to the western country in 1783, in quest of provision for a young and increasing family. He at this period considered his hopes *jeopardised*, and determined to look abroad for what he had not found at home. With this object he made a small equipment, and embarked on Kentucky river in April, 1787, and after escaping many perils from the savages, he arrived at New Orleans in June.

For the events which ensued, we beg leave to refer to the document A. This honourable testimonial will serve to illustrate a fact, which hundreds of living witnesses may be produced to sustain, viz. that General Wilkinson did procure to his fellow-citizens in the west, on his own risk and expence, the invaluable advantages of a free trade with New Orleans, years before that privilege was obtained by treaty. It is neither necessary nor obligatory, nor would it be honourable, to detail the means he employed to effect this object; it will suffice to say, that his country was accommodated and benefited by his enterprise, and that his personal speculations, in their nature politically innocent, were directed to the friendly correspondence, harmonious intercourse, and reciprocal interests of the two countries, and it will not be denied that he had the same right at that period to establish a mercantile connexion at New Orleans, which the merchants of the United States have, at present, to extend their commercial speculations to Vera Cruz and Laguira, or to Turkey, China, and the East Indies.

The General has acknowledged to the author of these remarks, that he originally contemplated removing to Natchez, and did favour the policy of the Court of Spain, at that time, to populate that district with emigrants from the United States, for motives too obvious to name.

Hie commercial engagements were exclusively with the Spanish government of Louisiana. As he never sold a cent's worth of property in the market, after his first voyage, of course the cash he received was from the government of the country, and this he either received *in person*, on *his bills*, or *by remittance* through various channels. The last payment was made him in the year 1796, through his *agent Philip Nolan*, being a balance which had arisen on the recovery of some tobacco which it had been believed was damaged, and lost in the year 1789.

On the General's *first engagement a cypher was formed*, more for the security of the communication of his friend, than his own, and when this friend left the country about the year 1790, their affairs being unsettled, he transferred the cypher to his successor, whom the General never saw, but with whom he recollects to have passed one or two letters in cypher, respecting his private business, about fourteen years since.

The last letter the General received from the Baron of Carondelet was dated in May, 1797. It was strictly official, and conveyed the Baron's protest against the descent of a body of troops, which the General had detached to demand possession of the posts on the Missisippi, agreeably to the treaty of friendship, limits and navigation. The General rebutted this protest, and the troops proceeded under Captains Guion and Heth, and for reasons of a confidential nature an order was passed by the General to the officer commanding at Massac,* to prevent the agent of the Baron from re-entering the United States by the Ohio. It is believed that the Baron de Carondelet came to the government of Louisiana about the year 1791, at which time the General left Kentucky, and has been since incessantly engaged in military life; and the documents (marked B) will exhibit Gen. Washington's sense of his services during three years of arduous duty; from whence it will appear that General Wilkinson was engaged in defending, instead of dividing the country.

General Wilkinson has never by word or deed endeavoured to incline a single individual to oppose the laws or injure the government of his country. He has never received nor employed a dollar for the purposes of corruption. He has never held a commission, nor received a pension from any foreign power. Nor has he ever given a test of allegiance but to his own country. He cannot prove a negative, but he has done what he could do, to purge himself of the slanders of his enemies; and the correspondence with his Excellency Governor Folch (marked C) and the voluntary declaration of Capt. Thomas Power (marked D) are offered as instances.

A KENTUCKIAN.

24th October, 1807.

(No. A.)

Extract from a Memoir submitted to the Honourable Timothy Pickering, when Secretary of State, by the Honourable Daniel Clark.

" About the period of which we are speaking, in the middle of the year 1787, the foundation of an intercourse with Kentucky and the settlements on the Ohio was laid, which daily increases. Previous to that time, all those who ventured on the Missisippi had their property seized by the first commanding officer whom they met, and little or no communication was kept up between the countries; now and then an emigrant who wished to settle in Natchez, by dint of intreaty and solicitation of friends, who had interest in New Orleans, procured permission to remove there with his family, slaves, cattle, furniture, and farming utensils, but was allowed to bring no other property except cash. An unexpected incident, however, changed the face of things, and was productive of a new line of conduct; the arrival of a boat belonging to Gen. Wilkinson, loaded with tobacco and other productions of Kentucky, is announced in town, and a guard was immediately sent on board of it. The General's name had hindered this being done at Natchez, as the

* Major Pike.

commandant was fearful that such a step might be displeasing to his superiors, who might wish to show some respect to a general officer—at any rate the boat was proceeding to Orleans, and they could then resolve on what measures they ought to pursue, and put them in execution. The government, not much disposed to show any mark of respect or forbearance towards the General's property, he not having at that time arrived, was about proceeding in the usual way of confiscation, when a merchant in Orleans, who had considerable influence there, and who was formerly acquainted with the General, represented to the Governor, that the measures taking by the Intendant would very probably give rise to disagreeable events; that the people of Kentucky were already exasperated at the conduct of the Spaniards, in seizing on the property of all those who navigated the Missisippi, and, if this system was persisted in, would, very probably, in spite of Congress and the Executive of the United States, take upon themselves to obtain the navigation of the river by force, which they were able to do; a measure for some time before much dreaded by this government, which had no force to resist them, if such a plan was put in execution. Hints were likewise given that Wilkinson was a very popular man, who could influence the whole of that country, and probably that his sending a boat before him, with a wish that she might be seized, was but a snare laid for the government, that he might have an opportunity at his return to inflame the minds of the people, and, having brought them to the point he wished, induce them to appoint him their leader, and then like a torrent spread over the country, and carry fire and desolation from one end of the province to the other. Governor Miro, unacquainted with the American government, ignorant even of the position of Kentucky with respect to his own province, but alarmed at the very idea of an irruption of Kentucky-men, whom he feared without knowing their strength, communicated his wishes to the Intendant, that the guard might be removed from the boat, which was accordingly done; and a Mr. Patterson, who was the agent of the General, was permitted to take charge of the property on board, and sell it free of duty.—The General, on his arrival in New Orleans some time after, informed of the obligation he lay under to the merchant, who had impressed the Governor with such an idea of his importance and influence at home, waited on him, and in concert with him formed a plan for their future operations. In his interview with the Governor, that he might not seem to derogate from the character given of him, by appearing concerned in so trifling a business as a boat load of tobacco, hams and butter, he gave him to understand that the property belonged to many citizens of Kentucky, who, availing themselves of his return to the Atlantic States, by way of Orleans, wished to make a trial of the temper of this government, that he on his arrival might inform his owners what steps had been pursued under his eye, that adequate measures might be afterwards taken to procure satisfaction. He acknowledged with gratitude the attention and respect manifested by the Governor towards himself in the favour shown to his agent, but at the same time mentioned that he would not wish the Governor to expose himself to the anger of the Court, by refraining from seizing on the boat and cargo (as it was but a trifle) if such were the positive orders from Court, and that he had not a power to relax them according to circumstances.—Convinced by this discourse that the General rather wished for an opportunity of embroiling affairs, than sought to avoid it—the Governor became more alarmed. For two or three years before, and particularly since the arrival of the commissioners from Georgia, who had come to Natchez to claim that country, he had been fearful of an invasion at every annual rise of the waters, and the news of a few boats being seen on the Ohio was enough to alarm the whole province, he resolved in his mind what measures he ought to pursue, (consistent with the orders he had from home not to permit the free navigation of the river,) in order to keep the people of Kentucky quiet, and in his succeeding interviews with Wilkinson, having procured more knowledge than he had hitherto acquired of their character, population, strength and dispositions, he thought he could do nothing better than hold out a bait to Wilkinson, to use his influence in restraining the people from an invasion of this province, till he could give advice to his Court, and require further instructions.—This was the point to which the parties wished to bring him, and being informed that in Kentucky two or three crops were on hand, for which, if an immediate vent was not found, the people would not keep within bounds, he made Wilkinson the offer of a permission to import on his own account to New Orleans, free of duty, all the productions of Kentucky, thinking by this means to conciliate the good will of the people, without yielding the point of navigation; as the commerce carried on would appear the effect of an indulgence to an individual, which could be withdrawn at pleasure. On consultation with his friends, who well knew what further concessions Wilkinson could extort from the fear of the Spaniards, by the promises of his good offices in preaching peace, harmony and good understanding with this government, until arrangements were made between Spain and America, he was advised to insist that the Governor should insure him a market for all the flour and tobacco *he might send*, as in the event of an unfortunate shipment he would be ruined, whilst endeavouring to do a service to Louisiana. This was accepted; flour was always wanted in Orleans, and the King of Spain had given orders to purchase more tobacco for the supply of his manufactory at home than Louisiana at that time produced, and which was paid for at about 9¼ dollars per cwt. In Kentucky it cost but two, and the profit was immense. In consequence, the General appointed his friend Daniel Clark his agent here, returned by way of Charleston in a vessel with a particular permission to go to the United States, even at the very moment of Gardogue's information, and on his arrival in Kentucky bought up all the produce he could collect, which he shipped and disposed of as before mentioned; *and for some time all the trade from the Ohio was carried on in his name, a line from him sufficing to insure to the owner of the boat every privilege and protection he could desire.* On granting this privilege to Wilkinson, the government came to a resolution of encouraging emigration from the western country, and offered passports to all settlers, with an exemption of duty on all the property they might bring with them invested in the produce of the country they came from.

" Under the denomination of settlers, all those who had acquaintances with a few persons of influence in Orleans obtained passports, made shipments to their address, which were admitted free of duty, and under pretence of following shortly after with their families continued their speculations; others came with their property, had lands granted them, which, after locating, they disposed of, and having finished their business returned to the United States: a few only remained in the province, and they were the people, who, in general, availed themselves the least of the immunities granted by the government; they possessed a few slaves and cattle, but had little other property, and they generally settled among their countrymen in the Natchez, and increased the cultivation of tobacco, at that time the principal article raised for exportation in the district. This encouragement given to emigrants and speculators opened a market for all the produce of the Ohio. Flour was imported from Pittsburgh; and the farmers finding a vent for all they could raise, their lands augmented in value, their industry increased, and they have exported annually to Louisiana for some time past from 10 to 15,000 barrels of flour, for which they generally find a ready market."

(No. B.)

SUNDRY EXTRACTS of letters from General KNOX, Secretary of War, to Brigadier General JAMES WILKINSON.

MARCH 3d, 1792.

" The steps you have taken to procure information of the state of the Indians were highly proper, and in future you will use every expedient to gain information of their designs.

" The President of the United States will be anxious to hear of your safe return from your excursion to the field of action; and this anxiety is in proportion to the risk you appear to encounter by so near an approach to the Miami towns, at and near which, if our information be just, near five hundred Indians may be collected in a short time.

Another Extract from the same letter.

" This defensive protection must be confided to you and General Scott, or the county lieutenants, *as you may judge proper.* A few scouts, at 5-6ths of a dollar per day, to each county ought to constitute, perhaps, the main part of this protection, aided by such a number of rangers, on the pay and rations of the troops of the United States, as shall be judged indispensable by you."

APRIL 3d, 1792.

" The expedition to the field of action is an honourable evidence of your military zeal, and I am happy that you returned safely.

" The President of the United States, whose orders I communicate to you on this and all other important points of your command, hopes, and is persuaded, that you will, to the utmost of your power, endeavour to give the surest effect to the measures of peace.

" I cannot close this letter, Sir, without expressing to you the entire satisfaction of the President of the U. States, of the vigilance and discretion you appear to have exercised since your command; and I flatter myself your judgment and talents will meet with all the approbation to which I am persuaded they will be entitled."

APRIL 21st, 1792.

" The zeal and promptitude with which you executed the wishes of the Executive are remarked with pleasure, and will not fail of receiving the approbation of the President of the United States.

" It is with sincere pleasure I transmit you the notification of an appointment of Brigadier General; and I ardently hope the other gentleman appointed to act with you, as well as the commanding General, will be perfectly agreeable to you."

APRIL 27th, 1792.

" The idea you have mentioned of employing about one hundred mounted volunteer riflemen, for escorts from post to post, is approved by the President of the United States; and you are hereby authorised to carry it into execution, upon the pay stated in the law herein enclosed.

" These volunteers are to be engaged for a period of three months, unless sooner discharged, and you will appoint the officers thereof: you will, however, observe, that this corps, as well as your other corps, are not to be employed in offensive measures pending the negociations for peace.

" I confess I shall be anxious to hear of your return from the establishment of Fort St. Clair, which will be an operation somewhat critical; however, the confidence I have in your intelligence and activity assures me that you will avoid all unnecessary hazard."

MAY 12th, 1792.

" I have not yet heard of your return from establishing Fort St. Clair, and therefore some anxiety is entertained upon that subject. But the confidence in your discretion is no small relief upon the occasion."

JULY 17th 1792.

" Although I have not received any information of the actual departure of Col. Hardin and Major Trueman, yet, from Mr. Hodgdon's information, they sat out from Fort Washington, upon Harmar's trace, about the 20th of May. That they were to proceed to a certain distance, and then to separate: Hardin to push for St. Duskey, and Trueman to the Rapids of Omie. I hope sincerely they may have arrived safely, and succeeded, so as to prepare the way for General Putnam.

" The terms you stipulated to Colonel Hardin shall be performed on the part of the public.

" The direction you gave Major Hamtranck, of endeavouring to persuade the Chiefs of the Wabash to repair to this city, was highly judicious, and it is desired that he may accomplish it.

" Your remarks of the disproportionate punishments of death, or one hundred lashes, are just———and the suggestions of hard la-hour seem to promise better success, and I shall communicate the same to Major General Wayne——this is within the power of a court, according to the present rules and articles of war."

JULY 27th, 1792.

" Your instructions to Colonel Hardin and Major Trueman, and your message to the Indians, are highly judicious.—I am extremely anxious to hear of their safety and success."

AUGUST 8th, 1792.

" The zeal and activity you have exhibited to further all the objects of public service is highly gratifying to me, and I have so expressed it, both to the President, who is in Virginia, and General Wayne."

JANUARY 4th, 1793.

" I regret exceedingly the sudden departure of this express, which prevents my enlarging at this time; but I cannot refrain from intimating the satisfaction repeatedly expressed by the President of the United States, at your activity and zeal to promote the several objects of the public service under your direction. I am persuaded this satisfaction will be increased with the experience of your further conduct."

MAY 17th, 1793.

" As the commanding General has descended the river to Fort Washington, it is unnecessary for me to reply particularly to your several letters, otherwise than to thank you heartily for the various, extensive and important information you have communicated from time to time; all of which was duly communicated to the President of the United States.

" Brigadier General Posey, who will deliver you this letter, is a gentleman, from whom I flatter myself the service will derive solid benefits. I suppose he will arrive time enough to descend with Mrs. Wilkinson, with whom you will be at the time of receiving this letter, and to whom please respectfully to present my homage.

" I have often expressed to her and Colonel Biddle the pleasure your conduct gave to the President of the United States. I am impressed with the conviction that you will persevere in the same paths.

" My God! what an uproar in Europe! If the French nation shall be united, and consolidate their force within their limits, they will be invincible, although they must differ immensely in the process. But a doubt rests upon their union. If they are divided almost equally, they will be conquered. What a scene the European theatre would be for your military talents."

December 4th, 1794.

" The difference between you and Major-General Wayne is considered as very unhappy, and tarnishing in a degree the military part of our national reputation. Indeed, my friend, there is no information, no complaint against you, by him, that has been transmitted to this office. In his public letter he pays you merited applause. This has been circulated through the United States and Europe. Cannot, therefore, some mode be suggested, to bury in oblivion all that is past, and which, indeed, appears to me to be more the effect of nice feelings, than any palpable cause. I am persuaded that such a conciliation would be highly acceptable to the President of the United States, for public considerations."

(No. C.)

New Orleans, Jan. 25th, 1807.

Sir,

I rest my apology for the intrusion of my personal concerns on your attention upon those sympathies, which connect military men throughout the civilized world, and that sensibility, which inclines every honest breast to resist persecution.

You have doubtless observed in the public prints of the United States, that my name and character have been slandered and stigmatised, for a criminal understanding imputed to me with the Spanish Governors of Louisiana; and that I am charged with holding a commission and drawing a pension from th government of Spain.

If my memory serves me, Sir, you were here, when I first visited this city in 1787, and I think you were the nephew of the deceased Governor Miro, and have lived on this station ever since; under those circumstances, and in your present station, it would seem probable, that if I am pensioned or commissioned by the court of Spain, the fact must come within your knowledge, and it is therefore, Sir, I presume to request from you the peculiar favour, to declare, upon the honour of a gentleman and an officer, whether such fact has ever come to your knowledge, or whether you believe it has existence.

" Your prompt and explicit declaration will oblige,
Sir, your most obedient servant,
JAS. WILKINSON.
His Excellency Governor FOLCH, Baton Rouge.

Mi GENERAL, *Baton Rouge*, 10*th February*, 1807.

Your favour of the 25th ultimo has come to hand, and so far from feeling any reluctance in complying with your request, it is with the greatest satisfaction that I answer the contents of your letter. The military life has become now-a-days a scientific profession, and those who embrace it, laying aside political or national prejudices, consider themselves as brothers, and under this point of view your present persecution cannot be indifferent to me.

I solemnly declare to you that I have resided in these provinces of Louisiana and W. Florida, with little or no interruption, since the 14th of July, 1783, (when I came to New Orleans, at the pressing invitation of my beloved uncle Don Estevan Miro, who was at that time Governor of them) to this period: and it being publicly known that, in the quality of a near relation and intimate friend, no person ever possessed his confidence in a greater degree than myself, it may be presumed that no person can give a more satisfactory answer to your queries than myself.

It is barely within the limits of possibility that, notwithstanding the unlimited confidence my uncle placed in me, he may have concealed from me, at that period, the circumstance of your holding a commission and enjoying a pension from the court of Spain ; but as *neither* the *one* nor the *other* is *ever* conferred without a commission, (patent or warrant,) since the records (or archives) of Louisiana have been in my trust, it is natural that I should have met not only a copy, but even the original documents with which they must have been accompanied from the court. For your satisfaction, and the utter confusion and shame of your calumniators, who availing themselves of the facility which the liberty of the press offers are endeavouring to wound your honour ; I do *asseverate to you and to them, under my sacred word of honour, that no such document, nor any other paper tending to substantiate such assertions, exists in the records in my possession ;* and should this declaration be insufficient to erase the unfavourable impressions that certain persons of weak minds may have received, persons who as implicitly and as blindly give credit to what they read in the newspapers as they do to the Bible, you ought not to forget that you are a soldier, and you must find in your unsullied conscience a source of consolation, and in the esteem and regard of an enlightened and liberal public your recompence.

I remain, with due consideration,
Your most faithful and affectionate servant,
(and kiss your hand)
((Signed)) VIS'TE. FOLCH.
His Excellency Gen. JAMES WILKINSON.

(No. D.)

New Orleans, 16th *May*, 1807.

SIR,

I cannot in silence behold my name employed to sanction the calumnies levelled at any man's character; and therefore, Sir, I make you a tender of the enclosed; and have the honour to be, with the highest consideration,

Sir, your most obedient servant,
THOMAS POWER.
General JAMES WILKINSON.

I, Thomas Power, of the city of New Orleans, lately an officer in the service of Spain, moved solely by a sense of justice, and the desire to prevent my name from being employed to sanction groundless slanders, do most solemnly declare, that I have at no time carried or delivered to General James Wilkinson, from the government of Spain, or from any person in the service of said government, cash, bills, or property of any species. I do most solemnly declare, that said Wilkinson, to the best of my knowledge and belief, had no participation, and was a perfect stranger to the mission on which I visited Kentucky in the year 1797, and do furthermore most solemnly declare, that my business at Detroit was to deliver an official letter from the Baron de Carondelet to General Wilkinson; that on my arrival at Detroit the General was absent, and I found the place under the command of Colonel Strong, by whom I was received with the greatest hospitality, and treated with kindness and civility, being left at perfect liberty to visit every part of the town and its neighbourhood, the fort excepted, during the few days that I remained there waiting for General Wilkinson's return from Michilimacinac; who immediately placed me under strict restraint, not permitting me to stir out of Colonel Strong's quarters without being accompanied by an officer, who was instructed to keep a watchful eye over me: that the

General delivered me his answer to the Baron de Carondelet's letter on the second day after his return to Detroit, and sent me in charge of an officer, by the nearest route, to Massac, and from thence to New Madrid, notwithstanding I protested against this step, and demanded that I might return by the Falls of the Ohio, where a boat and crew waited for me. I further declare, that I am ready to testify the truth of the preceding facts. Given in New Orleans, this 16th day of May, 1807.

THOMAS POWER.

*** *** ***

FROM THE INQUIRER.

Perceiving an oblique attempt in that oracle of truth, the Western World, to implicate Governor Harrison, for some undefined sympathy in relation to Burr, or his accomplice David Floyd——although Mr. Harrison's character and conduct will suffice to repel every foul insinuation——it is a matter of justice that the enclosed copies of two letters from Burr to that gentleman should be published——as they will not only evince Mr. H.'s ignorance of his nefarious projects, but will expose the base hypocricy and infamous falsehoods to which the little traitor could resort, to mask his villainous purposes, and cheat even those whom he called his friends.

JUSTITIA.

Richmond, October 26, 1807.

(COPY.)

Lexington, 24*th October,* 1806.

MY DEAR SIR,

By the hands of my friend and relation, Major Wescott, you will receive a newspaper containing the orders lately issued by General Jackson to the militia of West Tennesee, being the division under his command. It occurred to me that you might deem something similar to be addressed to the militia of Indiana not inexpedient at this moment, and that the perusal of this production might be acceptable.

All reflecting men consider a war with Spain to be inevitable; in such an event, I think you would not be at ease as an idle spectator. If it should be my lot to be employed, which there is reason to expect, it would be my highest gratification to be associated with you.

I pray you to believe in assurance of the very great respect and esteem, with which
I am,
Your Friend, &c.

(Signed)   A. BURR.
His Excellency Governor Harrison, Vincennes.

Louisville, November 27th, 1806.

Dear Sir,

Considering the various and extravagant reports which circulate concerning me, it may not be unsatisfactory to you to be informed (and to you there can be no better source of information than myself) that I have no wish or design to attempt a separation of the Union, that I have no connection with any foreign power or government, that I never meditated the introduction of any foreign power or influence into the United States, or any parts of its territories, but on the contrary should repel with indignation any proposition or measure having that tendency: in fine, that I have no project or views hostile to the interest, or tranquility, or union of the United States, or prejudicial to its government; and I pledge you my honour for the truth of this declaration.—It is true that I am engaged in an extensive speculation, and that with me are associated some of your intimate and dearest friends. The objects are such as every man of honour and every good citizen must approve. They have been communicated to several of the principal officers of our government, particularly to one high in the confidence of the administration. He has assured me my views would be grateful to the administration. Indeed, from the nature of them, it cannot be otherwise, and I have no doubt of having received your active support, if a personal communication with you could have been had. Accident and indispensible occupations have prevented me from visiting you for the purpose. This explanation seemed due to the frankness of your character and your responsible station, to my own feelings, and to the attachment with which your kindness and confidence had influenced me. If I have ascribed to you a solicitude you have not felt, you will impute it to the great value I place in your esteem, and I pray that you will always believe me to be   Your faithful and affectionate friend,

(Signed)   A. BURR.
His Excellency Gov. Harrison.

Vincennes, (I. T.) Dec. 2d, 1806.

I do hereby certify that the above is a true copy of the original letter written by Colonel Burr to his Excellency Governor Harrison, which at his request I have transcribed.

   (Signed)   WALTER TAYLOR.
 Copy of a copy.

NOTE No. 2.

DEAR SIR,

A FRIEND having proposed a Publication relative to services of eighteen or twenty years standing, I furnished him your extract from the memoir you transmitted Mr. Pickering in 1796-7. Being a public document, I could see no impropriety in this, and I hope you may concur in the same opinion, seeing that it was an introductory paper to me—assailed as I am by the worst, the meanest demons, that ever infested the earth—so soon as I have adjusted a single point here I shall be with you, and am,

      With respect and esteem,
        Your's,
          JA. WILKINSON.
Richmond, Oct. 27, '07.
The Hon. D. CLARK.

NOTE No 3.

(COPY.)

To all Persons to whom these presents shall come, Greeting:

KNOW ye, that James Wilkinson and Isaac B. Dunn, of the district of Kentucky, now in the state of Virginia, esquires, of the one part, and Daniel Clark, of the town of New Orleans, on the Missisippi, merchant, of the other part, do hereby consent and mutually agree to carry on a commerce between the said district of Kentucky and the town of New Orleans aforesaid—that is to say, That the said James Wilkinson and Isaac B. Dunn shall purchase in the district of Kentucky, or any other the settlements on the waters of the Ohio within the state of Virginia aforesaid—to wit. Tobacco, flour, butter, tallow, hogs-lard, beef, pork, bacon and bacon hams, on the joint account and risk of the said James Wilkinson, Isaac B. Dunn and Daniel Clark, *and the same to be sent down in good order*, (dangers of the river excepted) to the town of New Orleans, addressed to the aforesaid Daniel Clark, to be by him converted into cash, for the common benefit of the said James Wilkinson, Isaac B. Dunn and Daniel Clark, in the particular ratio hereafter written.

And likewise that the said Daniel Clark shall purchase and send to the Falls of Ohio, on account and risk of the aforesaid James Wilkinson and Isaac B. Dunn, such European and West-India commodities, as shall be jointly deemed necessary for the use and consumption of the aforesaid settlements on the Ohio, to be by them converted into cash or such articles of produce as are herein named, for the joint benefit of the said James Wilkinson, Isaac B. Dunn and Daniel Clark, in the particular ratio hereafter mentioned.

Now be it remembered, and it is hereby declared and made known, that the said parties are to be interested in the said commerce in the following proportions, viz. James Wilkinson to have and enjoy one fourth of the profits, which shall appear to arise from the said trade, to be carried on, agreeable to the letter and spirit of the contract, from Kentucky to this place and from this place to Kentucky, and also to sustain one fourth part of any loss that may happen to the parties in the said trade. In like manner shall Isaac B. Dunn share and enjoy one fourth part of the profits, which shall arise from the aforesaid commerce, and in like proportion bear any loss that may happen to the parties in the course of the said connexion. And likewise that the said Daniel Clark shall have and enjoy, of the profits which shall arise from the said trade, one half or equal moiety of the whole, or bear in like proportion any loss that may be sustained by the parties in the course of their said connexion.—Further, it is agreed by the contracting parties that this connexion shall take place on the first day of December next, and continue until dissolved by mutual consent of the said parties, or by prohibition of this government—Provided always that no tobacco which shall be sent down by James Wilkinson, esquire, antecedent to the first day of December next, shall be considered in any wise a property falling within the present connection. And whereas Daniel Clark is now preparing to make a shipment of merchandize to the aforesaid Falls of Ohio—Be it known that the merchandize is for account and risk of the aforesaid James Wilkinson, Isaac B. Dunn and Daniel Clark, in the proportions aforesaid.—Lastly, be it remembered that the said James Wilkinson and Isaac B. Dunn shall not charge commissions for what they buy or sell at any part of the settlements of Kentucky on the waters of the Ohio, for account of the parties in this concern. Nor shall the said Daniel Clark charge any commission for all or any business he shall transact at New Orleans for account of said concern.

In witness whereof the parties have hereunto interchangeably set their hands and seals, at New Orleans, this seventh day of August, one thousand seven hundred and eighty-eight.

For James Wilkinson and self,

ISAAC B. DUNN, (Seal.)
DANIEL CLARK, (Seal.)

Signed, sealed and delivered in
in presence of
A. HOOPS,
PHILIP NOLAN.

NOTE No. 4.

James Wilkinson's accountable receipt for our part of the cargo per the Speedwell's proceeds, and for a debt due by Craig and Johnston, for 318l. 13s. 7d.

I DO hereby acknowledge that I have not accounted with Daniel Clark for his half of the adventure of merchandise shipped per the batteau Speedwell, Jean Massey Patroon, from New Orleans to the Falls of Ohio, consigned to Wilkinson and Dunn, and that I will invest and ship the proceeds of the said adventure, which still remains in our hands, in good and merchantable tobacco, to him in the month of December next.

I also acknowledge that I have a debt due to the said Clark from Craig and Johnston, for three hundred and eighteen pounds thirteen shillings and seven pence, Virginia currency, under my direction, and that I will, or my heirs in case of my death, ship tobacco to him to the amount thereof, as soon as I or they shall recover the same, and when these several obligations into which I now enter are fulfilled by me or my heirs, that the articles of writing, declaratory of a connexion with the said Clark by Wilkinson and Dunn, bearing date the 7th of August, one thousand seven hundred and eighty-eight, shall be void and of no effect: and also that the power of attorney which I have had from said Clark shall be cancelled, and of no effect from this day, as witness my hand, at New Orleans, this eighteenth day of September, in the year of our Lord one thousand seven hundred and eighty-nine.

JAMES WILKINSON.

NOTE No. 5.

PERSONALLY appeared before me, the undersigned, one of the Justices of the Peace for the parish of New Orleans, Mr. John Ballinger, now resident in Cape Girardeau, Territory of Louisiana, late a member of the Kentucky Legislature, who, being duly sworn on the Holy Evangelists of Almighty God, did depose and say, that in the fore part of the winter of the year one thousand seven hundred and eighty-nine, as well as he recollects, his brother Joseph Ballinger brought two mules loaded with money from New Orleans to the state of Kentucky for General James Wilkinson; that, from the fatigue of the journey and indisposition, his said brother was unable to finish his journey, and got this deponent to conduct the said mules and money to General Wilkinson, at Frankfort, where he arrived on the twenty-sixth day of December, in the year aforesaid—the said money was in leather bags, and very heavy loads—and this deponent further declares, that the General expressed much satisfaction at the receipt of the money, having been under some apprehensions on account of the delay which had taken place on the journey, which said mules and money General Wilkinson receipted for, which receipt is among this deponent's papers, and further this deponent saith not.

JOHN BALLINGER.

Sworn and subscribed to, at the city of New Orleans, this 12th day of January, 1809, before me,

SAM. D. CARLE,
Justice of the Peace.

NOTE No. 6.

New Orleans, 16th February, 1809.

SIR,

IN answer to your letter of yesterday, I have to say, that I remember General Wilkinson's having stopped at my plantation in the fall of 1789, (as I think,) when he was on his way to Kentucky, accompanied by Philip Nolan. As I live on the west side of the Mississippi, and the General went up on the east, he stopped at some plantation nearly opposite to mine, and came over and spent a day or two with me.

In the course of our conversation, he told me that he had left a sum of money under the care of Nolan, who he spoke of as a man of great strength; saying he could take two thousand dollars

with one hand from off a mule or horse, and carry them with the utmost ease into a house. I do not remember whether the General mentioned to me the amount he was taking up with him; but, to to the best of my remembrance, he said he had two mules or horses for the purpose of carrying his money. This is all I can recollect of the transaction. I am, Sir,
Your most obed't serv't,
EVAN JONES.

DANIEL CLARK, Esq.

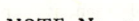

NOTE No. 7.

ON this twenty-ninth day of December, in the year one thousand eight hundred and eight, personally appeared before me, the undersigned, one of the Justices of the Peace for the county of Orleans, Monsieur Francis Langlois, a citizen of the United States and resident of New Orleans, who, being duly sworn on the Holy Bible, did depose and say, that in the year 1794 he was a lieutenant of militia in the service of his Catholic Majesty, and commanded the galliot the Flecha, then on station at New Madrid, having under his orders the gun boat the Taurean and batteau the Prince of Asturias; that whilst there a Mr. Owens arrived from New Orleans with a sum of money, entrusted to him by the Baron de Carondelet, to be delivered to General Wilkinson somewhere on the Ohio, and this deponent had directions from the said Baron de Carondelet to take measures, in concert with Don Thomas Portell, the commandant at New Madrid, and the aforesaid Owens, to have the sum entrusted to the charge of this latter conveyed in safety to its destination—in consequence thereof this deponent, at a council held at New Madrid, by Portell, Owens and himself, recommended that resident citizens of that place should be employed to accompany Owens, but his opinion was over-ruled by Portell and Owens, who thought it would be more economical, and consequently more agreeable to the Spanish government, to have a boat's crew furnished from the galliot of this deponent, which he furnished—and further he deposes, that the sum of six thousand dollars, which had been brought by Owens from New Orleans to New Madrid, and by him delivered to Don Thomas Portell, the commandant of the fort, was by Portell embarked on board the galliot of this deponent, to be conveyed to the mouth of the Ohio, at which place he furnished Owens with a patron, named Pepello, and six of his oarsmen, and shipped in his canoe the before mentioned sum of six thousand dollars, to be delivered to General Wilkinson, and he declares that the sum was packed by himself in three small barrels, but being apprehensive of some bad design on the part of Owens' crew, he took back the money into his galliot, and retained it twenty-four hours in his possession, when at Owens' pressing solicitations he re-delivered it to him, who then departed with it, and some short time afterwards he learned that Owens had been murdered by his crew, and the money made away with by them—and further he, this deponent, declares that he afterwards arrested, and sent to New Orleans for trial, one Vexerano, one of Owens' crew, who was concerned in the murder of said Owens and plunder of the money. He further deposes, that although it was agreed between the Spanish government and Owens, to save appearances, that the money should appear to belong to said Owens, yet he knows it was sent by the Baron de Carondelet, for the use of and to be delivered to General Wilkinson, and that knowing the interest which the Spanish government had in this transaction, he wrote an official account to the Baron de Carondelet of the part he had taken in it, and the advice he had given respecting the conveyance of the money safely to its destination, and in reply the Baron regretted that his advice had not been followed in every particular; and the deponent further declares, that Owens had no other money than the six thousand dollars above mentioned. In testimony of which he has signed.

F. LANGLOIS.

D. BOULIGNY, Justice of Peace.

Nouvelle Orleans, ce 28 *Janvier*, 1795.

J'AI apprit, monsieur, avec bien de la peine par votre lettre du 13 de 9bre. la mort de M. Owen; ce malheur est un de ces evenemens qui l'on ne scauroit prevoir, et que la Providence dispose a son gré sans qui toute la prudence humaine puisse l'eviter; je voudrois et j'espere encore que ce malheureux Vexerano sera arreté, car cette action est trop infame pour qu'il puisse trouver un asile.

Je compte que vous voirez M. Roasseau a la fin d'Avril que vous vous incorporerez avec l'escadre prenant le commandement d'un galere, avec la qu'elle vous desendrez ici a la fin de Juin, amoins que vous ne preferiez de rester encore avec la même commission dans ces parages; il paroit que vous vons y etes bien porté, ce qui n'est pas peu de choses dans des endroits aussi fievreux.

A'present que la fleuve sera haut, vous devez redoubler de soin pour ne laisser introduire porsonne, ni aucun papier par l'Ohio, tendant a troubler la province ; on est etonné en Europe de la tranquillité qui y reigne, et ceux que j'en ai ecarté au commencement de la guerre, ou qui en sont sorti pour leurs affaires, ecrivent presentement qu'ils voudroient etre encore a la Louisiane, et louent les soins que nous avons pris pour en ecarter les esprits turbulens, desorte que ces mêmes gens qui vituperoient autrefois nos dispositions sont ceux qui les exaltent actuellement, et nous exhortent a les continuer.

Je recommande a M. Portell de bien traiter les Francois Royalistes, Hollandois, Allemandes, &c. qui se presenteront, et dont je vais former un bel establissement dans le Ouachita, je vous fais le même recommendation, mais vous ne leur laisserez aucun papier, livres, ou manuscrits ayant rapport aux affaires du têms.

J'ai l'honneur avec la plus parfaite consideration,
    Monsieur,
        Votre tèrs humble et très obeissant serviteur,
            LE BARON DE CARONDELET.
Mons. LANGLOIS.

Nouvelle Orleans, 28 *Juin*, 1795.

J'ai reçu, monsieur, vos lettres du 25 Fevrier, 14 Avril, et 15 Maï, par lesqu'elles vous me parlez de M. de Vilemont comme d'un commissioné de la cour, ce qu'il vous aura sans doute fait entendre, mais il n'en etoit rien ; Don Louis de Vilemont etoit porteur d'un passeport de lar cour qui lui permet de voïager pendant quatre ans, et rien de plus, mais quand même il se seroit trouvé chargé d'une commission vous devez scavoir, qu'elle n'est valuble qu'autant que comme Commandant General de la province j'aurois expedié mes ordres aux Commandans particuliers de lui en permettre l'exercice, et qu'aucun commissionné ne peut agir sans m'avoir fait part auparavant de ses ordres ; puisque la chose est faite il n'y faut plus penser, mais vous voyez combien Don Louis Vilemont etoit peu fondé dans ses discussions avec vous.

J'ai été enchanté de la prise que vous avez fait du scélerat de Vexerano a qui on a fait ici le procés et qui sera probablement pendu : on pretend qu'il y en a un autre refugié de la province qui etoit du même complot.

Je viens de recevoir par M. Valé votre derniere lettre, je tacherai d'arranger avec M. l'Intendant le defaut de formalité de vos feuilles, mais je crains bien que si Don Thomas Portell ne consent

a les intervenir vous ne vous trouviez embarrassé, car au tribunal de *cuentas* de la Havane on ne les passera pas sans intervention: je ne comprends pas comment M. Portell ne vous a pas instruit a ce sujet. J'ai l'honneur d'etre très parfaitement,
 Monsieur,
  Votre très humble et très obeissant serivteur,
   LE BARON DE CARONDELET.

NOTE No. 8.

TRANSLATION.

ON the 16th day of the month of January, in the year 1809, personally appeared before me, the undersigned, a Justice of Peace for the city of New Orleans, Monsieur Dominique Bouligny, formerly Adjutant Major of the Regiment of Louisiana, in the service of his C. M. and now a member of the Legislature of the Territory of Orleans, who being duly sworn on the Holy Bible did depose and say, that in the year 1795, as well as he can remember, he exercised the functions of Adjutant Major in the Regiment of Louisiana, and was commissioned by the Governor, the Baron de Carondelet, to conduct the trial of one Pepillo, who was accused of having been one of the authors of the death of Mr. Henry Owens, (who had been assassinated on the Ohio, in the American Territory,) and of the robbery of a sum of money, of which this Mr. Owens was the bearer to General Wilkinson, and which had been delivered to him by the Spanish Government. And he has further declared, that it was public and well known among the officers under the Spanish Government that General Wilkinson was a pensioner of the Spanish Government, and that the major part of the people in office believed that there was no reliance to be placed on the promises which the General made to the Government, because they could not persuade themselves that his influence could induce the people of the Western States to separate from the American Confederation.

 (Signed)   D. BOULIGNY.
Sworn to and affirmed before me,
   F. DUTILLET, Justice of the Peace.

NOTE No. 9.

PERSONALLY appeared before me, the undersigned, one of the Justices of the Peace in and for the city of New Orleans, Mr. Thomas Power, who, being duly sworn, doth depose, that in the year 1794 Mr. Henry Owens arrived at New Madrid from New Orleans, with a sum of money to be delivered to General Wilkinson, as the deponent understands and believes, from the Spanish Government, that he left New Madrid in the Royal Galliot Flecha, commanded by Francis Langlois, accompanied by a King's Pirogue, the Galliot destined to the mouth of the Ohio, from whence the deponent understood Owens was to proceed up the Ohio in the Pirogue. And this deponent further saith, that some time after the departure of the said Owens one of the crew of the Pirogue, in which he had embarked at the mouth of the Ohio, returned to New Ma-Madrid, and gave information that Owens had been robbed and murdered by the rest of the crew, who had proceeded up the Ohio with their booty. And this deponent saith, that some time in the year 1795, this deponent being at New Madrid, Lieutenant Aaron Gregg, of the American army, arrived there, accompanied by Mr. Charles Smith, bearing a letter from Major Doyle, who then commanded at Fort Massac, to the Commandant of New Madrid; the letter stated the following circumstances, which were confirmed both by Smith and Doyle to the deponent—that three of the murderers of Owens, after a variety of adventures, were confined under General Wilkinson's orders at Fort Washington—that by his directions they were put in irons, and placed on board a flat, under the direction of Mr. C. Smith, to be conveyed to New Madrid—that a letter was given to him from Wilkinson to the Commandant of New Madrid, containing an order to pay five hundred dollars on the delivery of the prisoners—that Smith was proceeding with them, and attempting to pass Fort Massac by night, was stopped by Major Doyle, who commanded there, who would not permit them to be sent out of the territory of the United States to be tried for a crime committed in it. The letter, after stating these circumstances, requested Captain Portel to send an interpreter to examine the prisoners, who spoke no English—Captain Portel requested the deponent to go on this service, which he undertook, and returned with Lieutenant Gregg and Mr. Smith, the latter having presented his order for the five hundred dollars, the payment of which was refused, as the prisoners were not delivered. On this deponent's arrival, he found three of the boat's crew who had gone up with Owens. On the first examination they confessed the fact of having murdered and robbed him, and they gave to the deponent a circumstantial detail of their adventures afterwards. A few days afterwards the deponent went to Louisville with Lieutenant Gregg and Mr. Smith, for the purpose of interpreting for the prisoners, who were there delivered to a Justice of the Peace, (Capt. Harrison,) who transmitted them to another at Baird's Town, (Captain Frye,) but the men denying the fact before the Justices, they were detained for further evidence. And this deponent saith, that he did not divulge to the Justices the confessions made by the prisoners to him, because he knew it was the wish of the Spanish officers to have the men delivered to them, rather than tried in the territory of the United States, and that such wish arose from a fear of divulging the secret of Owens' mission on a public trial. And this deponent saith that he left the prisoners at Baird's Town, and afterwards understood that they had been sent to Frankfort, where they were afterwards discharged for want of evidence, and further this deponent saith not.

THOMAS POWER.

Sworn and subscribed before me,
in New-Orleans, the 18th March, 1809.
E. FITCH,
Justice of the Peace.

NOTE No. 10.

Farvors, Dec. 7th, 1808.

DEAR SIR,

I AM thus far on my return from Pascagola. My friend there has not any letter or receipt in the hand writing of W. that is of importance. In the latter end of the year 1794, he was sent to Orleans in company with Owens for money. He carried a sealed packet for the Governor, but had no power of attorney or order. In the sealed packet, he understood from W. were letters of introduction—on these he received from Gill-Bear 6333 dollars, and Owens received 6000 dollars. Owens went up the river, and C—ns went to New-York, and returned down the Ohio to Cincinnati, where he delivered his charge to W. in the month of August 1795. He asked W. for a receipt, but he refused to give him one—and called on Mr. J. Brown of Kentucky, who was present, to take notice that they had settled, and he C— owed him nothing——Mark the caution of an experienced villain.—Are mercantile transactions for such large sums settled in this way?——C—ns was sent for in Ap'l last, by Governor Folk, to Pensacola, and his deposition taken, and sent immediately to W—n. This dep'n, I suppose, was not laid before the court of inquiry, as in their report they say, It did not appear to them that he had received any money after the year 1792, at which time he entered the army.——I have been delayed so much longer in finding Capt. C—ns than I expected, that it is necessary I now go on to Natchez, otherwise I would cross the Lake and see you again—The business should not stop here; the money sent by Mr. Power and deposited in the store of Montgomery Brown can be proven in Kentucky. These three sums will amount to about 20,000 dolls. Add to this the depositions of three or four respectable men, with whom he has conversed on the subject of bringing the Kentuckians under the Spanish Govt. and to whom he has urged the advantages of such a measure—Such testimony can be procured in Kentucky—

I cannot yet say whether it will be in my power to meet you in the city of Washington, during the sitting of Congress—Should I be so fortunate, I again repeat to you that proofs will not be wanting to establish the fact—Unless I can raise or obtain the use of five or six thousand dolls. for the next season, it will be out of my power—I was in hopes of collecting cotton at Natchez, and by shipping it obtain bills on New-York, payable at sixty or even ninety days sight. On these bills I could raise money in Kentucky—but I am told by Mr. Harrogan, that cotton will not sell either in Orleans or New York—this, if true, augurs badly as to the continuance of the embargo——I am indeed at a loss what to do—

I write this in a hurry at Farvors—It will be handed you by the mail carrier—I will hope to hear from you at Natchez, by the first mail, or sooner, if you can—If you think of any thing that will be of advantage please to communicate it—

NOTE.—When C—ns received the money, he gave a receipt in the following words—

Received from Gilbert Leonard six thousand three hundred and thirty-three dollars, for the use of Gen. James Wilkinson, which I promise to deliver to him, the risk of the seas, &c. excepted——

I have not a doubt my friend C—ns was candid with me—He says he knows his deposition was not pleasing, or such as was expected—

Accept of my good wishes, and believe me to be sincerely your friend—

and Humble Servt.

JOHN ADAIR.

NOTE No. 11.

PERSONALLY appeared before me, the undersigned, one of the Justices of the Peace for the city of New Orleans, Mr. William Miller, of the county of Rapides, in the territory of Orleans, who, being duly sworn on the Holy Evangelists of Almighty God, did depose and say, that some time shortly after the hurricane which happened in this country in the month of August of the year 1794, he charter'd and fitted out, in company with Mr. Robert Cochran, of Natchez, a small vessel in the Bayou St. John, near this city, in which they both sailed for Pensacola and New-Providence, and at that time he formed an acquaintance with Mr. Joseph Collins, who shortly before arrived in this city with a Mr. Owen, from the Ohio—the said Collins was then occupied in fitting out a small vessel in the Bayou St. John, in which was shipped a sum of money, as said Collins informed the deponent, amounting to upwards of six thousand dollars, which he, said Collins, had received from the Spanish Government, for account of General Wilkinson; and he also informed this deponent, that a sum of nearly equal amount had been delivered to Mr. Owen, for the same purpose, with which he returned by way of the river; and this deponent further declares, that this step occasioned at the time much surprise, as it was contrary to law to ship cash, and subject to seizure and confiscation when discovered; and this deponent further declares, that the said Joseph Collins set sail a short time before him, with the aforesaid money on board his vessel, as said Collins informed this deponent; and he afterwards learned that he had arrived therewith in safety at the port of Charleston.

WM. MILLER.

Juré pardevant moi ce jour onzième du moi de Mars mil huit cent neuf:

DU COURNAUX.
Juge de Paix.

NOTE No. 12.

(COPY.)

New Orleans, 26th June, 1808.

DEAR SIR,

TO corroborate the facts that you have laid before Congress and the public, relative to Brigadier General Wilkinson, I offer you the following, as they occurred to me. The mean chicanery that has been used recently in this ever unfortunate country to procure affidavits has prevented me from coming forward in that shape. However, you may use this as you please, and I will solemnly declare to the *facts* as stated before any court of record, when legally called upon.

In the months of August and September 1797, I accompanied General Wilkinson on Lake Huron and up the Straits to Lake Superior; on our way down to Detroit, as we entered the river St. Clair, we met a command of men, with dispatches for the General; the same day, after his having read his letters, he invited me to go on shore with him, to shoot pigeons—while on shore, he told me that Mr. Thomas Power had arrived at Detroit in his absence, that Col. Strong, the Commandant, acting under an order of Major Gen. Wayne's, had him in confinement—that he was apprehensive that he would have to send Mr. Power out of the country—although he knew him to be an honest clever fellow, a man of talents, and one that had rendered him great services but unfortunately that Mr. P—— was suspected as a spy, and that the U. States suspected him, Gen. W———, and at the same time quoting the old adage—that it was more criminal in some to look over the hedge, than in others to steal a horse—asking me, " how I would like to take a trip to New Madrid with Mr. Power"—I answered very well; he then enjoined secrecy on me—We arrived at Detroit before the middle of Sept. 1797, and found Mr. P—— (as the Gen. had stated) in confinement—he was immediately set at liberty, and a few days after I dined with him at the General's table; a very short time after this (perhaps next day) I was sent for by the General, who informed me that he had other duty for me than that of escorting Mr. P. that Captain Shaumbaugh was selected for that command, that I must hold myself in readiness to proceed to Kentucky, there to procure money on bills, and pay the troops at Fort Massac and Fort Knox (at St. Vincennes) which order I obeyed, and left Mr. P. at Detroit. In the beginning of November following I met Captain Shaumbaugh at Fort Massac, on his return from New Madrid, where he had delivered Mr. Power, he showed me his instructions from the General relative to Mr. P. in which Capt. S—— was ordered not to permit Mr. P. to enter any of our forts, and denied him the use of pen, ink, pencil or paper, &c. on reading those instructions I expressed some surprise at this great precaution, when I knew that Mr. Power had travelled through that country on his way, and that he had his full liberty at Detroit. Captain Shaumbaugh, laughing, said it was a *bore*. In the month of February 1798 I met Mr. Joseph Collins in Philad. We spent some time together in that city Having been acquainted with Mr. Collins in the Western Country, and had known him to live in the General's family, our conversation turned much towards the events in that country; in the course of our being together, he gave me a detailed account of his having taken a large sum of money from New Orleans to Charleston, South Carolina, for General Wilkinson, valuing himself very much on the great risk he had run in the voyage—his statement was something in this way, he embarked at or near New Orleans in a small boat, with the money as above mentioned, with three or four hands, Spaniards or Frenchmen, that he coasted it round, that the boat proved leaky, he had to halt many times to repair her, and that finally he burned lime, out of which by a certain process he formed a certain cement, that effectually stopped the leak, and he fortunately terminated his voyage. During the many times he was obliged to lay on shore to repair he was under the necessity of taking out his bags or boxes of silver—the great apprehensions that he entertained of the dishonesty of his crew—his vigilance in watching, fearful lest they would attempt to rob and perhaps murder him, &c. &c.—— I again in the same year in the month of December met Mr. Collins at Cincinnati, on the Ohio, where he in part superintended the building a large flat boat for the accommodation of Mrs. Wilkinson and family, and in January 1799 set out in company with them for Natchez. Having provided a boat for my own accommodation, and Mr. Collins navigating and having the controul of all the boats for the family, I had little to say in the movement, except to give them whatever *aid* I could. During our passage, which according to my recollection was from 25th January to the 28th February, Mr. Collins and I were almost every day together— our conversation frequently turned on General Wilkinson's final arrangements—I myself believing that the expences he had to encounter, and his mode of living, could not be discharged by his pay and emoluments—to this Mr. Collins acceded, but always observed that the General had other resources, quoting the money he had delivered for him at Charleston as proof of it. Frequently speaking of himself (Mr. Collins) said that while in the General's employ he had become a Spanish subject, and that he would soon avail himself of it, and make the Spanish dominions his permanent residence, which he has actually done, and now resides near Mobile.

Accept, dear sir, my best wishes for your health and all its concomitant blessings.

Yours, respectfully,

JAMES STERRITT.

The Hon. DANIEL CLARK.

NOTE No. 13.

MY FRIEND, *August 7th, —95.*

I HAVE now, I intended to say this morning, rec'd your favour by Mr. M'Dowell. He has eat with me, but will return 20 miles this evening, which obliges me to rise from cool Madeira to drop you a hasty line—it will be disordered of course, for hurry always produces confusion.

I send that which is handed about here (and to me by Judge Turner) as the bottom of another memorable treaty—from the mo. Kentucky to the mo. of Ohio, we have a near neighbourhood with our old friends—will it be a good one? or will mutual aggressions soon throw open the temple of Janus once more?—the gov't here I am told scouts this important production of our Solomon—it is my business to keep my peace, which to a man of mercury, whose heart and tongue are in unison, is no easy thing. If my very damned and unparalleled crosses and misfortunes did not uncash me, I would be with you in flour, but as I have honour, of 6590 dollars rec'd for me in N. O. 1740 only have reached my hand, this independent of poor Owens' loss—the whole of this last sum is not lost, but is not within my controul, and will not be for 6 or 9 months. I am sorry for old M'Affod, for I think he was an honest man, but I am more sorry for his son, and if I can serve him respecting the property left behind, and you think him honourable, he may on your recommendation receive a letter to my friend—this " entre nous"—because I have refused many.

I know that an emotion of friendship induced you to give me the mare, and when I am outdone in that commerce may " perdition catch me"—yet I love the brute I must confess—if she runs, she must run your property, or she will certainly break a leg or a thigh—you understand me—I send you fifty dollars by Mr. M'Dowell—what was I to pay you for her? We must not misunderstand one another—if I lend the nag to you and any misfortune ensues, I shall not be pleased, nor will you be happy—but if she is essential to your pleasure or pasttime, although no other man should have the honour to cross her, she is yours at what she cost me—I make a single reserve, if you can make a match, and let me in for a bet of 100*l.* cash, I will divide the risque of her safety with you. Old Tony, tis currently said, will go to Philadelphia so soon as he finishes the *dependencies* of his treaty—this *entre nous also*—if this should be true, you will hear from me—in the mean time pardon this scrawl, which I have not time to examine, and believe me to the bottom your friend and obed't servant,

JA. WILKINSON.

Col. ADAIR.

NOTE No. 14.

TRANSLATION.

IN the Galley the Victoria, Bernardo Molina, Patron, there have been sent to Don Vincente Folch nine thousand six hundred and forty dollars, which sum, without making the least use of it, you will hold at my disposal, to deliver it the moment an order may be presented to you by the American General Don James Wilkinson. God preserve you many years. New Orleans, January 20th, 1796.

(Signed)   THE BARON DE CARONDELET.
To Senior Don TOMAS PORTEL.

I certify that the foregoing is a copy of the original to which I refer. New Madrid, 27th June, 1796.

(Signed)   TOMAS PORTEL.

NOTE No. 15.

Translation of a letter from Thomas Power to Don Thomas Portel, Commandant of New Madrid, dated June 27th, 1796, at New Madrid.

" HAVING received verbal instructions from Mr. James Wilkinson, the American General, to take charge of the money, which, by a letter he received from the Secretary of the government, D. Andres Armesto, under date the 7th or 8th March last, of which I was bearer, he has advice is deposited in this post, and being informed by the official letter which you have received on this business from the Governor General of the province, of which you will be pleased to furnish me a copy, that said money is not to be delivered without an express order from the said Mr. Wilkinson, I find myself forced to relate circumstantially some particulars, to smooth and remove the difficulty which the want of a written order on the part of the aforesaid General Wilkinson presents. Although this relation may appear an abuse of the confidence with which the Governor General of the province and the Governor of

Natchez, and particularly General Wilkinson, have honoured me, I am persuaded that the urgency of the case which offers will serve me as an excuse and justification. You are not ignorant of the fact, that Don *Manuel Gayoso de Lemos being here in the month of September of the year last past,* he entrusted to me some dispatches of the greatest importance for General *Wilkinson, which I carried to Cincinnati, and returned with the answers in the month of November.* By order of the said Don Manuel Gayoso, I made immediately another journey in the Ohio, and I ascended it to Red Banks, in search of Mr. Sebastian, who came with me to the mouth of the Ohio, where we met with the Governor of Natchez. At the end of December I accompanied this gentleman to Natchez, and went thence to New Orleans. The principal object of my going down was to take charge, by order of General Wilkinson, of the money which you have now in deposit for him, which is shown by the letters which he wrote to the Governors of this province and of Natchez; but at my arrival the money had been sent off in one of his Majesty's galleys for this place, which I learned from the Baron de Carondelet, the Intendant, and Don Andres de Armesto. I repeatedly (conversed) on this business with the two last of these persons, urging forcibly the necessity of sending sugar, coffee and powder, to New Madrid, to form a cargo to take to Kentucky with Wilkinson's money, hiding by this means the true intention of the voyage, and giving it the appearance of a commercial speculation. All this Wilkinson had before represented as indispensible, for many reasons, particularly in order to avoid a misfortune similar to that which had already occurred. At last the Secretary told me that the barge in which Mr. Aaron Gregg, the American officer, was to go up, was destined for this service, and that as for the crew, he would permit me to choose among the creoles, resident in this post, those who might appear to me most worthy of confidence, so that I left New Orleans with the belief, that at my return to this post I should find every thing disposed conformable to what I have just related. On arrival at Grenville I informed Gen. Wilkinson of the steps which I had no doubt had been taken, from whence has resulted, that he like myself was impressed with the belief that all the measures for executing this service with success had been taken. I cannot communicate all the motives why General Wilkinson has not given me an order in writing—but one of them was, that he did not know the sum of money which you had to deliver to his order, the Governor not having written a word to him on the subject; the Secretary only saying that his money was deposited in New Madrid, without expressing the sum. In the letters in cypher from General Wilkinson for the Governors, which are here enclosed, he tells them, that he has sent me to bring the aforesaid money, informing you that the No. 1 is for the Governor General of the province, and the No. 2 for Don Manuel Gayoso. I will add, that General Wilkinson, when I represented to him that, on presenting myself without his order in writing, some difficulty might arise, authorised me, if the case required it, to write an order that you should deliver his money, specifying the sum there might be, signing it in his name, and giving you a receipt therefor.

I cannot omit, that the commission of General Wilkinson was so sudden, so urgent, that it was extended even to limiting my return to my destination by the first of August, of which I advise you, that you may endeavour not to delay the service. I believe that the Governor General is not ignorant of the embarrassments of General Wilkinson, nor can he be ignorant that for a long time past he has been expecting this money, the delay of which has been the cause of much trouble to him, involving him in great difficulties; and I can assure you, confidently, that he will be very much disgusted with any delays in the expedition, which might be productive of serious injury. As for the mode of carrying the money, it is evident, that to take it openly would be too scandalous a thing, if I were not to say—madness! The unhappy result of the expedition of the unfortunate Henry Owens ought to serve us as a beacon, in order not to lose ourselves on the same rock, and to make us take another course less dangerous. I would wish to put a bag of one thousand dollars in a barrel of coffee or sugar, so that although the difference of the respective gravity, between silver, sugar and coffee, be very great, the quantity being so small, it would not be easily known. It will likewise be prudent to carry some barrels without money, in order to sell them before arriving at Cincinnati, if it should so happen that any one should offer to buy these goods; because not to sell them, when it might be done to advantage, would excite suspicion; and to complete the disguise, it would be well to take a certain quantity of powder and rum. If these dispositions should appear defective, I beg you may make such changes as may be to your mind.

God preserve you many years.

THOMAS POWER.

Don THOMAS PORTEL.

New Madrid, June 27, 1796.

NOTE No. 16.

Translation of a letter from Don Thomas Portel to Mr. Thomas Power, dated at New Madrid, June 27th, 1796.

"HAVING well considered the contents of your letter of this day, I mention that I agree in every thing, to the whole of the reflections you place before me; and although at first sight it appears that I ought to avail the decision of the Governor General, as he prescribes to me in his official letter of the 20th January, of the present year, and of which I enclose you a copy which you request of me, the circumstances which you expose are such, that they leave me nothing more to do than to tell you to forward me a memorandum of the number of pounds of coffee, sugar, barrels, in which to fill the powder and rum you desire for your expedition, because so soon as I receive it I will get it ready at your desire, informing you that for the merchandize you must sign me an acknowledgment of having received it, &c. and for the money a receipt, as the Attorney for General Wilkinson.

In order that the barge may be ready as you may want it, I have written an official letter to the Lieut. Col. Don Vincent Folch, that he may send it as soon as possible, because, as nothing was said to me of what you have now mentioned respecting it, Mr. F. Laughton asked it of me for an affair of service, and took it loaded with corn to the fort of Can Fernando, and it has not been returned, although I have required it, thinking it might be wanted here. Don Vincent Folch having answered me, that if I had not orders to keep it, there were none to return it. The two letters in cypher remain in my hands, which I shall forward by the first safe opportunity, with the distinction you point out, No. 1 to the Governor General, and No. 2 to the Governor of Natchez.

As for packing the money and arranging the barrels, as soon as they are ready, between you and myself, this all may be done without any one else acquiring a knowledge of it.

God preserve you many years.
New Madrid, 27th June, 1796.

THOMAS PORTEL.

To Don Thomas Power.

NOTE No. 17.

PERSONALLY appeared before me, the undersigned, one of the Justices of the Peace in and for the city of New Orleans, Mr. Thomas Power, who, being duly sworn, saith, that some time in the month of June, in the year of our Lord 1796, he arrived at New Madrid, after having had several conferences with Gen. Wilkinson, by order of the Baron de Carondelet, on the subject of a proposed separation of the Western Country from the U. S. under the protection and by the aid of Spain—that he was sent to New Madrid by General Wilkinson, for the purpose of taking charge of a sum of money which he had brought notice to the General was lying there for him from the Baron de Carondelet that on his first demanding the same in the name of Gen. Wilkinson, Captain Portel, the commandant, refused to deliver it without a written order—and that as he had none, he was obliged to write a letter to Captain Portel, entering into all the details which were necessary to show him that he, this deponent, was acquainted with the object of sending the said money; that the said Portel wrote him an answer, agreeing to deliver him the sum of money in question for General Wilkinson, and at the same time sent him a copy of the order from the Baron de Carondelet which accompanied the delivery of the money to him, Portel—that the said letter and answer are dated the 27th June, 1796, and the said order from the Baron de Carondelet is dated the 20th January, in the same year, and are the documents which have been laid before Congress by John Randolph and Daniel Clark, Esquires—and this deponent saith, that by virtue of the arrangement made by the said letters, he received from Don Thomas Portel the sum of 9640 dollars, which he packed up in barrels of sugar and coffee, and was proceeding up the Ohio with the same, when he was stopped and searched by Lieutenant Steele—that in consequence of this interruption he landed his cargo at Louisville, and went on horseback to Cincinnati, where he met General Wilkinson, and informed him of the circumstances that had occurred, on which the General directed him to deliver the dollars to Philip Nolan, which the deponent did—that the said Nolan conveyed the barrels of sugar and coffee in which the dollars were packed to Frankfort, where the deponent saw them opened in the store of Mr. Montgomery Brown; that the sum of nine thousand dollars was given by Gen. Wilkinson's direction to Philip Nolan, and the remainder, 640 dollars, was retained by the deponent, with the General's consent.

for the purpose of paying expences, but which he gave directions to secure for him from the Spanish government in the settlement of his account—and this deponent further saith, that he sold the sugar and the coffee in which the dollars were packed to Mr. Abijah Hunt, of Cincinnati—And this deponent further saith, that when he afterwards saw General Wilkinson, and informed him that he had delivered the money agreeably to his orders, he said it was well—and further this deponent saith not.

THOMAS POWER.

Sworn and subscribed to before me, in New Orleans, the 18th March, 1809.

E. FITCH,
Justice of the Peace.

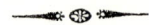

NOTE No 18.

TERRITORY OF ORLEANS.

City of New Orleans, sct.

PETER DERBIGNEY, of New Orleans, counsellor at law, being sworn on the Holy Evangelists of Almighty God, deposeth, that some time in the year 1796, this deponent being then a resident at New Madrid, on the Missisippi, Mr. Thomas Power, then employed by the Spanish government on a private agency, went up the Ohio as far as Cincinnati, as this deponent was told, and returned some time afterwards to New Madrid, in quest of a sum of money which was delivered to him by Don Thomas Portel, the then commandant of that post. That this deponent was informed by a Spanish officer, on whose veracity he had every reason to depend, that the said money was destined for General Wilkinson, who was in a secret correspondence with the Spanish government. That Mr. Thomas Power, in order to conceal the said money, which was, as far as this deponent can recollect, a sum of nine thousand dollars or thereabouts, bought from this deponent some barrels of sugar and coffee, in the centre of which the said money was packed up in small bags, which were made for that purpose in this deponent's family. That after these preparations were gone through,

Mr. T. Power set off on his way back to Cincinnati; and that on said Power's return from thence, this deponent was told that the said money had arrived safe, and had been delivered to General Wilkinson.

And this deponent further saith, that shortly after the surrender of Louisiana to the United States a rumour having circulated, that General Wilkinson had shipped in the vessel in which he returned to the Atlantic States a large quantity of sugar, the price of which he had paid him in dollars lately coined, contained in bags not yet unsewed, and such as they are when sent from the Spanish mint—this deponent grew suspicious that it was again money paid by the Spanish treasury to General Wilkinson, and felt it his duty towards the government, to whom he had of late sworn allegiance, to inform the Governor of this province of the facts to him known concerning the money sent up to General Wilkinson in 1796; that Governor Claiborne then requested this deponent to write to the President of the United States on the subject; that this deponent wrote accordingly to the President of the U. S. and delivered his letter into the hands of Governor Claiborne, after having shown him the contents, which he approved of, and that as the said letter was not signed, this deponent, by the advice of Governor Claiborne, mentioned therein to the President, that he might know the name of the writer from Governor Claiborne himself, if he should wish it.

And this deponent further swears, that in the winter of 1804 to 1805, this deponent, being then at Washington City, in the capacity of a deputy from the inhabitants of Louisiana to Congress, jointly with Messrs. Dostrehan and Sawis, he was introduced to Colonel Burr, then Vice-President of the United States, by General Wilkinson, who strongly recommended to this deponent, and, as he believes, to his colleagues, to cultivate the acquaintance of Colonel Burr, whom he used to call "the first gentleman in America," telling them that he was a man of the most eminent talents, both as a politician and as a military character; and this deponent further swears, that General Wilkinson told him several times, that Col. Burr, so soon as his Vice-presidency would be an end, would go to Louisiana, where he had certain projects, adding, that he was such a man as to succeed in any thing he would undertake, and inviting this deponent to give him all the information in his power respecting that country; which mysterious hints appeared

to this deponent very extraordinary, though he could not then understand them, and further this deponent saith not.

P. DERBIGNEY.

Sworn before me, at New Orleans, this 27th
of August, 1807

AS: BONAMY,
Justice of the Peace for the Parish of New Orleans.

COPIES.

Test.

WM. MARSHALL, Clk.

NOTE No. 19.

Territory of Orleans, sct.

JOHN MERCIER, jun. of the city of New Orleans, being duly sworn, maketh oath, that he was one of the clerks in the office of the Governor in the time of the Spanish dominion during a period of nine years, from the year 1792 to the year 1801. That whilst this deponent was employed in the said office, to wit, in the years 1795 and 1796, a secret correspondence was carried on in cypher between the said Governor, then the Baron de Carondelet, and some person of note, who then was in the western part of the United States, and, as this deponent believes, on the waters of the Ohio. That this deponent had no certain knowledge of the name of the said person, but that it was a matter of notoriety among those who were employed in the said office, that the said person was General Wilkinson. That this deponent was entrusted with the care or charge of decyphering some of the letters which were received from the said person, and of copying some of the answers which were made to them by the Governor. That the cypher was understood by means of a small English dictionary, and that, so far as this deponent recollects, the number of the page and line where the word was in the dictionary was made use of instead of the word itself. That this deponent very well recollects that the project treated of in the said correspondence was the dismembering of the western states and territories from the Union, but that he is not able to recollect the particulars. And this deponent further swears, that some time towards the end of the year 1795, Mr. Thomas Power, who was employed as the confidential agent of the Spanish government for this secret negociation, was entrusted with a sum of nine thousand dollars, or thereabouts, destined for the said person, which sum was delivered to said Power in the office of the Governor, in the presence of this deponent. That the said Power set off with it, and, as this deponent believes, with the dispatches which were prepared on that occasion for the said person.

J. MERCIER.

Sworn before me, at New Orleans, the 31st of August, 1807.

AIS: BONAMY, Justice of the Peace.

NOTE No. 20.

Nouvelle Madrid, 21 *Juin,* 1796.

MONSIEUR,

JE me suis rendu à ce poste hier après-midi. Comme ce n'est pas le moment à présent d'entrer dans le details rélatifs à mon voyage avec le Sieur S. ni de vous communiquer les observations sur les sujets auxquels vous m'avis si fortement recommandé de porter mon attention, je me bornerai. simplement à vous faire le récit de la situation ou je me par rapport à la commission que m'a donnée . . . . . de me charger de l'argent vous avez fait passer au commande de ce poste, pour lui etre envoyé.

Je suis arrivé à Cincinnati le 19 de Mai . . . . . de trouvait alors à Greenville—pour ne faire naitre de soupcons, j'ai cru qu'il etait prudent de ne point partir pour le quartier general sans avoir préalablement obtenir permission d'y aller du Gen. Wilkinson, qui y commandait—cette permission ne m'est parvenue que le 31—le 2 de Juin je m'y suis rendu, et j'ai remis à . . . . . les dépêches dont le Sieur S. s'etait chargé, et qu'il lui a ète impossible de lui faire tenir, d'une autre manière, sans les exposer à tomber entre les mains de ses ennemies—Je lui ai répété les conversations que j'avait eues avec le Mons. l'Intendant et Mon. Don Andres au sujet de l'argent il est a présent question, et des moyens dont nous nous etions avisé, pour le lui faire passer sans courir des risques; qui étaient que, sous prétexte de faire un voyage de commerce, je devais remonter l'Ohio jusque à la chute ou Cincinnati avec un cargaison de sucre, café, poudre, &c. le tout en barrils, chacun desquels devaient contenir une certaine quantité de piastres. Ces précautions lui ont paru si sages, qu'il m'a détenu le moins qu'il a pu, sans donner de l'ombrage, et m'a expèdié avec des ordres verbals de recevoir du command: de la Nouvelle Madrid l'argent qui était dèposé entre ses mains pour lui, et de lui en donner un recu. Lorsque je lui ai suggíré qu'il serait peut-étre nécéssaire que je présentasse au dit commandant un ordre de sa part, il m'a observé que ne sachant pas combien de piastres le dit command: recu pour etre livres à son ordre, il lui était impossible de spécifier la somme que je devais recevoir; ajoutant qu'il était surpris que Mons. Don Andrés ne lui eut pas marqué dans sa lettre, (qui ètait la seule de toutes celles qu'il avait recues dans laquelle il ètait fait mention de cet argent,) quelle ètait la somme qui avait ète envoye à la Nouvelle Madrid - d'ailleurs, m'a-t-il dit, " je me trouve dans une position " si critique, et suis environné de tant d'ennemis, que, vous donner " un ordre par écrit, se serait m'exposer à me perdre infaillible- " ment, et à faire manquer un projet auxquels nous travaillons de- " puis tant d'années." Il m'a même autorisé, puisqu'il n'osoit me donner l'ordre par ècrit que je lui demandais, et que le command: ne l'aurait pas compris s'il me leut donné en chiffres, d'ècrire moi-même une ordre en son nom, et de le présenter au command:t s'il arrivait qu'il fit des difficultés. Hier, comme j'ai déjà eu l'honneur de vous le dire, je me suis rendu ici, et ce matin j'ai fait application à Mons. le command:t pour l'argent de ..... pour toute réponse il m'a fait voir votre lettre officielle, en dâte du 20 Janvier 1796, dans laquelle vous lui donnés ordre de ne livrez les 9640 piastres qu'à celui qui présenterait un ordre du dit ..... à cet effet. Alors je lui ai fait part de ce qui s'etait passé entre ..... et moi : et pour lui donner une satisfaction complette et le convaincre que j'avais la confiance de ..... et son ordre pour recevoir l'argent en question j'ai cru qu'il ètait indispensablement a mon devoir d'entrer vis-à-vis lui dans certains details, pue dans toute autre circonstance je me serais pas permis—je présume que Mons. Portèl vous communiquera tout ce qui a eu lieu entre nous, avec une copie de la lettre que j'ai cru ne pas pouvoir me dispenser de lui écrire. J'espère, Mons. que vous ne laisserés pas que d'approuver la conduite que j'ai tenu dans cette circonstance épinecuse et embarrassante; et je vous prie d'ête persuadé qu'elle a été réglée uniquement par le zèle actif qui m'anime pour le service du roi, lequel j'ose me flatter m'attirera de plus en plus votre confiance.

La delicatesse me défende de vous tracer le tableau de la position de . . . . . —l'exposé que je pourrais vous en faire en même tems qu'il vous affligerait, veus convaincrait de la nécessité des démarchesque j'ai faites, ainsi que de la pureté et du désenteréssement de mes intentions. J'ai remis Mon. Don Thomas Portél pour qu'il vous le fasse parvenir, un billet de . . . . . il m'a prié de vous marquer que la multiplicité de ses occupations ne lui permittait, en ce moment, de s'étendre davantage, mais qu'il vous écrira a mon retour d'une manière plus dètaillée. J'ai également mis entre les mains de Mons. le command:t un billet dans le même genre, de . . . . . pour Mons. le Gouverneur de Natchez —les motifs qui m'ont guidé dans toute cet affaire, qui sont le dèsir de ne pas perdre du tems a voler au secours de . . . . . et la conviction dont je suis pénétré que par ce moyen j'entre complettement dans vos vues, ne me permettent de vous écrire avec toute l'ètendue que je m'etais proposée, mais je ne négligerai pas de le faire avant mon depart pour Cincinnati.— J'ai l'honneur d'être, Monsieur, avec le plus profond respect et le dévouement le plus parfait,

Votre très humble
Et très obeis't serv'eur.

Al Senior BARON DE CARONDELET, Caballero de la Religion de St. Juan, Marèscal de Campo de los Exercitos de S. M. Gobernor Gen'l. Vice-patrono de la Provincia de la Louisiana y Florida Occidental, è Inspector de sus tropas, Nueva Orleans.

TRANSLATION.

New Madrid, 22d June, 1796.
SIR,
I arrived at this port yesterday afternoon. As this is not a proper time to enter into the details of my journey with Mr. S. nor to communicate to you the observations on the subjects to which you have so strongly recommended to me to apply my attention, I shall confine myself simply to relate to you the situation with respect to the *commission (a) which* . . . . *gave me, to take charge*

. . . .

(a) In the original draft the following words were first written, but afterwards struck out, and those in italics inserted. " *Money which you sent to the commandant of this post for Gen. W.—and of which he begged me to take charge.*"

of the money which you sent to the commandant of this post, to be sent to him.

I arrived at Cincinnati the 19th of May—*(b)* was then at Greenville. Not to give rise to any suspicions, I thought it was prudent not to set out for head-quarters without having previously obtained permission from Gen. Wilkinson, who commanded there—this permission did not arrive until the 31st—the second of June I went there, and delivered to .... the dispatches which Mr. S. had taken charge of and he had found it impossible to send in any other manner, without exposing them to the risque of falling into the hands of his enemies—I repeated to him the conversations I had with the Intendant and Don Andres on the subject of the money in question, and of the means we had devised to send it him without running any risque, which were, that under pretext of making a commercial voyage, I should ascend the Ohio to the falls or Cincinnati, with a cargo of sugar, coffee, powder, &c. all in barrels, each one of which should contain a certain quantity of dollars. These precautions appeared to him so wise that he detained me as short a time as possible, without giving umbrage, and sent me off with verbal orders to receive from the commandant of New Madrid the money which was placed in his hands for him, and to give him a receipt for it; when I suggested to him that it would be necessary perhaps that I should present to the said commandant an order from him, he observed to me, that not knowing how many dollars the said commandant had received to be delivered to his order, it was impossible for him to specify the sum which I ought to receive—adding, that he was surprised that Don Andres had not designated in his letter (which was the only one of those which he had received in which the money was mentioned) what was the sum that had been sent to New Madrid. " Besides, he added, I find myself in so critical a position and surrounded by so many enemies, that to give you an order in writing would be exposing myself to infallible ruin, and to the failure of a project which we have laboured at so many years"—he authorised me even, since he could not give me the order in writing, which I asked from him, and the commandant would not have understood it if he had given me one in cypher, to write an order myself in his name, and to present it to the commandant, if it should happen that he made any difficulty. Yesterday, as I have already had the honour to inform you, I came here and

....

(b) In the original the words Gen. W. were first written, and afterwards struck out, but are still legible.

this morning I applied to the commandant for .... 's money. The only answer he gave was to shew me your official letter dated 20 Jan'ry, 1796, in which you order him to deliver the 9640 dollars only to the person who should present an order from the said .... to that effect—then I communicated to him what had passed between .... and me, and to give him complete satisfaction and convince him that I was in the confidence of .... and had his order to receive the money in question, I thought it my indispensible duty to enter with him into certain details, which under any other circumstances I should not have permitted myself to do—I presume that Mr. Portel will communicate to you all that took place between us, together with a copy of the letter which I thought I could not avoidw riting to him. I hope, Sir, that you will approve of the conduct which I have pursued in these difficult and embarrassing circumstances, and I beg you to be persuaded that it has been regulated solely by the active zeal which animates me for the service of the King, and which I dare flatter myself will more and more secure to me your confidence. Delicacy prevents my tracing to you the picture of the position of .... the detail which I could make, at the same time that it would afflict you, would convince you of the necessity of the steps which I have taken, as well as the purity and disinterestedness of my intentions. I have delivered to Dn. T. Portel, to be forwarded to you, a note from .... he begged me to inform you that the multiplicity of his occupations did not permit him at this moment to enlarge, but that he would write to you more in detail at my return—I have also put into the hands of the commandant a note of the same nature from .... for the Governor of the Natchez—the motives which have guided me in all this affair, and which the desire of not losing any time in flying to the relief of .... and the perfect conviction I have that in doing so I am completely into your views, do not permit me to write to you to the extent which I had proposed, but I will not neglect to do it before my departure from Cincinnati. I have the honour to be, Sir, with the most profound respect, and the most perfect devotion,

    Your most obed't servant, &c.

(Directed)

To the Baron Carondelet, Knight of the Order of St. John, Mareschal de camp of the armies of H. M. Gov. Gen. Vice Patron of the province of Louisiana and West Florida, and Inspector of the troops.

NOTE No. 21.

New Madrid, 27th June, 1796.

SIR,

I ARRIVED at this place yesterday afternoon—my return has been delayed nearly one month beyond the time I had calculated upon. Mr. S. and I parted at Cincinnati the 19th of last mo.—he was then not perfectly in health, and a good deal worsted by his journey ; which, owing to the uncommon severity of the weather, had been attended with more fatigue than we expected to encounter.— At some future and not distant period I will do myself the honour of laying before you some of the particulars of our travels, and the reflections that occasionally pressed themselves on our minds— the situation in which I am thrown by a concurrence of circumstances originating in a want of foresight, is far from being pleasant Indulge me in a few minutes patience and I will acquaint you with it. S... at Cincinnati gave me charge of the letters he had received for .... who was then at Greenville ; the vigilance and activity of his enemies made it unsafe to trust them to any ordinary conveyance : I therefore resolved to carry them myself— but not to attract the eye of suspicion, and to remove even the shadow of it, I judged it necessary to remain at Cincinnati until I obtained permission from General Wilkinson to visit head-quarters, where he commanded—having obtained it, I proceeded thither without delay, and arrived there the second of June, and delivered the letters.— ...... asked me what arrangements had been made to have the money forwarded to him. I informed him that I had agreed with Dn. Andres, who appeared to have the arrangement of that business, that I should proceed up the Ohio, in the barge in which Lieut. A. Gregg returned to Massac, with a cargo of sugar, coffee, &c. in barrels, and that, to elude the grasp even of conjecture, the money should be put up by small quantities into the barrels-- that I was to have the selection of the boat's crew from among the Creoles and Canadians living at this place, or on board the king's galleys—and that I understood the sugar and coffee had been sent up with the dollars. Pleased with these artful precautions, which to him appeared well calculated to lull suspicion, blind the inquisitive, avert danger, and ensure success, he gave me verbal orders to take charge of the money, proceed with all possible dispatch for New Madrid, and return speedily to Cincinnati. The reason for his not giving me an order by writing is obvious—it might fall into the hands of his enemies, an event that was within the scope of possible contingencies, and which would inevitably have involved him with perhaps some of his friends in destruction, and in one moment have blasted a scheme, in the prosecution of which he had devoted his talents, labour and time, and would have crowned the best founded hopes with the bitterness of disappointment. This, he thought, was putting too much at stake—and to have given me an order in cyphers would undoubtedly have been useless, for it would have been unintelligible to the command't——to obviate, as much as possible, these difficulties, he authorised me, if necessary, to write an order myself and sign his name. I cannot omit another cogent reason which would not allow ..... to give me such an order was, that he knew not what sum of money had been sent for him to New Mad'd, and could not therefore specify what I was to receive—he informed me that neither you nor the Baron had mentioned in your letters a syllable about sd. money : and that Dn. Andres alone writes him, that the money had been conveyed to N. M. without specifying the sum. This he was not a little surprised at. I left Greenville on the 9th and proceeded to this place. This morning I acquainted the command't with my commission ; on this, he showed me a letter from the Gov'or of the province, ordering him to deliver the money only to the person who should present him an order from ...... ; assuring me at the same time that neither coffee nor sugar had been sent for the purpose already mentioned. I expostulated in vain with him. Mortified and shocked with the thoughts of what .... would suffer by any further delay in this business, which by a hostile combination of events has been protracted so long, I thought it my duty to lay before the comm't certain circumstances, which the exigence of the case alone can warrant. This, however, had the desired effect by prevailing upon him to accede to my proposals. Inclosed you will receive a copy of what I have written to him. My conduct on this occasion I hope will meet with your approbation. I can with confidence assert, that it has been dictated solely by my zeal for the service of the King, my attachment to .... and a desire to serve him. As soon as the barge arrives from St. Fernando, and every thing got in readiness, I will proceed up the river without any loss of time. .... expects me by the first of August. I assured him so positively that my absence should not extend beyond that period, that, if he is disappointed, he will be tormented with the most painful anxiety. I am informed that you have been appointed Governor of the province—permit me to congratulate you on the event, and assure you that I rank amongst the foremost who sincerely rejoice at it. Not to detain the boat that is going to St. Fernando, I am obliged to close this, and defer writing to you more at length to a more leisure hour. I have the honour to be, Sir, with respect and consideration,

          Yours, &c.

Governor GAYOSO.

NOTE No. 22.

Nouvelle Madrid, 5 Janvier, 1797.

MONSIEUR,

 JE suis arrivé en ce poste le premier du mois passé. Je comptais vous annoncer cette nouvelle en personne : mais les évènemens les plus contrarians m'em ont empêché, et ne me permettent pas encore de partir pour la N. Orleans, pour vous rendre compte de ma mission, de laquelle je me suis acquitté avec succès, en dépit l'opposition de Wayne.—Je me serais déja rendu a la capitale si j'avais été moi-même porteur de lettres de * * * que j'ai recues il y a quelques jours par Mons. Nolan. Les gazettes que j'ai l'honneur de vous faire passer avec celle-ci vous apprendront le motif par lequel * * * * n'a pas ose m'en charger. Vous y verrez aussi la manière dont j'ai été traité pas les ordres du Gen. Wayne. Il y a certain details qu'il aura imprudent de mettre sous les yeux du public, mais que je vous communiquerai quand j'aurai l'honneur de voir votre Excellence. Dans les instructions qui ont accompagné les lettres de ..... il me donne l'ordre le plus pressant de me rendre sans délai a la Nouvelle Orleans, et de la a Philadelphie, où ma presence est indispensable : Et consequence j'ai fait application a Mons. le Command:t De Lassus par la berge dans laquelle j'ai fait mon dernier voyage, laquelle il a laissée a ma disposition ; et je serais parti le 22 de Décembre si une gelée la plus forte que l'on ait éprouvée en ce pays, ne fut survenue ; ce qui a glacé le Missisippi a la distance de plusieurs toises de son bord. La Rivière est encore dans le même état, et charie un quantité si prodigieuse de glacons, que entreprendre de la déscendre dans

quelqu' espèce d'embarkation que ce soit, hormis un petit canot, serait s'exposer a un naufrage inévitable—Aussitôt le froid rigoureux qu'il fait en ce moment aura cessé et que le fleuve sera assés débarrassé de glaçons pour qu'on puisse le naviguer, vous pouvez être persuadé que je ne retarderai pas mon départ d'un instant. Si je ne vous fait point tenir les lettres de * * * c'est pour ne pas me départir de ses ordres ; il m'a enjoint de la manière la plus urgente & la plus expresse me'n dessaisir, que pour vous les livrer in personne. J'ose me flatter que lorsque je vous aurai fait part des motifs de ma conduite dans toute cette affaire, si singulièrement, épineuse et delicate, vous ne me refuserez pas vous approbation : au moins je ne balancerai pas de vous assurer hardiment que mes intentions la méritent. Je crois qu'il est essentiel de ne pas vous laisser ignorer que les soupçons dont je vous ai fait part sur le compte du Gen. Colot, ne'étoient que trop bien fondés. " Il est en-évoyé par Monsieur Adet pour remplir la mission *manquéé* par le Sieur Egron." La personne de qui je tiens ceci, avait refusé de l'accepter—Vous dire qui c'est en ce moment, serait trop risquer. Lorsque je vous l'aurai nommé, vous ce douterez point de ce que j'avance.—Cette mê me personne m'a promis, qu' a mon retour à Philadelphie, elle me communiquirait certains détails très-intéressans pour cette province. Comme j'espère me rendre en ville presqu' aussitôt que ce courier, je ne me permettrai pas d'abuser plus long-tems de votre patience, et d'envahir votre tems precieux. J'ai l'honneur d'être avec dévouement et respect,
 Le très humble et treès obeissant serviteur de votre Excellence.
       THO.
Mons. le Baron de CARONDELET.

TRANSLATION OF NOTE No. 22.

New Madrid, 3d January, 1797.
SIR,
 I arrived at this post the first of last month. I intended to announce to you this visit in person : but the most contrariant events have prevented me, and do not yet permit me to set out for New Orleans, to render you an account of my mission, in which I have succeeded, in spite of the opposition of Wayne.—I should have already returned to the capital, if I had myself been the bearer of the letters of * * * which I have received some days since by Mr. Nolan. The gazettes which I have the honour to send you with this will in-

form you of the motives, which prevented * * * from putting them under my care. You will see there also the manner in which I have been treated by the orders of General Wayne. There are certain details, which it would be imprudent to exhibit to the eyes of the public, but which I will communicate when I have the honour of seeing your Excellency. In the instructions which accompany the letters of * * *, he gives me the most pressing orders to go without delay to New Orleans, and from thence to Philadelphia, where my presence is indispensable: In consequence thereof I have made an application to the commandant Lassus for the barge in which I made my last voyage, which he has put at my disposition; and I should have sat out the 22d of December, if a frost had not happened, the hardest ever known in this country, which froze the Missisippi the distance of several toizes from its banks. The river is still in the same state, and carries down so great a quantity of cakes of ice, that to undertake to descend it in any kind of vessel, except a little boat, would be exposing onesself to inevitable shipwreck. As soon as the rigorous cold which yet prevails shall have ceased, and the river shall be cleared of ice, so that it may be navigated, you may be persuaded that I shall not delay my departure an instant. If I do not send the letters of * * *, it is because I do not wish to go beyond his orders. He enjoined me, in the most express and urgent manner, not to part with them, until I could deliver them to you in person. I dare flatter myself, that when I shall have imparted to you the motives of my conduct in all this business, which is so very difficult and delicate, you will not refuse me your approbation; at least I do not hesitate to assure you that my intentions merit it. I believe it is essential that you should know, that the suspicions which I communicated to you on the subject of General Collot were but too well founded. He is sent by " Mr. Adet, to fulfil the mission in which Mr. Egron failed." The person from whom I have this refused to accept it. To tell you who it is, at this time, would be risquing too much. When I shall have named him, you will not doubt of what I advance. This same person has promised me, that at my return from Philadelphia he would communicate certain details, very interesting for this province. As I hope to be in town almost as soon as this courier, I will no longer abuse your patience, and take up your precious time. I have the honour to be, with devotion and respect,

Your most obedient servant,

Baron de CARONDELET.

NOTE No. 23.

New Madrid, 3d Jan. 1797.

Sir,

I ARRIVED at this place on the first of last month, and have been detained here by a concurrence of unlucky circumstances. * * * had ordered me to stay here until Nolan should arrive with the letters. Mr. Nolan did not arrive before the 17th or 18th of December. I was ready to set off on the 22d, when the severest frost ever known in this country suddenly froze the river for a great distance from the bank. It still continues frozen, and such vast quantities of ice float down the part that is not frozen, that to attempt to go down it in any thing but a small canoe would be rushing into the jaws of death. I enclose you two newspapers, by which you will learn the manner in which I have been treated in 'the U. S. and the reasons why * * * did not venture to trust me with any papers. I am happy, however, to acquaint you that I delivered my charge in safety. I do not transmit you * * *'s letters, not to depart from his orders, which are not to let them out my hands upon any consideration, but to deliver them personally to you; besides, I expect to be with you almost as soon as bearer of this. After I shall have explained to you at Natchez the motives of my conduct through the whole of this delicate and difficult business, I flatter myself it will meet with your approbation. I have the honour to be, with respect,

Your Excellency's most obedient and most humble servant.

His Excellency Governor GAYOSO.

NOTE No. 24.

Territory of Orleans, sct.

JOHN McDONAUGH, jun. being duly sworn, doth depose, that some time in the month of March, in the year 1804, Gen. Wilkinson consulted with this deponent as a commission merchant, on the probability of sugar or cotton shipped from this country to the Atlantic ports turning to advantage. The advice of this deponent was to ship sugars in preference, upon which the General requested this deponent to purchase for him sugars to the amount of nine or ten thousand dollars, payable in cash. This deponent accordingly purchased for the General, through Messrs. Dusan and Dubourg, brokers, one hundred and seven hogsheads of sugar, and chartered the ship Louisiana (in which the General took his passage), to transport it to New-York, the said sugar being shipped on the sole risk and account of the General. That the amount of the said sugars as invoiced was eight thousand and forty-five dollars and thirty-five cents, and this deponent gave the General a bill of exchange on New-York for one thousand dollars, the sugars not amounting to the sum which the General risked to be invested in them. That the amount of the said two sums, being dolls. 9045 35 cents, was paid to this deponent, by the General, in Mexican dollars, and that some of the bags containing the said money were Mexican bags, such as come from Vera Cruz, and this deponent recollects that the said purchase excited at the time much speculation among the American inhabitants of New-Orleans as to the resources of the General, which enabled him to pay so large a sum of money in cash, and the Governor himself, some time after the departure of the General, spoke to this deponent upon the subject, appearing to be desirous of ascertaining the amount of the sugars which had been purchased, and the means by which the General had been enabled to pay for them.

JOHN McDONAUGH, jun.

Sworn before me this 4th September, 1807,
at the city of New-Orleans.

JOHN LYND, Juſtice of Peace.

NOTE No. 25.

SOME time between the 10th and 20th days of January, 1807, in conversation with General Wilkinson, on the subject of publications in the Western World, I expressed a belief that some of the charges there brought against him (the General) were true, and remarked that they were generally credited in Kentucky. I noticed the immense sums of money he expended, as tending to impress a belief that he had some other resourse than his pay and emoluments as Commander in Chief of the army. I informed him that I had heard it very confidently asserted, that the money he paid to Mr. John McDonaugh, for sugars, when the Americans took possession of this country, was received from the Marquis de Casa Calvo. The General declared the report false, and raised to ruin him—That he had received the money from Lieut. Taylor, for extra services. Shortly after this conversation with General Wilkinson, I had one on the same subject with Governor Claiborne. He told me, that when he first heard of the purchase of sugars by the General, he was inclined to believe that he had come by the money with which he made the purchase corruptly—but that he had an explanation of the affair with General Wilkinson, who had removed every suspicion from his mind—and added, that the General received the money from Lieut. Taylor, then military agent, for extra services, in running lines.

Since writing the above, I have shewn it to Governor Claiborne, who agrees to the facts stated, with this correction—that instead of saying, he " was nclined to believe that he had come by the money with which he made the purchase corruptly"—he " believed all was not right"— And that instead of saying " the General received the money from Lieutenant Taylor, then military agent, for extra services, in running lines"—he said " the General received the money from Lieut. Taylor, for drafts on the United States,"—and he " had heard that the drafts were for extra services, in running lines, and making Indian treaties"— That he held these conversations frequently—and recollects one on this subject with the undersigned, in the winter 1807.

JAMES M. BRADFORD.

Sworn and subscribed to, at the city of New Orleans,
   this seventeeth day of March, 1809, before me,
SAMUEL D. EARLE,
Justice of the Peace in and for the parish of
the city of New Orleans.

NOTE No. 26.

COURT OF ENQUIRY.

Washington City, July 4th.

AFTER a full investigation of such evidence and circumstances as have come to the knowledge of the Court, in the course of its proceedings, a correct statement of which is hereunto annexed, and after mature deliberation upon the same, the following opinion, the amount of the testimony, is respectfully submitted:

It has been proved to the satisfaction of this Court, that Brigadier-General James Wilkinson had been engaged in a tobacco trade with Governor Miro, of New-Orleans, before he entered the American army in 1791; that he received large sums of money for tobacco delivered in New-Orleans in the year one thousand seven hundred and eighty-nine; and that a large quantity of tobacco was condemned, belonging to him, and stored in New-Orleans in that year; but it has not been proved, and after the fullest investigation and comparison of testimony in the possession of the Court, it does not appear that he has received any money from the Spanish government, or any of its officers, since the year one thousand seven hundred and ninety-one, or that he has ever received money from the government, or its officers, for any other purpose but in payment of tobacco and other produce, sold and delivered by him or his agents.

It has been stated by the General, that after his damaged tobacco had laid some years in the stores at New-Orleans, his agent there received for it, and transmitted to him, the several sums credited in the copy of an account current presented by him, and marked No. —; and under the impression that the letters accompanying said account were written by his said agent, Philip Nolan, the Court think it highly probable that statement is correct. They, however, do not consider the verity of it of the least importance in this case, since, if he did receive the money as stated, the transaction was fully justifiable, and if he did not receive it, there is no proof of his having received it at all.

It is therefore the opinion of this Court, that there is no evidence of Brigadier-General James Wilkinson having at any time received a pension from the Spanish government, or of his having received money from the government of Spain, or any of its officers or agents, for corrupt purposes: and the Court has no hesitation in saying, that as far as his conduct has been developed by this enquiry, he appears to have discharged the duties of his station with honour to himself, and fidelity to his country.

       H. BURBECK, President.
       T. H. CUSHING, ⎫
       JONA. WILLIAMS,⎬ Members.

City of Washington, June 28th, 1808.

  July 2d, 1808—Approved,
    (Signed)
      TH: JEFFERSON.

NOTE No. 27.

DR. JAMES WILKINSON, Esquire, in account current with CLARK & REES.

1787.	To balance of account this date,		4 0
Aug. 27.	To cash lent him, per note,		3000 0
1788.			
Apr. 17.	To cash paid William and Richard Thomas, per receipt,		90 0
May 15.	To cash paid Joshua Barbee, per receipt,		100 0
	To cash paid James Ferguson, per his order,	52 4	
July 12.	To cash paid his bill in favour of L. T. Beauregard,		1626 6
14.	To cash paid his bill in favour of Spoartsman,		861 0
	To cash paid his bill in favour of Ballenger,		360 0
29.	To cash paid Major Dunn, per account,	281 2	3389 0
Aug. 8.	To cash paid Wm. M'Faden, on account of Major Dunn, for 3 passages by schoo. Navaro,		180 0
		333 6	
	Dol. 333 6, ex. 152 p. cent.		219 0
	To cash paid Maj. Dunn, in full,		355 7
			10185 5

SUPRA,	CR.	
1788.		*Silver.*
July 29.	By nett proceeds of sales made for his account,	9835 5
	By a Negroe man named Jesse,	350 0
		10185 5

N. B. There is a quantity of tobacco on hand in bulk, weight unknown; also seven hogsheads full, which have not been weighed; for which we hold ourselves accountable, conformable to the sales we shall make thereof: We also hold ourselves accountable for one hogshead of tobacco, which was received among Mr. Christopher Thomson's tobacco, weight 913 lbs. when the King shall be pleased to pay for the same.

Errors excepted. New Orleans, 8th August, 1788.

CLARK & REES.

By virtue of the powers in me vested by James Wilkinson, Esquire, I do hereby acknowledge and declare that I have examined the above account, and that I have received from Messrs. Clark & Rees, of New Orleans, merchants, the several articles and payments in the said account,—balanced, as it stands, this 8th day of August, 1788.

ISAAC B. DUNN.

NOTE NO. 28.

DR. General JAMES WILKINSON, in account current with CLARK & REES.

1789.

Apr. 9. To cash remitted you by I. Ballenger,	1650	0
To our acceptance in favour of L. T. Beauregard,	2666	3
To ditto in favour of Reand & Fortier,	1333	3
To cash paid Benj. Fisher, per your order,	141	1
To ditto paid your order in favour of Thomas,	200	0
To ditto paid Mr. Moore,	50	0
To ditto paid boatmens' wages	948	5¼
To amount of your note for cash lent last year,	3000	0
To cash paid Parcells Parker,	41	6
To ditto paid A. M'Gilliwray's account against Philip Nolan,	99	2
To ditto for bacon, hams and rice, to be explained by Cn. Dunn,	33	4
Carried over,	10170	0½

Dr. General JAMES WILKINSON, in account current with
CLARK & REES.

Brought over,	10170	0
To ditto paid Mr. Ballenger, to defray his expences to Kentucky,	20	0
May 1. To cash paid Captain A. Dunn,	6251	0
	16441	0

SUPRA, CR.
1789.

Apr. 30. By nett proceeds of tobacco, as per sales,	16372	0
By six flats, at 8 dollars each, exchange at 23 per cent.	39	0
By two barrels of beef,	24	0
By two axes, at 3 dollars,	6	0
	16441	0½

N. B. We have not deducted 410 dollars, our commission on the above amount, being desirous to send forward to you as much money as we can by Capt. Dunn; but we have carried that charge to your debit in our books.

Errors and omissions excepted.   New Orleans, *May* 1st, 1789.
(Signed)   CLARK & REES.

I have examined the within account, and find it right; and do hereby acknowledge to have received of Meſſrs. Clark and Rees, the sum of six thousand two hundred and fifty-one silver Spanish milled dollars of Mexico, being authorised so to do by General Wilkinson's letter to Daniel Clark, bearing date 27th February last, having signed three receipts of the same tenor and date.

(Signed)   A. M. DUNN.

DR. General WILKINSON to MOSES & JOHN MOORE.

To an error in his account with Mr. Moore to his prejudice, and in favour of Gen. Wilkinson, 1564 lbs. tobacco, at five dollars,	77	4
By balance due J. Wilkinson, in account with Moses Moore,	30	1
To General Wilkinson's debit,	47	3

NOTE No. 29.

SALES of 342 hogsheads of tobacco, shipped by James Wilkinson, (on the purchase of which the sum of 729*l*. a balance due Daniel Clark, Esq. for his half of the proceeds of the batteau Speedwell, was invested, and in proportion thereto said Clark is interested) consigned to Philip Nolan, New Orleans.

Sold to .... 226,649 lbs. nett, at 80 p. 1000,		18131 7	
Charges.			
Paid for packing, in hard money,	149 0		
Lost, to procure this money, 11 per cent.	16 3		
		165 3	
Paid the pickers, in paper money,	88 0		
Lost, to procure this money, 6 per cent.	5 0		
		92 2	
Sundry expences, to be explained by P. Nolan,	105 0		
Lost, to procure this money,	10 4		
		115 4	
Mr. Ballenger's board for 30 days, at 1 dollar,	30 0		
Lost, to procure this money,	0 4		
		30 4	
Mr. Nolan's allowance, from the 27th July until the 25th September, 60 days, at two and a half dolls. per day,	150 0		
Lost, to procure this money, 10 per cent.	15 0		
		165 0	
Cooperage, per account,		541 4	
		1111 1	
Proportion of expence to be deducted,		329 5	
			781 4
			17350 3
Deducted from the invoice,			1500 0
			15850 3

Errors and Omissions excepted.

PHILIP NOLAN.

New Orleans, Sept. 21. 1790.

NOTE No. 30.

Lexington, Kentucky, May 20, 1790.

MESSRS. CLARK & REES,

GENTLEMEN,

I LAMENT that I should be obliged to address you at this late day, but the causes producing the delay have been insuperable.

This will be handed to you by my agent, Mr. Philip Nolan, who carries with him, and will exhibit to you for final settlement, the account of the unfortunate adventure by the Speedwell, he being specially authorised by me for that purpose. Amidst the embarrassments which result to me from this fatal expedition, it is with pleasure I reflect, that whilst I am obliged to abide by a dead loss on the sales, without remedy or consolation, you must feel yourselves indemnified by the advance you had upon the merchandize originally furnished from your store to the adventure, and for which you received cash. The proceeds of this adventure are invested in tobacco, at a very low price, which will I hope get to a good market. You will observe that I have consigned this cargo to Mr. Nolan, and authorised him to act for me in the storage, inspection, &c. because the quantity now shipped will overrun the claims of the owners of the Speedwell nearly two thirds, and I have determined to make no discrimination in the cargo, for fear of accidents to the boats, which might be assigned to the account of the Speedwell, or lest I should subject myself to the imputation of partiality to my private interest, and be charged with selecting the best tobacco. No difficulty can offer in the settlement, because when the costs and charges, and the nett profits of the whole cargo, are ascertained, the proportion due to the owners of the Speedwell can be readily established. This is the principle of settlement which I have directed my agent to take for his guidance, and to which I shall invariably adhere.

I am sorry to inform you that one of our flats, after being loaded with forty hogsheads, sprung a leak, and in spite of our endeavours sunk. The tobacco is wet, but I believe we shall be able to save the greatest part of it; though it will involve the inevitable detention of this tobacco until my next shipment, when it will go down on the same principles as the present cargo, of which it is indeed a part.

I have directed Mr. Nolan to require the original vouchers, on which the accounts rendered by you last year are founded, many of them being absolutely necessary to my own indemnity against the persons collaterally interested or connected in them.

I have the honour to be, Gentlemen,
Your most obedient servant,
JAMES WILKINSON.

Messrs. CLARK & REES, Merchants, New Orleans.

NOTE No. 31.

Louisville, June 20th, 1790.

GENTLEMEN,

YOUR surprise at hearing from me at this late date cannot exceed the mortification and regret I feel from the delay. My boats unfortunately grounded in Kentucky river, and were left by the flood. Mr. Nolan will give you the details, and will explain to you the personal hardships and risques I have been exposed to for three weeks past. Events have justified the propriety of my making no distinction in the tobacco shipped at this time, or allotting any separate portion for the account of the Speedwell, as three of the fleet which sailed are still aground in Kentucky river, with one hundred and eighteen hogsheads on board. The tobacco Mr. Nolan now takes down can be appropriated on the same equitable principles, and the same just scale of proportion, set forth in my letter of the 20th of May. The drowned tobacco is by this time completely recovered, I expect, at a loss of twelve or fifteen thousand pounds. I shall ship it, and it will go down with the three boats which are aground, so soon as the flood offers, which I expect must take place in the course of the month.

The stoppage of the boats has been attended with some additional expence, which was unavoidable in the measures necessary to get them out of the Kentucky river, and secure the tobacco. With due respect,

I am, Gentlemen,
Your most obedient servant,
JAMES WILKINSON.

Messrs. CLARK & REES.

NOTE No. 32.

Dr.   Messrs. WILKINSON & DUNN, in account current with CLARK & REES.

		Silver.
1788.	To their half adventure to Kentucky in company, per batteau Speedwell,	4087 7

Cr.

		Silver.
1788.	By cash received from the Governor,	3000 0
	Balance due on this account,	1087 7
		4087 7

Dr. Messrs. WILKINSON & DUNN,

		Paper.	Ex.	Silver.
1789.	To balance brought down,			1087 7
May 6.	To cash paid Moses and John Moore, on error discovered to their prejudice in account with J. Wilkinson, after we had adjusted accounts with Capt. Dunn, and paid him the balance,			47 3
	To cash paid Gen. Wilkinson's order in favour of G. I. A. Elkolm,			129 4
	Do. for 28 lbs. bacon supplied Mr. Ballenger, at 2½,	8 6	120	7 2
	Carried over,			1272 0

Dr. Messrs. WILKINSON & DUNN, in account current with CLARK & REES.

		Paper.	Ex.	Stiver.
	Brought over,			1272 0
June 4.	To cash paid Joseph Ballenger,	100 0		108 0
	Ditto,	8 0		6 0
July 20.	Do. paid P. Nolan,			96 0
	Ditto in paper,	121 7	127	150 0
21.	Do. paid your order in favour of R. McGillier,	267 6½		
25.	Do. paid Greenberry Dorsey,	377 4		
	Philip Nolan,	92 7		
31.	Mr. Minor, amount of your note,			
	A. White and Shoemaker,	29 6		
		767 7½	130	590 6
Aug. 2.	Do. paid Hipps Taylor,	12 6		
	Do. paid for four ells of silk,	12 0		
		24 6	125	19 6
	To our assumption to Mather and Strother, for a horse for Mr. Ballenger,			100 0
	To sundries supplied to Mr. Ballenger at Natchez, on his way to Kentucky, viz. One saddle,	40 0		
	Three quarters of a yard of blue cloth,	6 0		
	One pair of stockings,	3 0		
		49 0	150	32 6
	Carried over,			1103 2

Dr.   Messrs. WILKINSON & DUNN, in account current with CLARK & REES.

	Paper.	Ex.	Silver
Brought over,			1103 2
1789.			
Aug. 12. To cash you received for three flats,			14 0
To your order in favour of Col. Elzey, 14*l*. Vir. currency, at 6s.			46 4
To cash you received from the Governor of Virginia, £. 1004 15 10, Virginia currency, at 6s.			3382 3
To so much you received from the State of Virginia, 1256 3 6			
Deduct 20 per cent. 251 4 8			
£. 1004 18 10			
			3349 4½
Balance due Wilkinson and Dunn,			12464 7½
			21632 5

SUPRA, CR.
1788.
Dec. 31. By nett proceeds of sales of 5 casks of butter, 1 hogshead of tobacco, and 30732 lbs. tobacco loose, left by Mr. Dunn, 1479 4 160 924 6
1789.
May 17. By nett proceeds of sales of 38 casks of lard, per Capt. Dunn,   78 4
                                                                              1003 2

Messrs. WILKINSON & DUNN, in account current with CLARK & REES. Cʀ.

		Paper.	Ex.	Silver.
1789.	Brought over,			1003 2
June 13.	By cash returned by Mr. Ballenger,			1650 0
Aug 15.	By nett proceeds of sales of 27 casks of butter, per Capt. Dunn,			162 4
	By so much charged in an account rendered May 1st, for Mr. Nolan's expences through the Creek Nation,			99 2
	By cash paid Capt. Hoops, 280*l*. Virginia currency,			933 2½
	By first of adventures, with charges,			13991 0
	By adventures from Kentucky in Co. for your half gain,			3355 2½
	By amount of Philip Nolan's account,			374 0
	By Daniel, for deputy surveyor's fees paid in Richmond,			32 0
	By ditto, paid for advice in suit against Foster Webb,			32 0
				21632 5

Errors and Omissions excepted.

New Orleans, 29*th August*, 1789.

WILKINSON & DUNN.

DR. WILKINSON & DUNN, in account current with CLARK & REES.

1789.		Paper.	Ex.	Silver.
Sept. 2.	To cash paid G. M.			3000 0
3.	Do. paid Philip Nolan, for M. Duncan, per your order,			6800 0
	Do. paid John H. Craig, per Nolan's order,			471 5
4.	Do. paid Philip Nolan's order in favour of John Pickett,			1101 7
	Do. do. in favour of Mr. Pauling,			789 4
	Do. do. per receipt,			300 0
5.	Do. paid Philip Nolan, in full,			48 5½
				14511 3½

CR.

	By balance brought down,			12464 7½
	By note returned, which was charged to you, in favour of Col. Elzey, for 14l. Virginia currency,			46 4
				12511 3½

Errors excepted.

JAMES WILKINSON.

New Orleans, 5th September, 1789.

DEAR SIR, *September* 4, 1789.
WILL you be so good as to answer to Mr. Nolan the balance in your hands.
Your friend,

J. WILKINSON.

DANIEL CLARK, Efq.

RECEIPT.

New Orleans, 5th September, 1789. Received of Messrs. Clark and Rees forty-eight dollars and five and one half reals, the balance due James Wilkinfon, as stated in Messrs. Clark and Rees's account current, for James Wilkinson.

PHILIP NOLAN.

NOTE No. 33.

PHILIP NOLAN'S DECLARATION.

I, PHILIP NOLAN, Agent for James Wilkinson, Esquire, being applied to by Daniel Clark, junior, Attorney of Clark & Rees, to investigate an account settled the 5th of September, 1789, between Clark & Rees, merchants of this place, and the aforesaid James Wilkinson, Esquire, do declare that there is an error in said account, amounting to four hundred and seventy-three silver dollars two reals, to the prejudice of Clark & Rees, occasioned by their giving him credit twice in their account for the aforesaid sum of four hundred and seventy-three silver dolllars two reals, being my expences on my journey from hence to Kentucky in the year 1788. New Orleans, 10th September, 1790.

PHILIP NOLAN.

NOTE No 34.

In the year 1795 Governor Gayoso ascended the Missisippi, commanding the King's gallies and troops destined to erect and garrison the fort of San Fernando de las Barancas, (Chicasaw Bluffs) where he remained, I believe, about two months, or perhaps longer; and after having by his presence given spirit and activity to the works, proceeded to New

Madrid. Immediately on his arrival, which was in the beginning of September, 1795, he informed Captain Don Thomas Portell, the Commandant, that he had dispatches of the greatest importance to forward to Kentucky, and desired him to procure a person, on whom he could depend, to take charge of them. Portell spoke to me on the subject. As travelling was then my ruling passion, I proposed, without hesitation, to undertake the journey. It may not be improper here to observe, that I had already been sent by said Portell to Kentucky on two occasions; the first, at the beginning of 1794, to keep an eye on the movements and progress of what is generally known by the name of Genet's expedition against Louisiana, headed by Clark and La Chaise; and the second, to accompany the Spaniards that had murdered Mr. Henry Owen, the bearer of General Wilkinson's 6000 dollars, concerning which I have given my affidavit under this date. As I had acquitted myself of my commissions much to his satisfaction, he had recommended me strongly to the Governor.

Without loss of time, a perogue, hands and provisions were got ready, and I set off from New Madrid on the 6th of September, and reached Red Banks on the sixth day. Here I was detained by a bilious fever until the 24th, on which day I set off by land, and arrived at Cincinnati on the 3d of October, having delayed one day at Lexington. The day of my arrival I delivered my dispatches to General Wilkinson, agreeably to my orders. When I left New Madrid I was only half in the secret of the object of my mission; but the General disclosed the whole plot to me, which was a separation of the Western from the Eastern States, such as appears in Judge Sebastian's trial. After some days stay at Cincinnati, I proceeded up the Ohio as far as Galliopolis, in obedience to General Wilkinson's orders, which I had been instructed by Gayoso implicitly to follow. I returned to Cincinnati on the 8th of November, and left that place on the 14th, with Wilkinson's answers, having occasionally dined with the General, and having had several nocturnal conferences with him in Fort Washington.

In his letter in cypher to Gayoso, September 22d, 1796, he refers him to what I should verbally communicate to him, which was as follows: That I must immediately return to Red Banks, where I should meet the following gentlemen, or at least two of them, viz. Messrs. Benjamin Sebastian, Henry Innes, John Murray, and George Nicholas, whom I was to convey to the mouth of the Ohio, there to have an interview with Gayoso. I have already mentioned that the plan of separation was such as appears in Sebastian's trial; on which subject Wilkinson directed me to lay the following observations before Carondelet and Gayoso. However, before I proceed any farther, it will not be improper to state that Wilkinson ..:ived a letter some time after from Gayoso, expressive of much discontent and reproach, for having imprudently communicated to me the whole extent of their plots. This I had from Wilkinson himself. Here follow the observations. In this I am confident that I am perfectly correct, as I committed them to paper at the time, and which I will literally copy. " The various channels " through which the Western Country is to receive foreign commodi- " ties. Which the most advantageous? 1st. By the River St. Lau- " rence and the Lakes. 2d. By New-York, Hudson's or North River, " Mohawk River, and by Oswego into the Lake. 3d. By Baltimore, " up the Susquehannah, a portage to * * * * *, that empties into the " Allegheny, down into the Ohio. 4th. By * * * * *, up the Potow- " mack; portage to Cheete River, into the Monongahela, and down " the Ohio. 5th. By New Orleans and the Missisippi, &c. &c. &c. " An intelligent person ought to be sent to these different places, and " obtain every possible information on the spot, concerning the difficul- " ty or facility attending their navigation, &c. and by comparing them, " see which merits the preference. It might, perhaps, also be the means " of artificially giving the advantage to the Missisippi, in case it does not " possess it naturally. The free navigation of the Missisippi injurious to " the future population of Louisiana; because numbers who would have " migrated to it, for the sake of enjoying the privileges of Spanish sub- " jects, and from which foreigners were excluded, would now possess " those advantages, without moving to it.

" To ascend the Ohio with a cargo, the profits on which muſt be a " perquisite for the person entrusted with it. By these means the fol- " lowing advantages will be obtained. The money that it may be " judged proper to introduce into the country will be kept out of sight, " even of the crew, and the real object of the expedition kept secret. " It may draw the confidence of the people, and point out the channel " through which they must receive foreign commodities. The car- " go ought to consist of gun-powder, sugar, coffee, brandy, wine, se- " gars, &c. The mouth of the Ohio must be formidably fortified, and " works erected, of sufficient strength to arrest the progress of an army " during a whole campaign, and thus gain one year. Kentuckians must " be employed in raising these fortifications. This will help to do away " all national distinctions and prejudices, and to conciliate and fraternize " the two nations. The cannons wanted may be cast in Kentucky. A " Bank must be established in Kentucky, with a capital of one million " of dollars. The directors to be chosen among the most distinguished " and leading characters in the country. We shall thus secure a majo- " rity in the Councils and Assemblies of State. The fort of St. Fer- " nando must not, upon any consideration, be given up; for this would " lessen the power and importance of Spain, and the Americans would " immediately take possession of it. As the seeds of an approaching

" rupture are already cast, it is proper that all the necessary prepara-
" tions should be made in the province, by building forts on the fron-
" tiers, encreasing the number of Spanish agents in Kentucky, and de-
" positing funds in the country, to be enabled to face contingencies.
" Gen. Clark, and his adherents, who are in the pay of the French
" Republic, must be bought into the service of Spain. The French may
" hereafter be prevailed upon to take produce of Kentucky and the
" Western Country, for the use of their Colonies. It is absolutely ne-
" cessary that military magazines should be formed at New Madrid,
" well provided with arms, ammunition, and other military stores. A
" watchful eye must be kept upon Daniel Clark, senior, and his ne-
" phew Daniel Clark, Minor, Beauregard, Du Forĕt, Morales, and
" their friends. They must never be trusted in any thing that relates
" to Wilkinson and ―――――.

" Pounds of sugar mean hard dollars; Campbell, Carondelet; M'Cul-
" lough, Gayoso; Marietta, New Orleans; Post-Vincennes, Philadel-
" delphia; Store, Fortification; Monongahela, Mouth of the Ohio;
" Words, War; Silence, Peace; Cash, Spain; Corn, France; Pork,
" England; Whiskey, United States; Pounds of Coffee, Arms; Segars,
" Men; Bread, Ammunition."

Immediately on my return to New Madrid, a large perogue was purchased, and every thing provided that could contribute to the accommodation of the gentlemen, and I again set off for Red Banks towards the beginning of December. On my arrival at that place, I there found Mr. B. Sebastian, who had taken passage in a flat boat, bound to New Madrid. On my enquiring for the other gentlemen, he told me, that as Murray had for some time past been in a habitual state of inebriation, it was not judged proper that he should be of the party; that Mr. H. Innes could not leave his home, owing to some family concerns, or to indisposition, I do not well recollect which; and that the absence of Lawyer Nicholas would excite a degree of suspicion, that might defeat the object they had in view; but said that he was fully authorised to treat with the Governor in their names. We accordingly proceeded to the mouth of the Ohio, he in the flat, myself in the perogue. We arrived in a short time on the Missisippi. There we found Gayoso encamped, opposite the mouth of the Ohio, where he had amused himself in building a small triangular stockade fort, with the view of impressing the public with the idea that he had no other object in contemplation. Here the bad weather detained us a few days, during which time we had the visit of Julien Poydras and Mr. Bernoudi, jun. who were descending in a flat to New Orleans. We arrived at New Madrid, I think, on Christmas-day, and remained there but a short time, and continued our route to Natchez, Sebastian with the Governor in his galliot, and myself with Mr. Vandembemden in a King's barge. After an ordinary passage we arrived at Natchez, where we were hospitably entertained in the government house. I staid there but a short time; then proceeded to New Orleans, leaving Sebastian at the Governor's. They both reached Orleans together, a few days after me.

Mr. Sebastian and myself left Orleans, if I recollect right, in March, or the beginning of April, having taken passage for Philadelphia in the brig Gayoso, Capt. Jared Arnold, where we arrived, after nineteen days passage. We remained but a few days in Philadelphia, and proceeded to Shippensburgh in the stage. Here we put our baggage in a waggon, and for numerous reasons, unnecessary to expose, continued our journey to Redstone on foot. At Redstone we embarked in a flat, bound to Cincinnati, where we arrived on the 17th or 18th of May. The next day after our arrival, Sebastian took passage in a flat for Louisville. I remained at Cincinnati. On the 20th I wrote to General Wilkinson, who then had the command of the army, owing to General Wayne's absence, soliciting permission to travel by the line of forts to Grenville, and pursue my route from thence to the Illinois, by post Vincennes. The following is a copy of his answer.

[Duplicate.]

SIR *Head-Quarters, Grenville, May* 25, 1796.

The day before yesterday I had the honour to receive a letter from you, under date of the 20th instant, in which you request leave to visit this place, and to proceed by St. Vincennes and the Illinois to New Madrid. Permit me, Sir, to observe that this precaution was unnecessary, at a time when the United States of America are happily at peace with all the world. In this enviable situation, the officers of the American army have no concealments to make, and therefore our camps and our forts are free to the ingress and egress of all persons, who deport themselves with propriety. I beg you, Sir, to believe, that upon an unpleasant occasion, to which you are pleased to refer, my conduct was directed more by the delicacy of my own situation, than any sense of your demerit. Neither my sympathies nor my antipathies have ever gained such an ascendant over my reason, as to incline me to condemn upon hearsay, or to adopt the prejudices of any man. I thank you, Sir, for the trouble you have given yourself, in bringing forward the Segars committed to your care by my very worthy friends Governor Gayoso and Dr. Andreas; and have the honour to be, with due consideration, Sir,   Your most obedient servant,

JAMES WILKINSON.

Mr. THO. POWER.

Having obtained the General's permission to go to Grenville, Major

Mills. Adjutant-general, procured me a horse from the Quarter-master, to carry me to Grenville. There I staid five or six days, quartered on Capt. Prior and Lieut. Charles Hyde. As soon as I had received the General's instructions, and answers to my dispatches, I returned to Cincinnati; for my journey to the Illinois by Vincennes was a device, to avoid curiosity. I lost no time at Cincinnati, but proceeded with all possible haste to New Madrid, where I took charge of Wilkinson's 9640 dollars. For the details of the rest of this expedition, I refer to my deposition (No. 17) taken before Mr. Eliphalet Fitch.

THOMAS POWER.

New Orleans, March 18th, 1807. Personally appeared Thomas Power, and did solemnly swear that the preceding narrative is just and true.

E. FITCH, Justice of the Peace.

NOTE No. 35.

General Wilkinson's secret instructions to Power, in the hand writing of P. Nolan, General Wilkinson's agent.

TO proceed to Galliopolis, to make application and propositions to the leading characters there, to induce them to move to New Madrid, with all the French of the settlement; to urge this point in such measure as to attract the attention of the public officers there, whose report to the executive will immediately follow, and will account for his frequent missions to that place; to return as rapidly as possible, to load with flour, and proceed without a moment's delay to New Orleans; in the route to see Newman, and to enter on the subject of his desertion; to inform him of the facts which have transpired, and the opinions prevalent; to urge his return, at the request of all his friends; to assure him of safety, and of such rewards as he may demand. Also, that being pardoned for the imputed offence, no further process can be against him for the same; that the oath which he was suborned to take, being made while in ——— ———, is in itself a nullity, and cannot be offered in crimination of him—it will be necessary that he should take down his examination, founded upon the interrogations furnished him, and if they prove material to the examination of Wayne and his associates, then he must embark N——n under a fictitious name, at New Orleans, for Philadelphia, and having arrived there, must lodge him in some retired place, and call upon me, under cover of the night—for further advice; you will hear of me at ———. If N——n cannot be prevailed on to return under dispositions favourable to my views, then let his declaration on oath be circumstantially taken to all the points enumerated in the interrogations, in the presence of Dr. Flowers, Col. Bruin, Daniel Clark, or any three or four of the most notorious respectable Americans of the Natchez district; let these gentlemen certify to two copies and to the original, and let them be transmitted to me through different channels: P. to take charge of the original. Mr. P. must take with him credentials from the government of Louisiana, acquitting him of any political connexion or agency injurious or hostile to the interests of the United States. He must carry to Philadelphia testimonials of his family and character, addressed to as many of the native respectable merchants of that city as poffible: those may be readily procured from New Orleans and Havanna. It is indispensable that P. should meet me in Philadelphia; for the rest, let him rely on my friendship and address. To collect from Bradford every information respecting the Pittfburgh ———on, which may be employed, should it be found necessary, to disgrace certain persons: *to bear no paper upon him which carries my name upon it.*

Employ the 640 dollars *avec la cargaison* to pay expences and lay in a cargo of best flour—pour la ville—where it will help to reimburse. In making your settlement, take care to secure me the 640 dollars advanced, and bring them with you. I have urged peremptorily the necessity of your presence at the metropolis; bring me N—n, if upon examination you find his presence of more consequence than his deposition when taken as directed. I believe he was caused to desert by Ohara, probe him to that point—you are to bring me papers, but my name is not to be written or spoken. You must do the needful below to *expose and detect past treachery or indiscretion, and to prevent either in future; I have referred particularly on this head.* I shall expect you impatiently. Should I continue where I am, I shall wish you near me——— if I cross the water, you are to accompany. Bring every credential of family and fortune, to repulse the insinuations of ; trust something to my address, and put faith in my honour and affections to the grave.

NOTE No. 36.

Translation of a letter from Thomas Power, to the Baron de Carondelet, dated New-Orleans, 9th May, 1797.

ENCLOSED your Excellency will receive the documents relative to my last confidential expedition, made by your Excellency's order in the

Ohio; of which I have already given you a narrative, as well verbal, as in writing. The remarks which follow serve for its elucidation.

I left New Madrid with ten oarsmen and a patron; the provisions which were delivered to the crew were: Biscuit for a month, Meat for ditto, Rum for fifteen days.

To disguise, as far as possible, the true object of the expedition, we had hired the people under the same conditions as are common in commercial voyages, so that the monthly rations allowed by the king did not even last fifteen days. The reasons why I issued to the crew extraordinary allowances of liquour daily, counting from the day we left Red Bank until our arrival at the Falls of Ohio, was to encourage them to row with vigour, that lieutenant Steel, whom I thought in pursuit of me, might not again take me; because, had I fallen into his hands a second time, I was lost. As respects the 150 for the horse, which I bought to make the journey from Frankfort to Cincinnati, and the expences which occurred on this journey, they were indispensable, for a double motive; to carry my complaint against Steel, for having offered so great an insult to our flag, and to give advice of my arrival to the American general, Mr. James Wilkinson, that he might take the necessary measures. I have to add, that the motive which has induced me to dispose of the merchandize which I received of I. and A. Hunt, in exchange for the coffee and sugar, was to give credit to the opinion, which I myself had raised, that I had come to purchase horses to take to Natchez, in order to better the breed in that district. Besides this, as the occurrence with Steel had awakened suspicions, excited apprehensions, and attracted the attention of the inhabitants of the western country, all had their eyes on me, so that I found myself obliged to do something which should please them, that it might serve me as a safe conduct to quit those parts, which by this means I happily effected. The mare, of which the statement No. 1. makes mention, was lost on my arrival at New Madrid in the woods, where she died of thirst, the excessive frost having entirely frozen up the water. The stud horse I delivered on going down to Don Manuel Gayoso de Lemos, but he returned him to me a short time since, and I have him carefully kept, until your Excellency is pleased to make disposition respecting him. Of the sum of 9640 dollars which I was to deliver to Mr. James Wilkinson, I have only delivered him 9000, having retained the 640 dollars, to avoid the unfortunate result with which I was threatened, and likewise to provide what was necessary for the crew during the voyage. The following are the documents which are enclosed:

No. 1. The account sale of the merchandize laden, &c.

No. 2. Account of the expences for the crew.

No. 3. Account of the expenditures of the 640 dollars.

No. 4. Statement which shows in what manner the merchandize has been made use of.

No. 5. Ditto which shows what is due to me.

No. 6. Invoice of I. and A. Hunt.

All which are accompanied with the obligation of Mr. N. Welch, for 105 dollars, and the two receipts of Mr. Boyd, the one for 466 dollars, for the value of a horse, and the other for 200 dollars, for the value of a mare. The balance which appears in my favour, according to the statements 3 and 4, as well as the account of my monthly pay for fourteen months, I beg your Excellency will be pleased to direct that it should be remitted to me, or delivered Mr. Philip Nolan, to whom I have given advice on the subject. Mr. James Wilkinson, in the instructions which he has given me, directs that I should present to your Excellency the account of the expences to which the 640 dollars have been applied (and I have done so in the statement No. 3) that he may be reimbursed said account. The instructions say, " in making your settlement take care to secure me the 640 dollars advanced, and bring them with you."— Although he charged me to take them to him to the United States, I am of opinion that no one is better suited to remit them than Mr. Philip Nolan, as your Excellency has now resolved that I should remain in this province. Your Excellency will please suffer me to assure you, that in every particular I have acted with prudence, with honour, and the disinterestedness of an honest man, as well as with the zeal and fidelity which the King's service requires, and with the vigilance and activity—*(here there is a line unintelligible.)* I deserve nothing, and expect nothing for having fulfilled the obligations of a good subject to his majesty, unless your Excellency will be pleased to procure me opportunities of displaying the inclination I feel of sacrificing myself for the prosperity of my country and glory of my sovereign.

God preserve your Excellency many years.

THOMAS POWER.

New Orleans, 9th May, 1797.

NOTE No. 37.

Translation of the answer to the foregoing, dated New Orleans, May 28th, 1796.

THERE remains in my hands the six documents relative to the account of the last expedition which you made in the Ohio, and which you enclosed to me in your official letter of the 9th inst. and they are as follow:

No. 1. Account of sales of the effects laden at New Madrid.
No. 2. Another of the expences of the crew.
No. 3. Account of the expenditure of the 640 dollars.
No. 4. Statement which shows how the merchandize has been employed.
No. 5. Statement which shows the balance due to you, &c.
No. 6. Original invoice of I. and A. Hunt.

On account of it there will be delivered to you 1000, that you may make preparations for your journey, in the new commission which I entrust to your care. It is necessary to see how you can get rid of the horse, with the least possible loss, as well as to recover the debt of Nicholas Welch, or have it recovered; for which purpose I enclose you his obligation, and likewise the proceeds of the merchandize, which, to the amount of 353 dollars, you delivered to Pedro Derbigny, in order to give an account to the court without these balances, which cause trouble, and appear speculations, when they are no more than the effect of necessity; and the difficulty which these commissions cause in places where there are no resources, when you have to deceive the vigilance of spies. As you finish these matters, and as soon as your present commission is fulfilled, you will give me advice.

God preserve you many years.

New Orleans, 28th May, 1797.

THE BARON DE CARONDELET.

To Mr. Thomas Power.

Attestation of NOTE No. 38, which follows:

WE, whose names are hereunto subscribed, do severally swear and declare, that we were well acquainted with the hand writing of the Baron de Carondelet, late Governor General of the province of Louisiana, and that we have no doubt that the letters hereunto annexed, dated, severally, the 23d April, 1797, and 26th May, 1797, are in the proper hand writing of the said Baron de Carondelet, as also the signature to the same. And we do also declare, in like manner, that we are acquainted with the hand writing of Don Andres Armesto, late Secretary of the Government, and that the letter hereunto annexed, dated 28th May, 1797, is in the hand writing of the said Don Andres, and the signature thereto affixed is in the proper hand writing of the said Baron de Carondelet.

PIERRE PEDESCLAUX, Not. Pub.
STEPHEN DE QUINONES, Not. Pub.
NARCISSUS BROUTIN, Not. Pub.
J. J. BLACHE.
G. DUBUYS.

Signed, in my Presence, by Pierre Pedesclaux, Stephen de Quinones, Narcissus Broutin, J. J. Blache, and G. Dubuys, and duly sworn before me, this 17th March, 1809.

ELIPHALET FITCH,
Notary Public and Justice of the Peace.

NOTE No. 38.

N'lle Orleans, ce 26 *May,* 1797.

J'a recu, Monsieur, vos lettres du 5, du 7, 12, 13 et 16 de May, et j'y responds en deux mots en remplissant vos desires puis que je vous confie une commisson de la plus grande consequence, qui ne vous compromet en au eune facon, pourvu bien entendu que vous ne portiez aucuns papiers qui en fasse mention, et qu'elle vous procure de l'argent dont vous medites avoir grand besoin, enfin elle vous rend independant et me procure l'occasion de vous recommanderau Ministre d' Etat : personne n'en sera instruit pas même l'intendant, il n'y aura que Dr. Andres et moi qui enscauront le vrai motif.

Le General Wilkinson ayant prevenu le Commandant de la Nouvelle Madrid qu'il prepare un detachement de l'armeé qu'il a a ses ordres pour prendre possession des forts de Natches et Nogales, en conformité de l'article 2 du traité d'amitié, limites, et navigation, conclu avec l' Espagne, esperant qu'il sera fidellement observé, et lui ayant paru a propos de passer cet avis, in order tu prevent any misapprehension of the the motives which direct this movement of their troops, &c. il est tout natural que je lui reponde que s'etant suscité en premier lieu quelques doutes sur la facon dont les dits Postes devoient se retirer de la part de l'Espagne, c'est adire s'ils devoient etre remis avec leurs fortifications et edifices comme l'Entendent les Etats Unis, ou simplement evacués, rasés, et abandonnés, comme je le comprends, evitans de cette facon de nous compromettre avec les nations qui nous ont cedées les terreins des Ecors, de Nogales, et de la Confederation, sous la condition expresse que nous y batirions des forts pour empescher que leurs terres ne fussent invahis, j'avois resolus d'attendre la decision a cet égard de notre cour, ou de son Ministre Plenipotentiaire auprès des dits Etats, ainsi que la leur ; mais qu' instruit peude têms après que le Ministre susmentionné avoit informé le President qu'une expedition Angloise etant sortit de

Montreal, dans l'intention d'attaquer les Illinois avoit inverné sur les lacs, et devoit traversé le territoire des Etas Unis pour se porter contre la haute Louisiane, demandant qu'en vertu du dernier traité les dits Etats s' opposassent pardes moÿens efficaces a cette violation de leur territoire, j'avois determiné de garder les forts de Natches et Nogales pour mettre en sureté la Basse Louissiane jusqu' a ce que les mesures les plus efficaces de la part des Etats la missent a l' abris de ce danger, et qu'un corps de troupe suffisant, commandé par un officier d' un grade superieur, se presenta pour prendre possession de Natches, y maintenir le bon ordre, et contenir les vols et les vexations des nations Sauvages, conformement a l'article 5 du traité cité par le dit general : qu'en consequence je suis pret a evacuer les postes de Natches et de Nogales a l' arrivée du detachment, qu' il announce par sa lettre, datté du Fort Washington, toute et quante fois le Congrès sera convenu avec le Ministre Plenipotentiaire de S. M. de la facon dont la dit e évacuation doit avoir lieu ; mais qu'en attendant cette decision je le prie de faire suspendre la marche du dit détachement dont la presence ne pouirroit manquer de troubler la tranquillité de la province, et peut-etre la bonne intelligence que je desire maintenir entre les sujèts des deux puissance. Vous serez porteur de cette lettre, et si vous croyez pouvoir prevenir la descente du detachement Ameriquain, vous en remettrez le double au Commandant, en l'engageant a attendre de nouveaux ordres de son General.

Le second objet de votre commission, que personne ne doit penetrer. et que pour cette raison vous deverez retenier dans votre memoire, est de sonder et examiner les dispositions du peuple des Etats de l'ouest dont on ecrit que les milices ont reçu l'ordre d'etre pretes a marcher au premier avis ; et au cas que cela soit vrai, vous en ferez part au Commandant de la Nouvelle Madrid par la premiere occasion que vous trouverez ; mais afin de ne pas vous rendre suspect, vous vous contenterez de mettre la date de votre lettre en bas et ne traiterez que de choses indifferentes. Sil se fait des preparatifs hóstiles, vous mettrez avant votre signature une barre, comme celle dont use les framacons, et que vous voirez au bas de cette lettre ; le nombre des points audessus indiquera celui des mille hommes, et celui audessus celui des cent dont doit etre composée la dite expedition ; vous designerez celui des pieces d' artillerie par un nombre de points placé dans votre parafe, selon votre usage, dont les points de la gouche signifieront des dixaines, et ceux de la droite des unités. Cette lettre me sera envoiée sur le champ par l'Commandant de la Nouville Madrid d'apres les orders que je lui fais passer, vous pouvez même le lui marquer dans la votre en disant simplement qu'il convient que je sous informè sans delai de votre arrivée sur l'Ohio, et qu'il m' addresse votre lettre par un express : dans votre route vous ferez adroitement entendre aux personnes avec qui vous aurez occasion de parler que la remise des Postes, que les Espagnol occupent sur le Mississippi, aux

troupes des Etats, unis est directement opposeć aux interets de ceux de
l'ouest, qui devant un jour se separer des Etats Atlantiques, se trouve-
roient sans aucune communication avec la Basse Louisiane, d'ou ils doivent
s'attendre a recevoir de puissans secours en artillerie, armes, munitions,
et argent, soit publiquement soit secretement, toute et quante fois les
Etats de l'oust se desideront a une separation, qui doit assurer leur pros-
perité et leur independence ; que pour cette même raison le Congrèss se
decide a toute risquier pour enlever ces Postes a l'Espagne ; et que ce
seroit se forger des fers que d'appeüer sa pretention en lui fournissant
des milices et des moyens, qu'il ne puit trouver, que dans les Etats de
l'oust. Ces mêmes raisons repandues, dans les papiers publics, pour-
roient faire la plus forte impression sur le peuple, et le porter a secouer
le joug des Etats Atlantics, mais tout au moins si nous parven ons a le
dissuader de prendre part dans cette expedition, je doute que les Etats
Unis nous fassent la loi, avec les seules troupes qu'ils ont sur pied.

Si une centaine de mille piastres répandues dans le Kentuckee pouvoit
le soulever je suis bien sure que le Ministre dans les circonstances ac-
tuelles les sacrificroit avec plaisir, et vous pouvez sans trop vous hazarder
les promettre a ceux qui jouissent de la confiance du peuple, avec une
autre somme egale pour l'armée, en cas de necessité, et vingt pieces de
campagne.

Vous vous rendrez sans danger, commer porteur d'une depeche pour
le general jusqu' a l'armée, dont vous examinerez avec soin la force, la
discipline, les dispositions, et vous tacherez de decouvrir avec votre penetration naturelle, les dispositions du general ; je doute qu' une personne de son charactre prefere par vanité l' avantage de commander
l'armeé des Etats Atlantiques a celui d'etre le fondateur, le liberateur,
enfin le Washington des Etats de l'Ouest ; son role est aussi brilliant que
facile ; tous les youx sont attachés sur lui ; il possede la confiance de ses
concitoyens, et des voluntaires du Kentuckee ; au moindre mouvement
le peuple le nommera le general de la Nouvelle Republique ; si reputation lui formera une armée, et l'Espagne, ainsi que la France, lui four-
niront les moyens de soudoier, en s'emparant du fort Massack, nous lui
envoieront sur le champ des armes et de l'artillerie, et l'Espagde, se
reduisant a la possession des forts des Natchez et de Nogales, jusqu' a la
Confederation, cedera aux Etas de l'Ouest toute la rive orientale jusqu'
a l'Ohio, ce qui formera une republique tres etendue et tres puissante,
liée par sa situation et par son interest avec l'Espagne, qui d'accord avec
elle, forcera les Sauvages a en faire partie, et a se confondre avec le
têms avec ses citoyens. Le peuple est mécontent des nouvelles taxes,
l'Espagne et la France sont outrées des liaisons des Etats Unis avec
l'Angleterre ; l'armée est foible, et devouée a Wilkinson ; les menaces
du Congrés me mettent a même d esecourir sur le champ et sans deguise-

ment des Etats de l'Ouest; l'argent ne me manquera pas pour lors, car je depesherai sur le champ ma fregate a Vera Cruz pour en cherches, ainsi que des munitions; il ne faut par consequent qa'un instant de fermeté et de resolution, pour rendres les peuples de l'ouest parfaitement heureux. Si ils laissent echaper cet instant, et que nous soions forcés a remittre les postes le Kentuckee et le Tanesis, cernés par les dits postes et sans communication avec la Basse Louisiane, resteront a jemais sous l'oppression des Etats Atlantics.

Si vous representez avec force ces raisons a Wilkinson, Sebastien, La Cassagne, &c. si vous repandez ces notions dans le peuple, engagnant par des promesses, qui seront realisées fidellement, les meilleurs ecrivains, comme Brackenridge et autres, vous pourrez causer la commotion la plus glorieuse et le plus heureuse, vous vous couvrirez de gloire, et vous devez vous attendre a la fortune la plus brillante; si, ou contraire, vous echouez dans cette commission, je ne'en aurai pas moins l'occasion de vous faire obtenir du ministre quelque traitement, qui vous rendra independent de la haine et de la jalousie.

Il faut que vous partiez sans delai, et par terre, vous dirigeant droit a Cumberland, tant pour eviter le fort Massack, comme pour tacher de couper le detachement Ameriquain, et l'engager a attendre la reponse ou de noveaux ordres du General Wilkinson; car s'il arrive aux Natches, il y a tout a croire qu'en enviendra aux mains, n'etant pas d'humeur de souffrir des insultes. L'Intendant envôie l'ordre de vous compter mille piastres.

Si vous pouvez engager le Commissaire, Don Andrés Ellicot, a descendre a la Capitale, je ferai sa connaissance avec le plus grand plaisir, et en lui montrant sans detour la copie des ordres que j'ai envoié a M. de Gayoso, depuis son arrivée a Natches, il voira que ma conduite vis avis des Etas Unis est francke, fondée sur la prudence et la bonne foi, et sans autune idée de rompre, ni manquir au s'articles du traité; qu'enfin le louche qu'il trouve dans la conduite de Governeur de Natchez ne provient que des changemens que de son chef il a fait a mes dispositions. Enfin, vous pouvez asseurer Don Andres Ellicot que je suis persuadé, que dans un mois ou deux toutes les difficultés seront arrangés par le Congré et par le Ministre Plonipotentiaire de S. M. Don Carlos Martenez Yrujo, et que par consequent il feroit très mal de se retrier; il puit au contraire, descendre commodément dans ma chaloupe avec Mr. Guillemard, qui desire passer icy un mois ou deux, en attendant la reponse du Congrés. Mr. Ferrusola a egalement l'ordre de venir en ville.

Je marque a Mr. Gayoso que vous etes porteur de la reponse de la lettre qu'a ecitr le General Wilkinson au Commandant de la Nouvelle Madrid, et que j'ai disposé qu'on vous compte mille piastres a compte de votre dernier voiage, et de celui que vous allez faire. Cela suffit.

Le champ qui vous est ouvert est assez brillant, mais il faut autant de prudence que de capacité pour sa reussite.

J'ai l'honneur d'etre, avec la plus parfaite consideration,

Monsieur,

Votre très humble et très obeissant serviteur,

LE BARON DE CARONDELET

M. Thomas Power.

Nueva Orleans, 28 de Mayo, de 1797.

Segun la intruccion que tengo dado á vmd, luego que reciba del Sor. Brigadier Don Manuel Gayoso, los auxilios que le mando dar à vmd, para su comision, se poudrà en viage por tierra, para entregar al General Don James Wilkinson, la repuesta de la carta, que derigiò al Comandante de Nuevo Madrid, acerca de tomar posesion con un destacamiento de tropas, de los Fuertes de Nogales y Natchez ; por si aun encontrare vmd el destacamiento que no hubiere pasado de Masac, lleva vmd simple copia, de la misma carta, para que se la entregue, y obre en consequencia, de biendo vmd, continuar su viage hasta el Fuerte Wafhington, ò al quartel General en que se hallare el Comandante en Xefe, Don James Wilkinson, cuya contestacion esperará vmd y se regresara con ella immediatamente por agua y con la mayor prontitud. Dios nuestro Senor gde. a vmd mos anos.

EL BARON DE CARONDELET.

Sr. Dn. Thomas Power.

TRANSLATION of NOTE No. 38.

New Orleans, 26th May, 1797,

I HAVE received, sir, your letters of the 5th, of the 7th, 12th, 13th, and 16th May, and I briefly answer them in fulfilling your wishes, because I entrust to you a commission of the greatest consequence, which does not compromit you in any manner, it being however well understood that you carry with you no paper which may make mention of it, and as it procures you a sum of money which you state to me you are in great need of—in fine, it renders you independent, and procures me the opportunity of recommending you to the Minister of State. No one will be informed of it, not even the Intendant. There will be none but Don Andres and myself, who will be acquainted with the true motive.

General Wilkinson having informed the commandant of New Madrid that he is getting ready a detachment of the army, which he has at his orders, to take possession of the forts of Natchez and Walnut Hills, in conformity to the 2d article of the treaty of friendship, limits and navigation, concluded with Spain, hoping that it will be faithfully observed; and it having appeared proper in him to give this advice, in order to prevent any misapprehension of the motives which direct this movement of their troops, &c. it is very natural that I should answer him, that, in the first place, some doubts having arisen respecting the manner in which the posts are to be withdrawn on the part of Spain, that is to say, if they ought to be delivered with their fortifications and edifices, as the United States understand it, or simply evacuated, razed and abandoned, as I comprehend it, avoiding in this way to compromit us with the nations who have ceded to us the territories of the Bluffs, Walnut Hills and Confederation, under the express condition that we should build forts there, to prevent their lands being taken from them, I had resolved, in regard to this point, to await the decision of the court, or of the Minister Plenipotentiary near the United States, as well as theirs, but being informed shortly afterwards that the abovementioned Minister had informed the President, that an English expedition had left Montreal, with the intention of attacking the Illinois, had wintered on the lakes, and was to traverse the territory of the United States, in order to attack Upper Louisiana, and had demanded that, in virtue of the last treaty, the said states should oppose by efficacious means this violation of their territory, I then determined to retain the forts of Natchez and Walnut Hills, to place Lower Louisiana in safety, until the most efficacious measures on the part of the United States should put it in safety from this danger, and until a sufficient corps of troops, commanded by an officer of superior rank, should present himself, to take possession of Natchez, maintain good order there, and restrain the robberies and difficulties with the Indians, conformable to the 5th article of the treaty cited by the said General; that, in consequence, I am ready to evacuate the posts of Natchez and Walnut Hills, on the arrival of the detachment which he announces by his letter dated from Fort Washington, as soon as ever the Congress shall have agreed with the Minister Plenipotentiary of his Majesty on the way in which the said evacuation is to take place; but until this decision is made, I request he will suspend the march of the said detachment, whose presence could not fail to disturb the tranquility of the province, and perhaps the good intelligence which I wish to maintain between the subjects of the two powers. You will be the bearer of this letter, and if you believe you can prevent the American detachment from descending the river, you will deliver a duplicate of it to the commandant, requesting him to wait new orders from his General.

The second object of your commission, which no one must penetrate, and which for this reason you must retain in your memory, is, to sound and examine the dispositions of the people of the western states, whose militia, it is reported to me, have received orders to be ready to march on the first advice; and in case that should be true, you will inform the commandant of New Madrid of it by the first opportunity you find. But in order not to render yourself suspected, you will content yourself with putting the date of your letter at bottom, and will only treat of indifferent subjects. If hostile preparations are making, you will put before your signature a stroke (une barre) like that which Free Masons use, and which you see at the bottom of this letter; the number of dots above will designate that of thousand men, and that below the hundreds, of which this expedition is to be composed. You will point out the number of pieces of artillery by a number of points placed in your flourish (parafe) according to your custom, the points on the left signifying tens, and those on the right units. This letter will be immediately sent me by the commandant of New Madrid, in consequence of the orders I shall give him. You may even mention it to him in yours, saying simply, that it is proper that I should be informed without delay of your arrival on the Ohio, and that he should send me your letter by express. On your journey you will give to understand adroitly, to those persons to whom you will have an opportunity of speaking, that the delivery of the posts, which the Spaniards occupy on the Missisippi, to the troops of the United States, is directly opposed to the interests of those of the west, who, as they must one day separate from the Atlantic states, would find themselves without any communication with Lower Louisiana, from whence they ought to expect to receive powerful succours in artillery, arms, ammunition and money, either publicly or secretly, as soon as ever the western states shall determine on a separation, which must insure their prosperity and their independence; that for this same reason Congress is resolved on risking every thing to take these posts from Spain, and that it would be forging fetters for themselves to furnish it with militia and means, which it can only find in the western states. These same reasons diffused abroad, by means of the public papers, might make the strongest impression on the people, and induce them to throw off the yoke of the Atlantic states; but at the very least, if we are able to dissuade them from taking part in this expedition, I doubt whether the states could give law to us, with such troops alone as they have now on foot.

If a hundred thousand dollars distributed in Kentucky could cause it to rise in insurrection, I am very certain that the minister, in the present circumstances, would sacrifice them with pleasure; and you may, without exposing yourself too much, promise them to those who enjoy the confidence of the people, with another equal sum to arm them, in case of necessity, and twenty pieces of field artillery.

You will arrive without danger, as bearer of a dispatch for the General, where the army may be, whose force, discipline and disposition, you will examine with care; and you will endeavour to discover, with your natural penetration, the General's dispositions. I doubt that a person of his character would prefer, through vanity, the advantage of commanding the army of the Atlantic states, to that of being the founder, the liberator, in fine, the Washington of the Western states; his part is as brilliant as it is easy; all eyes are drawn towards him; he possesses the confidence of his fellow-citizens and of the Kentucky volunteers; at the slightest movement the people will name him the General of the new republic; his reputation will raise an army for him, and Spain, as well as France, will furnish him the means of paying it. On taking Fort Massac, we will send him instantly arms and artillery, and Spain, limiting herself to the possession of the Forts of Natchez and Walnut Hills, as far as Fort Confederation, will cede to the Western States all the Eastern bank to the Ohio, which will form a very extensive and powerful republic, connected, by its situation and by its interest, with Spain, which, in concert with it, will force the savages to become a party to it, and to confound themselves in time with its citizens. The public is discontented with the new taxes; Spain and France are enraged at the connexions of the United States with England; the army is weak and devoted to Wilkinson; the threats of Congress authorise me to succour on the spot, and openly, the Western States; money will not then be wanting to me, for I shall send without delay a ship to Vera Cruz in search of it, as well as of ammunition; nothing more will consequently be required, but an instant of firmness and resolution, to make the people of the West perfectly happy. If they suffer this instant to escape them, and that we should be forced to deliver up the posts, Kentucky and Tennesse, surrounded by the said posts, and without communication with Lower Louisiana, will ever remain under the oppression of the Atlantic states.

If you represent forcibly these reasons to Wilkinson, Sebastian, La Cassagne, &c. and if you diffuse these notions among the people, gaining by promises, which shall be faithfully realized, the best writers, as Brackenridge and others, you will be able to effect the most fortunate and the most glorious commotion; you will cover yourself with glory, and you may expect the most brilliant fortune; if, on the contrary, you should fail in this commission, it will not deprive me of the opportunity of obtaining for you from the Minister an appointment, which will render you independent of hatred and jealousy.

You must set off without delay, and by land, going straight to Cumberland, as well to avoid Fort Massac, as to endeavour to fall in with the American detachment, and persuade it to wait the answer or new orders from General Wilkinson; for if it arrives at Natchez, there is every reason to believe that we may come to blows, not being of a humour to put up with insults. The Intendant sends an order to pay you one thousand dollars.

If you could persuade the commissioner, Mr. Andrew Ellicott, to descend to the capital, I should with the greatest pleasure form an acquaintance with him, and by shewing him without disguise the copy of the orders which I have sent to Mr. Gayoso, since his arrival at Natchez, he will perceive that my conduct towards the United States is frank, founded on prudence and good faith, and void of the idea of breaking or failing in the articles of the treaty; that, in fine, the unaccountable part of the conduct of the Governor of Natchez only proceeds from the alterations which he has made, of his own accord, in my arrangements. Lastly, you may assure Mr. Andrew Ellicott that I am persuaded, that in a month or two all the difficulties will be settled by Congress and by the Minister Plenipotentiary of his Majesty, Don Carlos Martinez de Yrujo, and that consequently he would do very ill to withdraw; on the contrary, he may come down conveniently in my barge with Mr. Guillemard, who is desirous of spending a month or two here, whilst we are waiting the answer of Congress. Mr. Ferrezola has also orders to come to town.

I inform Mr. Gayoso that you are the bearer of the answer to the letter which General Wilkinson has written to the Commandant of New Madrid, and that I have given directions to pay you one thousand dollars on account of your last journey, and that you are about to undertake. This suffices. The field which is opened is brilliant enough, but as much prudence as capacity is required, in order to succeed.

I have the honour to be, with the greateſt consideration,
Sir, your very humble and very obedient servant,
LE BARON DE CARONDELET.

Mr. Thomas Power.

New Orleans, the 28th May, 1797.

According to the instructions which I have given you, that as soon as you receive from the Brigadier Don Manuel Gayoso, the assistance which I have ordered to be afforded you for your commission, set off by land, to deliver to General James Wilkinson, the answer of the letter he wrote to the Commander of New Madrid, relative to the taking possession with a detachment of troops, of the forts Nogales and Natchez ; but if you should meet the detachment, which may not have departed from Massac, take a mere copy of said letter, that it may be delivered to him, and act in conformity ; and you continue your journey as far as Fort Washington or to Head-Quarters, where you will find the Commander in Chief, Don James Wilkinson, whose answer wait, and return with it immediately, by water, with all speed. God preserve you many years.

Thomas Power, Esq.
BARON DE CARONDELET.

NOTE No. 39. UNIMPORTANT

NOTE No. 40.

Natchez, 4 *Juin,* 1797.

J'ai reçu hier la lettre du 26 Mai, que vous m'avez fait l'honneur de m'ecrire, à la quelle les preparatifs de mon voyage ne me permettent pas de répondre que trés succintement. J'ai reçu de M. Gayoso la depêche pour le Gen. Wilkinson, et sa copie, a fin de m'em servir selon que les circonstances pourront le demander. Quant au second objet de mon expedition, qui est les plus interressant, comme puet ne rein cadrer plus complètement avec mes inclinations, vous pouvez compter que je m'en acquiterai avec toute la fidélité et tout le zéle, que vous me connaissez, et avec cette intelligence, qui doit resulter d'une connassance parfaite du local et de personnages avec qui nous avons a faire. Pour èviter la possibilité d'une méprise, dans le communications que je serai dans le cas de faire au Commandant de la Nouvelle Madrid, je vais expliquer ce que je prétends vous faire comprendre par ma signature. A celle ce, cette barre ⎯·⎯·⎯·⎯·⎯ avec les points avant la signature, signifie quatre milles six cent. hommes. ⎯⎯⎯⎯⎯⎯ Dans la parafe, les points a gauche de la petites raie sont des dixaines, ceux de la droite des unites; de sorte qu'ils indiquent trente cinq pieces d'artillerie. La datte mise en bas de ma lettre, signiefiera, que les milices sont sur pied, et prêtes a marcher. Les réflexions que contient votre lettre sont parfaitement de nature à faire la sensation la plus forte dans la Kentuckey, tant sur le peuple, que sur le General Wilkinson et autres, charactéres distingués, et je ne manquerai pas de les leur exposer sous le point de vue les plus frappant, et les appuierai de celles, que pourront me sugirer l'étude qua j'ai faite de leurs intérets, et l'ardeur avec la'quelle je desir de voir leur decision. Cependant, je mettrai de la sagêsse et de la prudence, dans mes démarches, pour ne pas me compromettre, et il faudra toutes les precausions imaginables, de mon côté, de rien laisser échapper qui puisse jetter de jour sur moin dessein ; car toutes les fois qu'ils me voient entrer dans leur territoire, leur mefiance et leur jalousie leur font croire que j'ai quelqu' objet secret en vue. Je dirai a Wilkinson, que la difficulté et le danger de porter de l'argent par terre ne vous ont pas permis de lui envoyer les 640 piastres. L'ambition et la politique de ce General me sont un garant certain, qu'il appuyera nos plans (qui ont toujours été les sien) de tout son influence ; et nous pouvons faire fonds sur Nicholas, Sebastian, Innes, Murray, Clarke ; en un mot, sur tous ceux qui sont attachés à W. ainsi que ceux qui devoient composer l'armée de Clarke. Les principaux du pays, tiennent à nous par l'ambition et l'intérêt ; et une gallomanie forcenie, et un amour pour le changemement, nous répondent de l'appuie du peuple, qui donnera tête baissée dans votre projet. Si j'en croyois mes présentimens, notre succés est immanquable. Il y a tant de motifs puissans, qui devroeient porter les états de l'ouest a cette démarche, qu'il nous seroit permis de croire qu'ils ont perdu la tête, s'ils réculent. Quant à moi, j'en épargnerai ni pienes ni travail pour faire rèussir cette revolution importante ; et j'ai a vous, prier de daigner agréer l'expression de ma plus vive réconnaissance, tant de m'avoir lanceé dans une carriére aussi brillante et glorieuse, que de m'avoir soustrait à la haine, et a la jalousie. J'ai vu Ellicott. Je lui est fait part de ce que vous m'avez communiqué à son sujet, et il en a été trés satisfait. Il á parlé de vous dans les termes les plus flatteurs, et m'a prié de vous presenter les respects, et de vous assurer, que de quelque maniére que les affaires se terminent, il n'abandonnera pas la province sans avoir eu le plaisir de vous voir. Les mille piastres m'ont été comptées, et je n'attends qu'un cheval pour partir. Ne cesséz de compter sur mon zéle, ma vigilance, et mon courage. J'ai l'honneur d'etre, avec le plus profound respect, et la reconnaisance la mieux sentie,

       Monsieur, &c.

      ·:·:·:·:— THOMAS POWER.

Monsieur Le Baron de Carondelet.

TRANSLATION OF NOTE No. 40.

Natchez, 4th June, 1797.

I RECEIVED yesterday the letter of 26th May, which you have done me the honour to write me, and which the preparations for my journey do not permit me to answer but very briefly. I have received of Mr. Gayoso the dispatch for General W. together with the copy, in order to make use of it as circumstances may require. With respect to the second object of my expedition, which is the most interesting, as nothing can coincide better with my inclination, you may depend that I will acquit myself of it with all the fidelity and zeal which you know me to possess, and with that good understanding, resulting from a perfect knowledge of the place and personages with whom we are concerned. To avoid the possibility of a mistake, in the communications which I shall have to make to the Commander of New Madrid, I will explain what I mean to give you to understand by my signature. This bar, with the dots  before the signature, signifies 4,600 men. In the flourish, the dots to the left of the small stroke are tens, and those of the right are units, so that they mean thirty-five pieces of artillery. The date at the bottom of my letter will simply signify, that the militia are on foot, and ready to march. The remarks which your letter contains are well adapted to cause the strongest sensations in Kentucky, as much on the people, as on General W. and others, distinguished characters; and I will not fail to represent them in that point of view which is most striking, and I will strengthen them with those, which the study I have made of their interests, and the ardour with which I desire to see their decision, may suggest. However, I will use wisdom and prudence in my measures, not to compromise myself, and all imaginable precautions will be necessary on my part, in order not to let slip any thing which may give light to my design; for whenever they see me enter their territory, their mistrust and their jealousy causes them to suspect that I have some secret object in view. I will tell W. that the difficulty and the danger of carrying money by land have prevented you from sending him the 640 piastres. The ambition and politics of this General are a certain guaranty to me, that he will support our plans (which have always been his) with all his influence; and we may rely upon Nicholas, Sebastian, Innes, Murray, Clarke; in a word, on all those who are attached to W. and also those who were to compose the army of Clarke.

The principal characters of the place are united to us by ambition and interest; and an excessive gallicism, and a love of change, ensure the support of the people, who will willingly submit to your project. If I give credit to my presentiment, our success is infallible. There are so many powerful motives, which should lead the western states to take this step, that we should be permitted to believe that they had lost their senses, if they flinch. As to myself, I will spare neither pains nor labour for the success of this important revolution; and I have to request of you, that you will deign to accept of my most sincere acknowledgment, as well for having launched me into a career so glorious and so brilliant, as for protecting me from jealousy and hatred. I have seen Ellicott. I told him what you communicated to me about him, and he was very well satisfied with it. He spoke of you in the most flattering terms, and requested me to present you his best respects, and to assure you, that however affairs may turn out, he will not leave the province without seeing you. The 1000 piastres have been delivered to me, and I only wait a horse to set off. Do not cease to trust in my zeal, vigilance and courage. I have the honour to be, with the most profound respect, and most sincere acknowledgment,

Sir, &c.

THOMAS POWER.

Monsieur LE BARON DE CARONDELET.

NOTE No. 41.——See No. 11.

NOTE No. 42.

Head-Quarters, Detroit, September 5th, 1797.
SIR,

I HAVE the last moment received your letter of the day, which occasions me much surprize.

At our first interview, the night before the last, I expressed to you the necessity of your speedy return by the shortest route to the Baron de Carondelet, with my answer to the letter which you bore me from him. You offered no objection to this proposition, except the incapacity of your horses for the journey, which I immediately agreed to remove, by furnishing others.

You at the same time complained to me of the violence and outrage which you had experienced on your journey to this place, being at one time stopped, and another time pursued, seized and examined, in every particular of person, baggage and papers. It seems a little singular, that you should incline to retrace a route in which you had suffered such abuse, when a secure and convenient one is proposed to you.

As no man can more highly appreciate the rights of treaties and of individuals than myself, and as I am well apprized of the obligations subsisting between the United States and his Catholic Majesty, I am among the last men on earth, who would wantonly or capriciously question the compacted rights of the two sovereignties, their citizens, or subjects.

But as you have approached me in a public character, and on national business, which requires my speedy answer to the letter of the Governor of Louisiana, whose messenger you are, I cannot consider you so far a free agent, as to elect the time or route for your return, but that you stand bound by motives of political import, as well to Spain as to the United States, to consummate the objects of your mission with all possible promptitude; and, of consequence, that all objects of a private or personal nature must yield to the obligations of public duty.

I therefore, Sir, cannot recede from my purpose, and will hope you may be prepared to take your departure early to-morrow morning, in the company of Captain Shaumburgh, who will be instructed to attend you to New Madrid, and who will receive and forward any letter you may wish to send to the Falls of Ohio, from the most convenient point of your route.

With due consideration, I am, Sir,
Your most obedient servant,
JA. WILKINSON.

NOTE No. 43.

El dia 3 del mez de Junio po. po. recibi la carta del Senor Baron de Caroudelet, con fha de 28 del mes anterior, acompanado de la instruccion anunciada, en ella de que incluyo copias, Nos. 1 y 2. En execucion de las ordenes é intenciones que en su primera se ha servido prevenirme en ellas, hize las prevenciones correspondientes para el viage, y me puse en marcha el 8 del mismo mes. Por haber perdido mis caballos el dia que salí del Bayou Pierre, y por otros incidentes imprevistos é inevitables, tardé llegar a Nashville (capital de Cumberland) hasta el 5 de Julio, donde tuve que permanecer algunos dias, tanto para desenpenar con acierto micomision reservada, y examinar con cuidado las disposiciones de sus habitantes en lo tocante á las desavenencias que entonces existian entre los Estados Unidos y nosotros, y aviriguar definitivamente el partido que intentan tomar en la actual crisis, como para allanar los impedimientos que me estaban susitando, precaver las dudas, y evitar los riesgos que no dexarian de resultar de las voces esparcidas en le publico, por lo respectivo al verdadero objecto de mi viage: me detuvo el Magistrado, J. Gordon, algunos dias.

Habiendome desenredado y vencido estos embarazos, proseguì mi viage para Louisville, donde me aboqué con Don Benjamin Sebastian, á quién como previene la citada instruccion, communiqué el motivo aparente, como asi mismo la causa verdadera de mi mision. Ademas de las proposiciones expresadas en mis instrucciones, para no perder el fruto de mi viage, me ví en la precision de anadir las seguientes, pues sin la primera. Advertí que ni el ni los demas sujetos interados é interesados en este asunto importante no huvieran hecho los movimientos indispensables para su feliz exíto. En primero lugar he pactado, que siempre que alguno de los que avorecieren á fomentar el proyecto del Sor. Baron, viniera por este motivo a perder su empleo, reciberâ del Rey una indemnizacion comensurada con los emolumentos de que gozaba.

En 2º lugar la linea divisoria septentrional, entre el territorio de S. M. y el de los Estados Nuevos del Oriente, ha de empezar a la embocadura del rio Yazou, y extenderse en tal direccion hacia el Tombecbé; que el nltimo pueste fuerte, ó estabelicimiento Espanol sobre dho rio quede seis millas dentro del territorio de S. M.

3º. Que el puesto de San Fernando de las Barancas, con todo el terreno concedido á la Espana por la nacion Chicacha en el tratado hecho con ella por el Sor. Don M. G. de Lemos, hade quedar en posesion de S. M.

4º. Que el Rey no ha de mesclarse, ni directa ni indirectamente, en la formacion del Gobierno ó de las leyes que ellos tuvieren por conveniente establecer.

Conseguiente á estos objetos, resolvimos que el los participaria á los

Sres. Nicholas, Innes, Todd, y otras personas de su confianza, practicas y zelozas del adelantamiento, prosperidad, é independencia del Kentucky, y rehusanda absolutamende se hablar sobre el asunto con Murray y Brackenridge, porque de ambos desconfiaba. Pues el primero está entregado crapulosamente á bebidas, la mala fé y perfidia ; del otro son notorias para tener con ellos conferencias, derigidas á verificar los deseos del Baron, y concertar las operaciones á este fin. Mientras yo continuaria mi viage hasta Detroit, en donde estaba el General Wilkinson, tanto para entregarle la carta del Senor Baron, como para ocultar el objeto principal de mi mision, y evitarlo que se estabo tramando contra mi en Louisville, cuyos habitantes estaban muy alborotados con mi llegada en el pays, y me estaban amenazando abiertamente. Quedamos tambien en que á mi regreso pasaria por Greenville, Cincinnati, Newport, Georgetown, Lexington, Frankfort, &c. para ver los Sres. ya citados, y interarme de las resultas de sas conferencias, y que él (Sebastian) con otro deputado, me acompânaria hasta la Neuva Orleans. Sin embargo de que Don B. Sebastian está persuadido qne por aora todos los medios y conatos para estimalur los habitantes de los Estados del Oriente á separarse de la federacion serán infructuosos, con todo no dexará de hacer todos sus esfuerzos para conseguir lo que con tanta ansia deseamos todos.

Volviendo pues á mi viage. Salí de Louisville el dia   de Julio, para ponerme con la brevidad posible en Detroit, y el dia seguiente me aconteció lo que manifiestan los documentos No.
Nota, que 16 de Julio escribí al Capt. Don Isaac Guyon, encaminandole la copia de la carta del Sor. Baron de Carondelet al Gen. Don James Wilkinson ; incluyo copia de la mia al dho. Capt. Guyon, No.
No se ofreció novedad alguna en el curso de mi viage, y llegué en la vicindad de Detroit el 16 de Agosto. Noticioso de que el General Wilk..... habia salido para Michilimakinak, no entré en el puerto hasta el 24, dia en que le estaban esperando ; pero no regresó sinó el 3 ó el 4 de Setiembre. Antes de su llegada, luego que supo que yo estaba allí, me mando quedan arrestado en el quartel de los officiales. El dia 6 me entregó su respuerta á la carta del Sor. Gobernador obligandome contra *(jus gentium)* a regresar al Neuvo Madrid por el Wabash baxo una guardia, mandada por il Capitan Don Bartolomé Shaumburgh, como lo evidencia no solamente mi correspondencia con él, sobre el asunto, la que está copiada en No.   , No.   , y No.   , sinó tambien la declaracion adjunta de Shaumburgh No.   . A mi llegada al puesto Vincennes despaché un proprio a Louisville, con una carta para Don Benjamin Sebastian, cuya copia va inclusa No.   , dandole aviso de lo que me habia succedido, enterandole de los motivos que no me dexaban

complir con la palabra que le habia dado. El 10 de Octobre llegamos en el Neuvo Madrid sin otra particularidad alguna. Permanecí en ese puerto 15 dias, aguardando á Monsieur Sebastian. Por fin, viendo que no venia, y no recibiendo noticia alguna de èl, me puse en deriva el 24 de Octobre; peropor motivo de las aguas baxas, los malos tiempos, y vientos del sud, no me restituí á esta capital antes del 30 del mes proxo. paso. El Capt. Shaumburgh, por order del Gen. Wilkinson, y por cuenta de los Estados Unidos, hizo todos los gastos de neustro viage desde Detroit hasta el Neuvo Madrid. Pero bolvamos al objeto de mi mision.

El General Wilkinson me recibió con bastanse frialdad. En la primera conferencia que tuve con el, prorumpió con decirme amargamente, " somos perdidos, vmd y yo sin poder sacar provecho alguno de mi viage, y sequidamente me preguntó si le habia traido 640 pesos; anadio, que el executivo le habia dado orden al Gobernador del Territorio del Nord Oueste para que me prendiese y me embiase á Philadelphia; que no me quedaba otro recurso para escaparme, que el dexarme conducir immediamente baxo una guardia al Fuerte Massac, y de alli al Nuevo Madrid."

Y habiendole enterado de las proposiciones del Sor. Baron, proseguió diciendome, que era un proyecto chimireco, que era imposible executar; que los habitantes de los Estado del Oueste, habiendo logrado por el tratado todo lo que deseaban, no querian formar otros enlaces politicos ó de comercio, y que ya no tenian motivo de separarse de los intereses de los otros Estades de la Union, aunque la Francia y la España les hagan las proposiciones las mas ventajosas; que la fermentacion que reynaba en el pueblo hace 4 anos ya esta asosegada; que las depredaciones y las vexaciones que padecia el comercio de los Americanos de parte de los corsarios Franceses les habia infundido un odio implacable contra su nacion; que algunos del Kentucky le habian propuesto levantar 3000 hombres, para invadir la Louisiana en caso que se declrarase la guerra entre los Estados Unidos y la Espana. Esta no tenia otro rumbo que seguir en las circunstancias actuales, que dar complido efecto al tratado, el que ha trastornado todos sus planes, é inutilizado, el trabajo de mas de diez anos, &c. &c. En quanto á el, dixo que habia hecho pedazos sus cifras, y toda su correspondencia con nuestro gobierno, y que su deber y su honra no le permitian continuarla; que con todo el Sr. Gobernador no debe tener recelos de que el abùse de la confianza que ha hecho de él; enfin, que en entregando la Espana á los Estados Unidos el territorio de Natchez, &c. puede qne le nombren Gobernador de ello, y que entonces no le faltarán occasiones para tomar medidas mas eficaces para efectuar sus proyectos politicos. Se quexa mucho de que el secreto de sus relaciones con neustro gobierno se ha divulgado, por falta de prudencia y recato de nuestra parte; que supo en el mez de Setiembre del ano prox. pas. por uno de sus oficiales, que la Espana no tenia intencion de entregar los puestos; pues dicho official vió en el puesto Vincennes una carta, escrita por un *oficial Espanol de los Ilinois*, y derigida ó un vecino del puesto, in que se lo dice, pues M. Audrain tiene una correspondencia con Don Z. Trudeau (o lo hace créer) y que este le comunica asuntos reservados de gobierno, de suerte que Audrain suele hacer correr noticia que a todo riesgo podran causar un rompimiento, en las fronteras, de otro; que el M. Trudeau se ha comportado con mucha imprudencia, habiendo empleado emisarios entre los Indios en el terretorio de los Estados Unidos, combidandoles a establecerce en el de la Espana, diciendoles, que su padre, el Espanol, estaba en guerra con los Ingleses, y que en breve laharia á los Americanos, &c. &c.

Por lo que toca a las disposiciones de los habitantes de Kentucky, el parecer de Mons. Sebastian discrepa mucho del del Gen. Wilkinson. Dice, que aurique se declare la guerra entra la Espana y los Estados Unidos, no tendremos nada que temer de los Kentuckianos; y no ha omitido insinuar que seria uno de los medios los mas eficaces de empujarles á tomar un partido violento contra los Estados del Este. Sin embargo de las repetidas representaciones, que de palabra y por escrito que he hecho á V. S. y al Signor Baron de Carondelet, sobre esto asunto, recapitularé en pocas palabras las resultas de mis muchas observaciones, hechas con la atencion la mas escrupulosa.

Una gran porcion de los notables de Kentucky, Cumberland, y North West territory, han sido motores, de la expedicion de Genet y Clarke contra esta provincia, por consegiente, enemigos de los que lo son de los Franceses; mas dela mitad de los dimas son los, que toman el mayor interes en qui los Estados del Orieste se enlacen mas intimamente con nosotros; y muchos de los que quedan, como no tiene granansia de hacer conquistas sobre la Epana, y si solo conservar los limites, y los privilegios senalados por el tratado, haran lo que cabe en ellos, para que no lleguen las cosas á hostilidades. La plebe se dexa gobernar implicitamente ò por los unos ó los otros de los referidos, de suerte, que attendidas estas circumstancias, podemos deponer todo recelo en esta parte. Para otras causas mas graves se oponen a que se declaren independientes de los Estados del Este. Me contentaré con exponer le mas *importante*:—Mientras estaran haciendo un tratado con el Gobierno de la Louisiana, que seguridad tendrán de que el Gabinete de Madrid no esté haciendo al mismo tiempo otro muy opuesto á lo que habran pactado aqui? la experiencia les ha ensenado, disgraciadamente, que esto no es una mera conjectura. Solo tres motivos les podran impelir a romper la confederacion con los otros Estados, que son :

1º. La guerra con la republica de Francia.

2º. La prohibicion de naviger el Missisippi, y de establecerse en los dominios el Rey.

3º. El no poder pagar en plata lo que les toca de los derechos generales (28000 pesos) ó ver que el Gobierno intente cobrarlo por fuerza. Estos son los exes sobre que gira su politica. Mi queda aun que decir algo de la fuerza militar de los Estados Unidos. Su exercito ascende acerca de 3000 hombres; consiste de 4 regimentos de infanteria, 1 regimento doble de artilleria, y dos compania de caballaria; in cada regimento hay 8 companias, cada compania se compone de 65 hombres, inclusos un Capitan, un Teniento, y un Alferez, pero no hay ni una que esté completa. Se debe observar, que las dos de caballaria ascenden á 180 hombres, pero solo hay unos 60 de montados. Cada regimento tiene un Coronel, y dos Sargentos-Mayores. El primero regimento, mandado por el Coronel Hamtramk, se halla en Fort Wayne, y los demas tuertos hacia Fort Washington; el segundo, mandado por el Coronel Strong, está in guarnicion en Detroit, Michilimakinack, Niagara, Presqu-ile, Oswego, &c. el tercero, mandado por el Coronel Gathers, guarnece pour los Fuertes de Massac, las Barrancas, &c. una ó dos companias quedando in Georgia; el 4to. mandado por el Coronel Butler, esta en el Tenesse; los artilleros estan repartidos en los fuertes, aunque la mayor parte no sale de Stony-Point, en los Estados del Este; la cabelleria esta parte en el Tenesse, parte en Detroit, y los demas en Fort Washington. Por lo respectivo á sus fuertes, como es un asunto de ninguna importancia para nostros, no quiero molestar á su Senoria con una discripcion enfadosa de ellos. Se observa en el exercito una disciplina muy rigoroso; los soldados son casi todos mozos do 16 a 26 anos; executan algunas evoluciones militares con bastante precision. En quanto á los officiales, desde el primer hasta el ultimo (exceptuando muy pocos) carecen de todas calidades que deben adornar un buen militar, menos la braveza, y estan submergidos en la ignorancia, y los vicios los mas verguenzosos.

La influencia del General Wilkinson en el Kentucky ha llegado a ser muy corta; y en el exercito, por querer reformar muchos abusos y establecer algunas innovaciones, pierde de dia en dia mucho de ella. Esperode lo que va dicho sobre el asunto di mi mision, que V. S. quedará convencido, que si no ha tenido una salida mas feliz y ventajosa, no debe de ningunmodo atribuirie á indiscrecion ó otro defecto mio, pues es patente que ha dimanado de causas que ninguna penetracion humana podia alcanzar, y que ninguna prudencia podia precaver; y si he carecido de inteligencia y capacidad que pedia el desempeno de mi comision, no será atrevimiento en mi, el decir, que la prontitud y el zelo, el sigilo y fidelidad, que in otros ocasiones aun de mas intedad he manifestidad en el services de S. M. nu me han abandonado en esta. Dios guarde a V. S mos. anos. 5 de Decembre, 1797.

P. D. Incluyo, con los otros documentos, la cuenta de los gastos del viage No. 11. La de los 640, que pide con tanta instancia el General Wilkinson, y que me ha encargado de reciber por su cuenta, la remetí al Segnor Baron de Carondelet en el mes de Mayo del presente ano. No. 3, acompanado de otros documentos, los que recibió, como consta por su oficio de 28 del mismo mes y ano, de que tambien incluyo copia, No. 12.

San. Don Manuel Gayoso Lemos.

TRANSLATION OF NOTE No. 43.

ON the 3d of June last I received the Baron de Carondelet's letter, dated 28th of the preceding month, accompanied by the instructions therein announced, of which I enclose copies, No. 1. and 2. In consequence of the orders and intention which his Excellency has deemed proper to advise me of in them, I took the necessary steps for the journey, and set out on the 8th of the same month. Having lost my horses the day I set out from Bayou Pierre, and by other unforeseen and unavoidable accidents, my arrival at Nashville (capital of Cumberland) was retarded until the 5th of July, where I was compelled to remain some days, as well to execute with exactness my private instructions, carefully to examine the dispositions of its inhabitants with respect to the difference then existing between the United States and us, and to ascertain definitively the part which they intend to take in the present crisis, as also to lessen the difficulties which were rising, to provide against doubts, and avoid the dangers which would not fail to result from the rumours spread among the public as to the true object of my journey; the magistrate, Mr. J. Gordon, detained me some days.

Having done away and overcome these difficulties, I pursued my journey to Louisville, where I had an interview with Mr. Benjamin Sebastian, to whom, as the above letter mentions, I communicated the apparent motive, and likewise the true cause of my mission. Besides the propositions expressed in my instructions, not to lose the fruit of my journey, I found myself compelled to add the following, since, without the first, I perceived that neither he nor the other persons interested in this important undertaking would have taken the necessary measures for the happy issue of it. In the first place I have agreed, that whenever one of those who favoured the fomentation of the projects of the Baron should by this means lose his office, he shall receive from the King an indemnification, with the emoluments which he enjoyed.

2d. That the boundary line on the north, between the territory of his Majesty and that of the new States of the East, must begin at the mouth of the river Yazou, and extend in that direction as far as the Tombecbe; that the last strong post or Spanish settlement on said river be six miles within his Majesty's territory.

3d. That the place called St. Fernando de las Barrancas, with all the land granted to Spain by the Chicacha nation in the treaty made with her by Mr. M. G. de Lemos, must remain in his Majesty's possession.

4th. That the King is not to interfere, either directly or indirectly, in the formation of the government or laws which they may think proper to establish.

Consequent to these objects, we resolved that he should make them known to Messrs. Nicholas, Innes, Todd, and other persons in whom he confided, who were zealous for the improvement, prosperity, and independence of Kentucky, and absolutely refusing to speak to Murray or Brackenridge on the subject, as he mistrusted both. The first is given to drink, infidelity and perfidy; the other is known to hold conferences with them, tending to fulfil the wishes of the Baron, and to concert measures to that effect. In the mean time I should continue my journey to Detroit, where General Wilkinson was, as well to deliver him the Baron's letter, as to conceal the object of my mission, and avoid what was plotting against me at Louisville, whose inhabitants were much alarmed at my arrival in the country, and were openly threatening me. We agreed also, that on my return I should pass through Grenville, Cincinnati, Newport, Georgetown, Lexington, Frankfort, &c. to see the gentlemen above mentioned, and inform myself thoroughly of the result of their conferences, and that he (Sebastian) with another appointed person, should accompany me as far as New Orleans. Notwithstanding Mr. B. Sebastian is persuaded, that for the present all the means and endeavours used to stimulate the inhabitants in the Eastern states to separate themselves from the confederation will be useless, still he will not fail to exert his utmost to obtain what we so anxiously desire.

To return to my journey. I sat out from Louisville the —— of July, to reach at Detroit as soon as possible, and the following day I met with the accident manifested in the document No. ——. Note, that on the 16th of July I wrote to Capt. Isaac Guyon, forwarding him the copy of the Baron de Carondelet's letter to General James Wilkinson; I enclosed a copy of mine to said Capt. Guyon, No. —. Nothing new presented itself in the course of my journey, and I arrived in the neighbourhood of Detroit on the 16th of August. I was informed that General Wilkinson had sat out for Machilimakinac, in consequence of which I did not enter the post until the 24th, which was the day they expected him; but he did not return before the 3d or 4th of September. Before he arrived, as soon as he knew that I was there, he ordered me to remain arrested in the quarters of the officers. On the 6th he delivered me his answer to the Governor's letter, obliging me (contra jus gentium) to return to New Madrid, by Wabash, under a guard, commanded by Capt. Bartholomew Shaumburgh, as is proved, not only by my correspondence with him on the subject, which is copied in No. —, No. —, and No. —, but also by the annexed declaration of Shaumburgh, No. —. On my arrival at Post Vincennes I dispatched an express to Louisville, with a letter for Benjamin Sebastian, a copy of which goes enclosed, No. —, advising him of what had occurred, and informing him minutely of the motives which prevented me from complying with my promise given him. On the 10th of October we arrived at New Madrid, without any particular occurrence. I remained in that place fifteen days, waiting for Mr. Sebastian. Finally, seeing that he did not come, and not hearing from him, I departed on the 24th of October, but by low tides, bad weather, and winds from the southward, I did not arrive at this capital before the 30th of last month. Capt. Shaumburgh, by order of Gen. Wilkinson, and on account of the United States, defrayed all the expences of our voyage from Detroit to New Madrid. But let us return to the object of my mission.

General Wilkinson received me very coolly. During the first conference I had with him, he exclaimed very bitterly, we are both lost, without being able to derive any advantage from your journey, and then asked me if I had brought him the 640 dollars; he added, that the Executive had given orders to the Governor of the North-Western Territory to take and send me to Philadelphia; that there was no other resource for me to escape, but by permitting myself to be conducted immediately under a guard to the Fort Massac, and from there to New Madrid. Having informed him of the proposals of the Baron, he proceeded to tell me that it was a chimerical project, which was impossible to execute; that the inhabitants of the Western States, having obtained by treaty all they desired, would not wish to form any other political or commercial alliances, and that they had no motive for separating themselves from the interests of the other States of the Union, even if France and Spain should make them the most advantageous offers; that the fermentation which existed four years back was now appeased; that the depredations and vexations which American commerce suffered from the French privateers had inspired them with an implacable hatred for their nation; that some of the Kentuckians had proposed to him to raise 3000 men, to invade Louisiana, in case war should be declared between the United States and Spain; that the latter had no other course to pursue under the present circumstances, but to comply fully with the the treaty, which had overturned all his plans, &c. and rendered useless the labours of more than ten years; that as to him, he said he had destroyed his cyphers, and torn all his correspondence with our government, and that his duty and his honour did not permit him to continue it; that, with all, the Governor ought not to be apprehensive of his abusing the confidence which he had placed in him; finally, that Spain, by delivering up to the United States the territory of Natchez, &c. might perhaps name him Governor of it, and that then he would not want opportunities to take more effectual measures to comply with his political projects. He complains very much that the secret of his connexions with our government had been divulged, for want of prudence on our part; that he knew in September of the last year, by means of one of his officers, that Spain had no intention to give up the posts, as the above-mentioned officer saw a letter at Post Vincennes, written by a Spanish officer of the Ilinois, and directed to an inhabitant of that place, in which he tells him, that Mr. Audrain had a correspondence with Z. Trudeau (or makes it to be believed) and that he communicates to him private affairs of the government, so that Audrain is accustomed to spread news that at all events may cause a rupture on the frontiers; that Mr. Trudeau has conducted himself with a great deal of imprudence, having sent emissaries among the Indians in the territory of the United States, inviting them to come and establish themselves in that of Spain, telling them that his father, the Spaniard, was at war with the English, and that he would soon make it with the Americans, &c. &c.

With respect to the dispositions of the people of Kentucky, the opinion of Mr. Sebastian differs very much from that of General Wilkinson. He says, that, even if war is declared between Spain and the United States, we will have nothing to fear from the Kentuckians; and he has not omitted to insinuate, that it would be the most efficacious mode to spur them on to take a violent part against the Atlantic States. Without considering the many representations, which, verbally and in writing, I have made to your Excellency and to the Baron de Carondelet on this subject, I will recapitulate in a few words the result of my many observations, made with the most scrupulous attention.

A great portion of the principal characters in Kentucky, Cumberland, and the North West Territory, have been instigators of the expedition of Genet and Clarke against this province, consequently they are enemies of those who are of the French; more than one half of the rest are those, who take the greatest interest in a more intimate union of the Western States with us; and many of those who remain, as they are not very desirous of gaining conquests over Spain, but only to preserve the limits and privileges marked in the treaty, will do what they can, in order to avoid hostilities. The people permit themselves to be implicitly governed by one of the parties mentioned, so that, considering these circumstances, we may labour under no apprehensions on this account. But other more weighty reasons oppose to their declaring themselves independent of the Eastern States. I will content myself with relating the principal one: Whilst they will be making a treaty with the government of Louisiana, what certainty will they have that the Cabinet of Madrid is not making a treaty at the same time, very different from what they may have agreed to here? Experience has taught them, to their misfortune, that this is not a mere conjecture. Three motives alone would be able to impel them to break the confederation with the other States, viz.

1st. War with the republic of France.

2d. A prohibition to navigate the Mississippi, and to establish themselves in the dominions of the King.

3d. Their incapacity to pay in cash their share of the common duties, (28000 dolls.) or to see the government intent on recovering it by force.

These are the axis upon which their policy turns. It now remains for me to say something of the military forces of the United States. Their army amounts to near 3000 men; they consist of four regiments of infantry, one double regiment of artillery, and two companies of cavalry. In each regiment there are eight companies; each company is composed of 65 men, including a Captain, a Lieutenant, and an Ensign, but there is not one complete. It must be observed, that the two companies of cavalry amount to 180 men, but there are only 60 mounted. Each regiment has a Colonel, and two Serjeant-Majors. The first regiment, commanded by Colonel Hamtramk, is at Fort Wayne, and the other forts towards Fort Washington; the second, commanded by Colonel Strong, is encamped at Detroit, Michilimakinac, Niagara, Presq-Isle, Oswego, &c. the third, commanded by Colonel Gathers, fortifies the Forts of Massac, Barrancas, &c. one or two companies remaining in Georgia; the fourth, commanded by Colonel Butler, is in Tenessee; the artillery men are divided among the forts, although the greatest part does not go from Stony-Point, in the Eastern States; the cavalry is divided between Tenessee, Detroit, and Fort Washington. With regard to their forts, as it is a subject of little importance to us, I do not wish to trouble your Excellency with a tedious description of them. There is a strict discipline observed in the army; the soldiers are almost all youths, from 16 to 26 years of age; they go through some military evolutions with sufficient precision. With respect to the officers, from the lowest to the highest (excepting very few) they are deficient of those qualities which adorn a good soldier, except fierceness, and are overwhelmed in ignorance, and in the most base vices.

The influence of General Wilkinson in Kentucky has become very limited: and in the army, by wishing to introduce some innovations, it lessens from day to day. I hope, from what is said on the subject of my mission, that you will be convinced, that if it has not had a more happy issue, it ught not to be attributed in any manner to indiscretion, or other deficiency, on my part, since it is evident that it sprung from a cause which no human penetration could foresee, and no prudence prevent; and if I have been deficient in the intelligence and capacity, which the discharge of my commission required, it will not be boldness in me to say, that the promptitude and zeal, silence and fidelity, which, on more important occasions, I have manifested in the service of His Majesty, have not been of any avail on the present. God preserve you many years. December 5, 1797.

P. S. I enclose you, with the other documents, the account of the expence of the journey No. 11; that of the 640 dollars, which Gen. Wilkinson so anxiously solicits, and which he has charged me to receive on his account, I remitted to the Baron de Carondelet in the month of May of this year. No. 3, with the other documents, those which I received, as stated in his official letter of the 28th of the same month and year, of which I also enclose a copy, No. 12.

M. Manuel Gayoso de Lemos.

NOTE No. 44.

Nouvelle Orleans, ce 23 Avril, 1797.

J'ai reçu, Monsieur, la lettre que vous m'avez fait l'honneur de m'ecrire, et a la qu'elle je n'ai pu repondre plustot enayant été empeché, par un surcroit d'occupations. Que m'a donné la nouvelle que j'ai reçu de notre Envoié auprès des Etats Unis, que les Anglois vont attaquer les Illinois, ceci m'oblige a changer de nouveau les dispositions que j'avois prises, pour commencer la demarcation des limites; car, si l'expedition est assez consequente pour s'emparer de St. Louis, qui, comme vous ne l'ignorez, pas n'a qu'un très meauvais fort, propre uniquement a en imposer a des Sauvages. Il ne nous reste rien jusqu' a Nogales, pour arreter l'ennemi, et couvrer la Basse Louisiane; en consequence j'ordonne a M. de Gayoso de faire scavoir a M. Elicot, et au Commandant du detachement Ameriquain, que je me trouve forcé de mettre Nogales en etat de defense, et d'y transporter toute la troupe et l'artillerie existans a Natchez, ou je ne laisserai que cinquante hommes, commandés par Don Manuel Lanzos, M. de Gayoso devant passer egalement a Nogales, avec Ms. Guillemard et Perchet, pour hater les traveaux. Enfin, je vais faire monter une compagnie de grenadiers en sus audit Nogales. Comme il convient, qu'il y ait aux Natchez une personne intelligente, qui veille, et soit instruite, des demarches du Comisaire et de d'Officer Commandant, j'ai disposé que vous serviriez d'Interprete et Secretaire a M. Lanzos, qui ne manque pas de finesse ; et que Vidal accompagne M. de Gayoso a Nogales, ou passe aux Illinois, avec de l'argent et des depesches que j'y envois. Vous me rendrez compte exactement de tout ce qui se passera, digne d'etre mandé, et tacherez de vous insinuer dans la confiance du Commandant Americain, que vous ferez ensorte de mettre en opposition avec Elicot ; quand il devroit en couter quelques cent piastres en present au Roy, que cela ne vous arrete, et je vous promets qu'ils seront satisfaits ; par ce moyen nous reduirions Elicot a l'impuissance d'agir par lui meme, et nous serions tranquilles de ce coté.

L'Envoyé de S. M. a intimé au Ministre des Affaires Etranges, que l'expedition Angloise ne pouvant parvenir a St. Louis d'Illinois, qu'en violant le territoire Ameriquain, el esperoit que les Etats Unis s'opposeroient a son passage, et observeroient exactement le dernier traité conclu avec l'Espagne. S'il arrive le contraire, je ne donte pas qu'il sera annulé. On attend a la Havane douze mille hommes de troupes Espagnoles. La reception que vous avez reçu de M. Gayoso n'a rien qui m'etonne, mais je suis absolument du même avis que vous sur les suites qu'elle aura. Il est impossible que les habitans sensés des Natches puissent se decider a une demarche, qui, en insultant une puissance jalouse de son pouvoir, les exposeroit a une ruine certaine, et a etre desavoués par les Etats Unis, qui n'entreprendroient certainement pas une guerre contre l'Espagne et contre la France, pour soutenir une demarche faite contres les loix de l'equité, et le droit des nations. Je crois la chose si peu possible, que je retire, comme je vous, l'ai dit les troupes, et n'y laisse qu'un detachement, pour y maintenir le bon ordre, et etre a l'abris d'une insulte des Sauvages. Quant a M. Elicot, dont la conduite a monégard est des plus irreguliere, il pourroit très bien etre rappellé, ou tout au moins restraint a la seule commission des limites, car j'en ai ecrit fortement a l'Envoié de S M. et au Prince de la Paix.

Il paroit que le principe de la mesintelligence entre M. Gayoso et Elicot, d'apres ce que m'en a dit M. Nolan, provient de ce que, des Sauvages Chactaws ayant bū avec exces, ont cherché dispute aux gens de la suite du dernier, qui s'est figuré que le Gouverneur les avoit enivré, pour les porter a faire main basse sur lui et sur ses gens au point que Nolan a été obligé, pour le rassurer, de passer deux nuits dans son camp. Qu'elle petitesse dans un homme, qui s'arroge le titre de representant d'une nation.

C'est moi qui ai ordonné, qu'on laissa le detachement Ameriquain s'etablir auprès de M. Elicot, et j'ai desaprouvé, dés le premier instant, l'opposition qu'en y avoit mis. Si M. Elicot m'eut fait scavoir d'office son entrée dans ma province, comme cela est d'usage, et se fut addressé a moi pour les motifs de plainte qu'il croioit avoir, j'aurois agis avec franchise a son égard, et rien tout cela ne seroit arrivé, hors la suspension de l'evacuation des postes qui dimane de moi, ne me croyant pas autorisé a les remettre, avec leurs fortifications et edifices, comme l'exigent le General Wayne et Don Andres Elicot.

J'ai trouvé etrange qu'on ait laissé arborer le pavillon Ameriquain devant la porte d'Elicot. Mais je suis censé l'ignorer, et je n'ai pas crûs devoir aigrir davantage les esprits en la faisant oter

Je viens d'ecrire a W. en remettant ma lettre a M. Nolan, garçon charmant, et dont je fais le plus grand cas. Il m'adit qu'il avoit une occasion sure pour la lui faire passer. Il y avoit très long tēms que je ne lui avois écrit, faute d'occasions et crainte de le comprometre.

Portez vous bien; donnez moi de vos nouvelles, et disposez de celui, qui a l'honneur d'etre, avec la plus parfaite consideration,

Monsieur,
Votre très humble et très obeissant serviteur,
LE BARON DE CARONDELET.

P. S. L'Envoié de S. M. aux Etats Unis a fait passer aux Illinois l'ingenieur Francois, M. Finiels, pour le fortifier, si on en a le tēms; mais il y aura trouvé Vandenbenden, occupé au même objet. Connoissez vous le premier?

TRANSLATION of NOTE No. 44.

New Orleans, the 23d April, 1797.

Sir,

I HAVE received the letter you honoured me with, which I have not been enabled to answer sooner, on account of a multiplicity of occupations. In consequence of the news which I have received from our Envoy near the United States, that the English are going to attack the Illinois, I am compelled to change anew the arrangements I had taken, to begin the delineation of the limits; because, if the expedition is of sufficient consequence to take possession of St. Louis, which, as you know very well, has but a very bad fort, only calculated to silence the Savages, we have nothing remaining, as far as Nogales, that could stop the enemy, and protect Lower Louisiana; in consequence of which I have ordered Mr. Gayoso to make known to Mr. Ellicot, and to the commander of the American detachment, that I find myself compelled to put Nogales in a state of defence, and to forward there all the troops and artillery existing at Natchez, where I shall leave but fifty men, commanded by Don Manuel Lanzos, Mr. Gayoso being compelled to go with Messrs. Guillimard and Perchet to Nogales, to hasten the preprarations. Finally, I am going moreover to send up to Nogales a company of grenadiers. As it is requisite, that at Natchez there should be an intelligent person, who should watch, and be informed of, the steps taken by the Commissary and Commanding Officer, I have ordered that you should serve Mr. Lanzos as Secretary and Interpreter, who is not deficient in finesse; and that Vidal shall accompany Mr. Gayoso to Nogales, or to the Illinois, with money and dispaches which I send there. You must send me an exact information of all that passes, worthy mentioning, and endeavour to insinuate yourself into the confidence of the American commander, whom you must endeavour to put at variance with Ellicot; even if it should cost the King some hundreds of dollars in presents, let that be no obstacle, and I assure you that they will be satisfied; by these means we will render Ellicot unable to act by himself, and we would be safe on that quarter.

The Envoy of his Majesty has intimated to the Minister of Foreign Affairs that the English expedition could not arrive at St. Louis de Illinois, without violating the American territory, and that he expected that the United States would be opposed to their passage, and observe exactly the last treaty concluded with Spain. If the contrary happens, I doubt not but it will be annulled. At the Havanna are expected 12,000 Spanish troops. The reception you met with from Mr. Gayoso does not astonish me, but I am exactly of your opinion relative to the consequences which will follow. It is impossible that the wise inhabitants of Natchez can agree to a step, which, by insulting a nation jealous of its power, would expose them to certain ruin, and to be disavowed by the United States, who assuredly will not undertake a war against Spain and France, to maintain a step taken against the law of equity, and of the rights of nations. I believe it so very improbable, that I cause to retire, as I told you, the troops, and only leave a detachment, to maintain good order, and to repel the insults of the Savages. As to Mr. Ellicot, whose conduct towards me has been very unbecoming, he might be recalled, or at least restricted to the commission alone of the limits, because I have written strongly to the Envoy of his Majesty and to the Prince of Peace.

It appears that the beginning of this misunderstanding between Mr. Gayoso and Eilicot, as Mr. Nolan told me, proceeds from the following cause: that some Chactaw savages, having drank to excess, got in dispute with some of the servants of the latter gentleman, who thought that the Governor had made them inebriated, to cause them to put him and his people to the sword; so much so, that Nolan has been compelled to remain two nights in his camp, to tranquilize him: what littleness in a man, who boasts of the title of the representative of a nation. It was I who ordered, that the American detachment might remain near Mr. Ellicot, and I disapproved, from the first moment, the opposition which was made. If Mr. Ellicot had officially informed me of his entering my province, as it is customary, and had addressed himself to me on account of motives of complaint which he thought just, I should have acted with frankness towards him, and nothing of that kind would have happened, except the suspension of the evacuation of those posts which depend on me, not thinking myself authorised to deliver them up, with their fortifications and edifices, as Gen. Wayne and Mr. Andrew Ellicot exacted.

I have thought it very strange that the American flag should be permitted to be hoisted before the door of Ellicot. I could not help observing it, although I do not wish to sour them, by commanding them to be taken away.

I have just written to W. and delivered my letter to Mr. Nolan, a fine young man, and of whom I think highly. He told me he had a secure conveyance to forward it to him. It had been a long time since I wrote him, for want of an opportunity, and for fear of committing him.

Farewell; let me hear from you, and command him who has the honour to be, with the greatest consideration,
    Sir, your very humble and obedient servant,
      THE BARON DE CARONDELET.

P. S. The Envoy of his Majesty near the United States has sent to the Illinois the French engineer, Mr. Finiels, to fortify it, if there is time; but he will have found there Vandenbenden, occupied at the same thing. Do you know the former?

NOTE No. 45.

MR. CLARK'S STATEMENT TO CONGRESS.

I ARRIVED from Europe, at New Orleans, in December, 1786, having been invited to the country by an uncle, of considerable wealth and influence, who had been long resident in that city. Shortly after my arrival I was employed in the office of the Secretary of the Government. This office was the depository of all state papers. In 1787 General Wilkinson made his first visit to New Orleans, and was introduced by my uncle to the Governor and other officers of the Spanish government.

In the succeeding year, 1788, much sensation was excited by the report of his having entered into some arrangements with the government of Louisiana, to separate the western country from the United States; and this report acquired great credit upon his second visit to New Orleans in 1789. About this time I saw a letter from the General to a person in New-Orleans, giving an account of Col. Connolly's mission to him from the British government in Canada, and of proposals made to him on the part of that government, and mentioning his determination of adhering to his connexion with the Spaniards.

My intimacy with the officers of the Spanish government, and my access to official information, disclosed to me shortly afterwards some of the plans the General had proposed to the government for effecting the contemplated separation. The general project was the severance of the western country from the United States, and the establishment of a separate government, in the alliance and under the protection of Spain. In effecting this, Spain was to furnish money and arms; and the minds of the western people were to be seduced and brought over to the project, by liberal advantages resulting from it, to be held out by Spain. The trade of the Missisippi was to be rendered free, the port of New Orleans to be open to them, and a free commerce allowed in the productions of the new government with Spain and her West-India Islands. I remember about the same time to have seen a list of names of citizens of the western country, which was in the hand writing of the General, who were recommended for pensions, and the sums proper to be paid to each were stated; and I then distinctly understood that he and others were actually pensioners of the Spanish government. I had no personal knowledge of money being paid to General Wilkinson, or to any agent for him, on account of his pension, previous to the year

1793 or 1794. In one of these years, and in which I cannot be certain until I can consult my books, a Mr. Le Cassagne, who I understood was postmaster at the Falls of Ohio, came to New Orleans, and, as one of the association with General Wilkinson in the project of dismemberment, received a sum of money, four thousand dollars of which, or thereabouts, were embarked by a special permission, free of duty, on board a vessel which had been consigned to me, and which sailed for Philadelphia; in which vessel Mr. La Cassagne went passenger. At and prior to this period, I had various opportunities of seeing the projects submitted to the Spanish government, and of learning many of the details from agent, employed to carry them into execution.

In 1794, two gentlemen, of the names of Owens and Collins, friends and agents of General Wilkinson, came to New Orleans.—To the first of these was entrusted, as I was particularly informed by the officers of the Spanish government, 6,000 dollars, to be delivered to General Wilkinson, on account of his own pension and that of others. On his way, in returning to Kentucky, Owens was murdered by his boat's crew, and the money, it was understood, was made away with by them. This occurrence occasioned a considerable noise in Kentucky, and contributed, with Mr. Power's visits, at a subsequent period, to awaken the suspicions of General Wayne, who took measures to intercept the correspondence of General Wilkinson with the Spanish government, which failed through the address of Power.

Collins, the co-agent with Owens, first attempted to fit out a small vessel in the port of New Orleans, in order to proceed to some port in the Atlantic states, but she was destroyed by the hurricane of the month of August, in 1794. He then fitted out a small vessel in the Bayou St. John, and shipped in her at least 11,000 dollars, which he took round to Charleston.

This shipment was made under such peculiar circumstances, that it became known to many, and the destination of it was afterwards fully disclosed to me by the officers of the Spanish government, by Collins, and by General Wilkinson himself, who complained that Collins, instead of sending him the money on his arrival, had employed it in some wild speculations to the West-Indies, by which he had lost a considerable sum, and that in consequence of the mismanagement of his agents, he had derived but little advantage from the money paid on his account by the Spanish government. Mr. Power was a Spanish subject, resident in Louisiana, and the object of his visits to the western country became known to me in 1796, when he embarked on board the brig Gayoso, at New Orleans, for Philadelphia, in company with Judge Sebastian, in which vessel, as she had been consigned to myself, I saw embarked, under a special permission, four thousand dollars, or thereabouts, which I was informed were for Sebastian's own account, as one of those concerned in the scheme of dismemberment of the western country.

Mr. Power, as he afterwards informed me, on his tour through the western country, saw General Wilkinson at Greenville, and was the bearer of a letter to him from the Secretary of the government of Louisiana, dated the 7th or 8th of March, 1796, advising that a sum of money had been sent to Don Thomas Portel, commandant of New Madrid, to be delivered to his order. This money Mr. Power delivered to Mr. Nolan, by Wilkinson's direction. What concerned Mr. Nolan's agency in this business I learned from himself, when he afterwards visited New Orleans.

In 1797 Power was entrusted with another mission to Kentucky, and had directions to propose certain plans, to effect the separation of the western country from the United States. These plans were proposed, and there rejected, as he often solemnly assured me, through the means of a Mr. George Nicholas, to whom among others they were communicated, but who spurned the idea of receiving foreign money. Power then proceeded to Detroit, to see General Wilkinson, and was sent back by him, under guard, to New Madrid, whence he returned to New Orleans. Power's secret instructions were known to me afterwards, and I am enabled to state, that the plan then contemplated entirely failed.

At the period spoken of, and for a long time afterwards, I was resident in the Spanish territory, subject to the Spanish laws, and without any expectation of becoming a citizen of the United States. My obligations were then to conceal, not to communicate, to the government of the United States, the projects and enterprizes, which I have mentioned, of the Spanish government.

In the month of October, 1798, I visited General Wilkinson, by his particular request, at the Camp at Loftus's Heights, where he had shortly before arrived. The General had heard of remarks made by me on the subject of his pension, which had rendered him uneasy, and he was desirous of making some arrangement with me on the subject. I passed three days and nights in the General's tent. The chief subjects of our conversation were the views and enterprizes of the Spanish government, in relation to the United States, and speculations as to the result of political affairs. In the course of our conversation, he stated that there was still a balance of 10,000 dollars due him by the Spanish government, for which he would gladly take in exchange Governor Gayoso's plantation near Natchez, who might reimburse himself from the treasury of New Orleans.—I asked the General if this sum was due on the old business of the pension. He replied that it was; and intimated a wish that I should propose to General Gayoso a transfer of his plantation for the money due him from the Spanish treasury. The whole affair had always been odious to me, and I declined any agency in it. I acknowledged to him that I had often spoken freely and publicly of his Spanish pension, but told him I had communicated nothing to his government on the subject. I advised him to drop his Spanish connexions. He justified it heretofore from the peculiar situation of Kentucky, the disadvantages that country laboured under at the period when he formed his connexions with the Spaniards, the doubtful and distracted state of the Union at that time, which he represented as bound together by nothing better than a rope of sand; and he assured me solemnly that he had terminated his connexion with the Spanish government, and that they never should be renewed. I gave the General to understand, that as the affair stood, I should not in future say any thing about it.

From that period until the present I have heard one report only of the former connexion being renewed, and that was in 1804, shortly after the General's departure from New Orleans. I had been absent for two or three months, and returned to the city not long after General Wilkinson sailed from it. I was informed by the late Mayor of New Orleans, that reports had reached the ears of the Governor, of a sum of ten thousand dollars having been received by the General of the Spanish government, while he was one of the commissioners for taking possession of Louisiana. He wished me to enquire into the truth of it, which I agreed to do, on condition that I might be permitted to communicate the suspicion to the General, if the fact alledged against him could not be verified. This was assented to. I made the enquiry, and satisfied myself, by an inspection of the treasury books for 1804, the ten thousand dollars had not been paid. I then communicated the circumstance to a friend of the General, Mr. Evan Jones, with a request that he would inform him of it. The report was revived at the last session of Congress, by a letter from Colonel Ferdinand Claiborne, of Natchez, to the delegate of the Missisippi Territory. A member of the House informed me, that the money in question was acknowledged by General Smith to have been received at the time mentioned, but that it was in payment for tobacco. I knew that no tobacco had been delivered, and waited on General Smith for information as to the receipt of the money, who disavowed all knowledge of it; and I took the opportunity of assuring him, and as many others as mentioned the subject, that I believed it to be false, and gave them my reasons for the opinion.

This summary necessarily omits many details, tending to corroborate and illustrate the facts and opinions I have stated. No allusion has been made to the public explanations of the transactions referred to, as made by General Wilkinson and his friends. So far as they are resolved into commercial enterprizes and speculations, I had the best opportunity of being acquainted with them, as I was, during the period referred to, the agent of the house who were the consignees of the General, at New Orleans, and who had an interest in his shipments, and whose books are in my possession.

DANIEL CLARK.

Washington City, Jan. 11, 1808.

[To the above statement is annexed the oath of Mr. Clark, taken before Judge Cranch, in which he swears, that the foregoing, so far as it regards the matter of his own knowledge, is true; and so far as it regards matters whereof he was informed by others, he believes to be true.]

NOTE No. 46.

DR. CARMICHAEL'S TESTIMONY.

DOCTOR Carmichael has also been examined. The Doctor lived in General Wilkinson's family at the period when Mr. Clark declares he made his visit at Fort Adams, and partook of the General's hospitality in his tent for three days and nights. The Doctor's testimony is expresly contrary to that which Mr. Clark offers on the occasion.— The General " was not encamped at the time, but slept on board his boat."

NOTE No. 47.

TERRITORY OF ORLEANS.
Parish of Rapide, sct.

ON this 30th of October, in the year 1808, before me, Richard Claiborne, of said parish, personally appeared William Miller, Esquire, of the settlement of Bayou Boeuf, in the parish and territory aforesaid, who, being duly sworn, made oath, that in the fall of the year, 1797, he, this deponent, was at Loftus's Heights, in the Missisippi territory, at which time General James Wilkinson was also there, and lived in a tent or marquee: This deponent perfectly recollects, that on his arrival at Loftus's Heights he found Daniel Clark, Esquire (who at present represents this territory in the Congress of the United States) at the General's marquee, and in company with the said General, and while he staid there to have parted with him late in the evening, and on his return on the ensuing morning to have again met with him, the said Daniel Clark, Esquire, at the same place, viz. the tent or marquee of the General, and in his the General's company: This deponent further recollects, that Mr. Clark told him that he had been, for several days and nights preceding, living with the General, and engaged with him in the transaction of business.

WM. MILLER.

Subscribed and sworn to before me; in testimony
of which I place my own signature, and affix
the seal of the parish hereto, the day and date
first above written.

R. CLAIBORNE,
Judge of the parish of Rapide.

NOTE No. 48.

MISSISIPPI TERRITORY,
   Adams County, sct.

PERSONALLY appeared before me, a Justice of the Peace in and for the county aforesaid, Isaac Guion, late an officer in the United States army, and being sworn on the Holy Evangelists of Almighty God, he deposeth and saith, that on the twenty-second day of October, in the year one thousand seven hundred and ninety-eight, he joined the army at head-quarters, then at Loftus's Heights, on the Missisippi river, encamped, commanded by General James Wilkinson; that the General then lived in his marquee, in the swamp, or bottom, on the right of the infantry; that on the day of his arrival at head-quarters, to the best of his recollection and full belief, he was introduced to Mr. Daniel Clark, jun. who was there on a visit, from New Orleans, as he was informed; Mr. Clark remained in the camp two or three days after the arrival of this deponent, and then left it, and went on an excursion of twelve or fifteen days towards the Natchez; and on his return visited the camp again, and was there on the twentieth day of November in that year. But how long he remained this deponent cannot now be certain, but, to the best of his recollection, his visit was short, perhaps only one or two days. That from the time this deponent joined the army on the twenty-second of October, until after Mr. Clark's visit in November, in the year 1798, General Wilkinson lived in his marquee; having only changed its position from the right of the infantry in the bottom, to the hill near the house (or boat) then fitting up for him; and afterwards occupied by him; that he is very certain the General did live in his marquee at the time when Mr. Clark made both those visits, for he well recollects having been in company with them in the General's tent, and his memory, as to dates, is assisted by papers and writings now in his possession, which were written and dated by Mr. Clark, in the General's tent, in the presence of this deponent.

I. GUION.

Sworn to and subscribed this 22d day of July,
    in the year 1808, before me,
        SAMUEL BROOKS, Justice of the Peace.

NOTE No. 49.

ADAMS COUNTY, SCT.

    PERSONALLY appeared before me, a Justice of the Peace in and for the said county, David Michie, of the city of Natchez, and, being first sworn, deposeth and saith, that in the autumn of the year one thousand seven hundred and ninety-eight, he was at the encampment of the army of the United States, commanded by General James Wilkinson, at Loftus's Heights, on the Mississippi river, and while there he did see Mr. Daniel Clark, jun. of the city of New Orleans, there, in the tent or marquee of the General, then pitched in the swamp near the encampment of the troops; that he well remembers that the General then lived in his marquee, and that Mr. Clark was there in it in company with the General; and to the best of his recollection it was in the month of October or November in that year.

D. MICHIE.

Sworn to and subscribed before me, this
    22d day of July, 1808.
        SAMUEL BROOKS, Justice of the Peace.

NOTE No. 50.

New Orleans, 6th July, 1808.

MR. DANIEL CLARK,

DEAR SIR,

I RECEIVED your letter of the 4th inst. and would have answered it sooner, but have been much engaged and somewhat indisposed. I have no hesitation in saying, that the first time I had the pleasure of forming an acquaintance with you was in Gen. Wilkinson's tent or marquee, at Loftus's Heights, some time in the latter part of October, 1798. I was on my way from the Ilinois to this city, and stopped at the Heights to visit General Wilkinson, and to endeavour to procure some bills of exchange. I was advised by the General to wait your arrival at camp for that purpose, which he stated would be in a day or two. You appeared the next day. I was introduced to you by the General, and we dined with him in his tent or marquee, in company with several officers. I do not recollect whether Dr. Carmichael dined with us on that day, but I well recollect that the Doctor had then just returned from Pittsburgh, or some of the upper forts; that he was in camp while you and myself were there, and I well recollect your sleeping in the General's tent, where a bed had been prepared for myself the night before. I also recollect Captain Shaumburg and Captain Guion having dined with us in the General's tent, and have no doubt, on application to them, that their relation of the circumstances you wish to substantiate will prove more satisfactory, than the particulars with which my memory serves me. After spending several days at the Heights, I set off to this city, and about two weeks after my arrival you came down.

I am, very respectfully, your obedient servant,
(Signed)   JOHN CLAY.

NOTE No. 51.

EPHRAIM H. MARSALIS'S AFFIDAVIT.

PERSONALLY appeared before the subscriber, one of the Justices of the Quorum for Wilkinson County, in the Mississippi Territory, Captain Ephraim H. Marsalis, who, being duly sworn, on oath, says, that being a non-commissioned officer in the service of the United States, he was Standing Orderly to General Wilkinson several days (to the best of his recollection) in the months of October or November, in the year 1798, and that during the time he acted as Orderly to the Geneneral, which was in the months of the year aforesaid, a gentleman, by the name of Daniel Clark, visited General Wilkinson, who then lived in a marquee, near where Fort Adams now stands; and this deponent declares that the said Clark remained with the General three or four days, and that there appeared a degree of intimacy (unusual with the General) between him and Mr. Clark; that the General was accustomed to call him Dan; that during the time Mr. Clark remained in the marquee, the General once gave this deponent leave of absence, by saying he should not want him until such an hour; and he further states, that when Mr. Clark was going away, the General came out to the front of the marquee, and insisted on his staying till the next day, and that he would send Marsalis and the dragoons with him; that a brother of this deponent was the Serjeant commanding some dragoons, called in camp the General's life guard.

E. H. MARSALIS.

Sworn and subscribed to at Wilkinsburgh, Wilkinson county, Missisippi Territory, on the 4th day of August, 1808.

NAT. EVANS.

NOTE No 52.

GOVERNOR SALCEDO'S EVIDENCE.

QUERIES.

Whether the Governor's situation with the government, and the Secretary of the government, Don Andres Armesto, in the years 1795, 96 and 97, did not give him an intimate acquaintance with the public and private affairs of that government?

Whether he knows any thing of the payment of any pension, particularly 9640 dollars, by the agency of Thomas Power, or any other person, to General Wilkinson; and if not of a pension, of any money in mercantile or other transactions.

Whether, had such transactions taken place, he considers it probable or possible he should not have been informed of them.

Whether he knows of Daniel Clark, or Thomas Power, separately, or together, having had access to the archives of the Secretary of the government, any circumstance attending it, and at what time, and, generally, of the character and conduct of the above named, under the notice or knowledge of Governor Salcedo?

Any other information which the Governor may conceive will elucidate the transactions of that period, or the conduct of Gen. Wilkinson?

The estimation in which General Wilkinson was held by the officers of his Most Catholic Majesty?

ANSWER.

Translated from the Spanish.

Governor Salcedo cannot, nor ought not, to answer the foregoing queries, excepting that part which refers to the character and conduct of Mr. Daniel Clark, and hereby declares that this gentleman was universally known at all times in Louisiana as a zealous patriot of the United States, an upright man, and of the highest integrity, both in his public and private affairs, always preferring the good of his country to his own interest.

N. B. The original of the foregoing queries and answer are in General Wilkinson's possession.

NOTE No. 53.

Washington, January 2d, 1808.

I WAS this day called upon to be present at an explanation between Mr. Daniel Clark, of New Orleans, and General Smith, of Maryland, relative to a conversation had between them during the last session of Congress, in relation to a report then in circulation of General Wilkinson's having received in 1804 ten thousand dollars from the Spanish government.

Mr. Clark began, by observing that he had been informed that General Smith had reported this conversation different from what was the fact; that he now reminded him again, as he had done during the last autumn in the Coffee-house at Baltimore, when General Smith had brought to his (Mr. Clark's) recollection this conversation, which the General must certainly remember, that it related only to one specific fact, viz. as to General Wilkinson's having received the particular ten thousand dollars in 1804, which had been stated in a letter from Col. F. Claiborne to the Delegate from the Mississippi Territory, and shewn in the House of Representatives; that about the time of the receipt of this letter Mr. Willis Alston mentioned to him, that General Smith had acknowledged that General Wilkinson had received from the Spanish government this sum of money, but that it was for tobacco; that he (Mr. Clark) knowing it could not be for tobacco, was induced to call on General Smith, to enquire into the truth of the fact; that upon General Smith's declaring he neither knew or had said any such thing, he (Mr. Clark) thought it due to General Wilkinson to state that this subject had been mentioned to him by the late Mayor of New Orleans, as having come to Governor Claiborne's ears, and an enquiry made whether the fact could be ascertained; upon which he (Mr. Clark) undertook to investigate it, and accordingly went to the Spanish treasury in New Orleans, where he examined the book for that year, and no trace of any such charge appeared upon it. This he had stated to General Smith, but the conversation went exclusively to the particular ten thousand dollars mentioned in Mr. Claiborne's letter, and said to have been received by General Wilkinson in 1804; for that it would have been the height of absurdity in him to state a general negative, applying to General Wilkinson's whole life, or what he, General Wilkinson, had never done.

General Smith observed, that Mr. Clark had volunteered the conversation alluded to, by making enquiries as to what he, General Smith, had said on the subject of Colonel Claiborne's letter, and authorised him to use his (Mr. Clark's) name; that he had noted down the conversation some days afterwards, he would not say how many, perhaps a considerable number; that Mr. Clark had held the same conversation with Governor Wright; that he (General Smith) had intended to send Mr. Clark a copy of his note of it; that the conversation referred to had been impressed upon his mind of a more general nature; that he understood Mr. Clark as saying that he had examined the books of secret service money in the Spanish treasury, from one end to the other, and found no charge of any money advanced to General Wilkinson, or General Wilkinson's name upon them, upon which he considered Mr. Clark as saying he did not believe General Wilkinson had received the money, or any money, from the Spanish government.

To which Mr. Clark replied, the latter was not the fact; that it was true he had satisfied himself at the time, that Gen. Wilkinson did not receive the ten thousand dollars in 1804, but that the books at the Spanish treasury are made up from year to year, one for each year; that he had only examined the book for 1804, in which, if in any, this ten thousand dollars must have been entered, and with a view only to this specific charge, at the instance of the Mayor of New Orleans.

General Smith observed, that this explained the ground of misunderstanding between them; *that he must have misapprehended Mr. Clark as to the extent of the enquiry made at the treasury of New Orleans;* that he had not before supposed that Mr. Clark had examined only one of the books of the treasury, but had been impressed with an idea that he had gone through the whole of the books.

To which Mr. Clark replied, that his impression had been very erroneous then.

General Smith observed, he wished to have no personal difference on this subject; that Mr. Clark and General Wilkinson had fallen out, but that it was nothing to him.

Mr. Clark answered, neither did he wish any personal difference; that he respected General Smith, but would support this statement at the risk of his life, as he knew it to be true, and could not avoid noticing any contrary statement that might be published, sanctioned by General Smith's name.

To which the General replied, he had no intention of publishing any thing about it, and that upon the explanation, it appearing that Mr. Clark had examined only the treasury book for 1804, there was little or no difference between them.

I hereby certify that the above was committed to writing immediately after the conversation, to which it alludes, between Daniel Clark, Esquire, and General Smith, at which I was present, in the Senate Chamber; and that it is in substance, and, as nearly as I was able to recollect, in language, the particulars of that conversation.

SAMUEL WHITE.

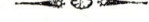

NOTE No. 54.

MR. R. G. HARPER'S EXAMINATION.

PERSONALLY before me, one of Associate Justices of the Supreme Court of the United States, at Baltimore, in the district of Maryland, on the 12th day of May, 1808, appeared Robert Goodloe Harper, of the said city, Counsellor at Law, who being duly sworn by me, on his oath did say, that on this day he did deliver to Brigadier General James Wilkinson, at Baltimore aforesaid, an original letter from Walter Jones, junior, of which the following is a true copy, viz.—

May 6, 1808.

Sir,

I have the honour to notify you, that on the 12th instant, at the house of Samuel Chase, a Judge of the Supreme Court, in the city of Baltimore, between the hours of seven and eight o'clock, P. M. Robert G. Harper, Esquire, Counsellor at Law, will be examined, on behalf of the United States, and his deposition reduced to writing, before the aforesaid Samuel Chase, one of the Associate Justices of the Supreme Court of the United States, to be read in evidence before the military court of enquiry, in the case in which you are a party. Mr. Harper will be examined on the following interrogatory, viz.

Have you had any conversation with Daniel Clark, Esq. in relation to any report or allegation of Brigadier General James Wilkinson having ever been a pensioner to the Spanish government, or having any illicit connexion with that government or its officers? If so, please state, circumstantially, the time, place and occasion of holding such conversation, and the language used by Mr. Clark; in particular, whether, in explaining or giving any opinion upon such reports or allegations, there was any discrimination between a specific charge (mentioned in a letter from Colonel Claiborne, or otherwise promulgated) of General Wilkinson having received the sum of 10,000 dollars, while acting as a commissioner under the Louisiana convention, and the general charge of having been, for several years before, in the receipt of an annual pension from the Spanish government?

Your obedient servant,

(Signed) W. JONES, jun.
Officiating Judge Advocate.

Addressed—Brigadier General James Wilkinson, Washington.

Sworn before me the day aforesaid,
(Signed) SAMUEL CHASE.

State of Maryland.
Baltimore, sst.

Be it remembered, That on this 12th day of May, 1808, before me, the subscriber, one of the Associate Justices of the Supreme Court of the United States, appeared R. G. Harper, Esquire, of Baltimore aforesaid, Counsellor at Law, at my house in the city of Baltimore aforesaid, at the hour of seven o'clock, P. M. and that Brigadier Gen. James Wilkinson then and there attending, pursuant to the notice contained in the foregoing letter, the said Robert G. Harper was by me then and there examined, on oath, upon the interrogatory in the said letter contained, and on his said examination did answer and say as follows, viz.

Some time in the latter part of February, or beginning of March, 1807, being at Washington, attending the Supreme Court of the United States, I heard it reported that Brigadier General James Wilkinson had received 10,000 dollars from the Spanish Government, at New Orleans, in the year 1804, as a bribe. In what manner this report arose, or came to my ears, I do not recollect. I had also heard it reported that General Wilkinson had formerly received a pension from the Spanish government; but I do not recollect whether any particular sum or payment was mentioned. Having at the time above mentioned become intimately acquainted with Daniel Clark, Esquire, of New-Orleans, and supposing, that, from his situation at New Orleans, he probably had some knowledge of these transactions, I one day, at his lodgings, took the liberty of asking him whether there was any truth in these reports, particularly in that respecting the 10,000 dollars in 1804; and he replied to this effect, and, as nearly as I can recollect, in these words— "Whatever may have happened at other times, I have reason to believe, and do believe, that no money was received by General Wilkinson from the Spaniards in 1804."—Perhaps Mr. Clark said that he knew that no money had been so received in 1804. On this point I cannot speak positively, but I perfectly recollect that the answer of Mr. Clark satisfied me as to the allegation of General Wilkinson's having received from the Spanish government in 1804; and that I made no further enquiry from Mr. Clark on the subject of General Wilkinson's supposed connexions with the Spanish government.

I afterwards heard Mr. Clark speak to the same effect to other persons, respecting the 10,000 dollars in 1804; but I never heard him, until after his first communication to Congress on the subject, say any thing more particular than I have stated above, respecting any former pecuniary or other transaction between General Wilkinson and the Spanish government; on the contrary, he seemed to me studiously to avoid saying any thing on the subject, which I several times heard mentioned in his presence. I recollect nothing further on this subject.

(Signed)   ROBT. G. HARPER.

CROSS INTERROGATORIES.

1st. Did you not voluntarily mention to the Judge Advocate, Walter Jones, Esq. the information you have now deposed to, and request to be permitted to depose to it?

2d. In making this proposition, did you not indulge an emotion of friendship to Mr. Clark?

[3d Query omitted by mistake in the copy; for its import see answer.]

4th. When Mr. Clark mentioned to you that General Wilkinson had received no pension or money from the Spaniards in 1804, had the previous conversation turned on General Wilkinson's general conduct, or only certain parts of it?

5th. Did Mr. Clark intimate to you during that communication, or at any other time previous to the late session of Congress, that General Wilkinson had received a pension from the Spanish government?

6th. Did you hear Mr. Clark then, or at any other time previous to his last arrival from New Orleans, speak injuriously of General Wilkinson, or imply, by his language, that a friendly understanding did not subsist between them?

7th. Did you see Mr. Clark on his journey from Richmond to Philadelphia last autumn, as he passed through this city, and had you any conversation with him respecting Colonel Burr's trial, then pending at Richmond, and which he had been subpœned on the part of said Burr to attend as a witnesss; and if so, be pleased to state it?

8th. Have you any knowledge of a letter written by John Randolph, Esq. to the Hon. Joseph Nicholson, in which mention is made of General Wilkinson; and if so, will you please to state the particulars?

9th. Had you any knowledge of the documents delivered by John Randolph, Esq. to the House of Delegates of the Congress, calculated to criminate General Wilkinson for an illicit connection with the Spanish government, previous to their exhibition by Mr. Randolph, and do you know from whom Mr. Randolph received those documents?

10th. Did you at any time hear Mr. Clark speak of the practicability of subverting the government of the Mexican provinces, and erecting a separate empire there?

11th. Did you ever hear said Clark speak of the dismemberment of the union, of the erection of a western empire, and having Colonel Burr for President there?

  (Signed)   JAMES WILKINSON.

And the said Robert Goodloe Harper, being further examined by me, on the annexed cross interrogatories, exhibited by the said General James Wilkinson, answered thereunto as follows, viz.

1st. To the first he answers—" I did not—Mr. Jones first mentioned the subject to me, and asked me what I knew about it, adding, that he intended to call on me as a witness, and that he thought it due to Mr. Clark to do so."

2d. " I did not make the proposition—But I certainly at that time, and ever since I knew him, felt warm and strong emotions of friendship towards him. If it be meant to insinuate by this question, that my friendship for Mr. Clark would induce me to discolour the truth, I have only to answer, that such an insinuation merits no reply.

3d. To the third he answers—" I became acquainted with Mr. Clark first at Washington, during the session of Congress which he attended. I had never seen him before; I was introduced to him by the gentlemen of the mess to which I had been invited to dine, on the day of the introduction."

4th. To the fourth he answers—" The conversation which I have related in my answer to the direct interrogatory, respecting the money in 1804, was introduced by myself, and before by a question from me to Mr. Clark, whether this report was true? Mr. Clark's answer put an end to the conversation on that subject. There was no previous conversation respecting General Wilkinson's conduct, as far as I can now recollect, and as I believe. This conversation took place at Mr. Clark's lodgings, during the same session of Congress, and some time, but I do not recollect how long, after I first became acquainted with him.

5th. To the 5th he answers—" Mr. Clark did not during that conversation intimate to me, further than what I have stated in my answer to the direct interrogatory, that General Wilkinson had received a pension from the Spanish government. Mr. Clark then, and at other times, whensoever the subject was mentioned or alluded to in his presence and mine, previous to his first communication to Congress, seemed anxious to avoid any conversation on the subject. But I did conjecture, from his manner of answering my questions, on the occasion alluded to, and especially from his discriminating between the money in 1804—and " what might have happened at other times"—that he knew more on the subject of other money transactions than he wished to explain. My belief that he wished to avoid further explanation, as to other transactions, prevented me from pressing the matter any further. I had no conversation with Mr. Clark afterwards on these subjects, previous to his first communication to Congress; but have heard the subject afterwards mentioned in his presence, and he always appeared desirous of avoiding any explanation concerning it, further than to say, that no money had been received by General Wilkinson from the Spaniards in 1804—which I think I frequently heard him say."

6th. To the sixth he answers—" I never did hear Mr. Clark, previously to his first communication to Congress, speak injuriously of General Wilkinson, further than I have already stated, nor intimate that a friendly understanding did not subsist between them. I think that when the account of General Wilkinson's proceedings at New Orleans, in the winter of 1806 and 1807, was received at Washington, and mentioned in the presence of Mr. Clark, he expressed his disapprobation of those measures, on the ground of their being unnecessary and unconstitutional, but of this I am not confident."

7th. To the seventh he answers—" I cannot certainly recollect, but I believe that Mr. Clark did not call on me, and that I did not see him on his way from Richmond to Philadelphia, in the autumn of 1807. If he did call, it was merely for a few minutes, and I had no conversation with him, on the subject of this interrrogatory. If I saw him, he probably mentioned to me, as he has done at other times, that he was not called as a witness, by reason of a decision of the Court, that no investigation on General Wilkinson's conduct, unconnected with his testimony against Col. Burr, could be permitted. I have not at any other time had any conversation with Mr. Clark on the subject of the interrogatory."

8th. To the 8th he answers—" I have no knowledge of any such letter. During the session of the Court of Appeals of this state, at Annapolis, in the summer of 1807, while the case of Colonel Burr and his associates was before the Court at Richmond, I did hear Judge Nicholson speak of a letter which he had received from Richmond, giving him an account of the result of the grand jury's deliberation respecting General Wilkinson; but I did not hear, nor do I know, by whom that letter was written. I might have conjectured, and may perhaps have mentioned my conjecture, from the known intimacy between Judge Nicholson and Mr. Randolph, that the letter was written by the latter gentleman."

9th. To the 9th he answers—" I had no particular knowledge of those documents, or of their existence, before they were communicated to Congress by Mr. Randolph; but I did learn, soon after the trial of Col. Burr was concluded at Richmond, that Thomas Power had in his possession some original documents, tending to prove that General Wilkinson had received money from the Spanish government corruptly in 1796. This information I obtained from Power himself. After the trial he passed through Baltimore, on his way to Philadelphia, and called on me, to deliver a letter of introduction from a gentleman in New Orleans, not Mr. Clark. I asked him to dine with me in a family way, and he came. During dinner he told me that General Wilkinson had violated a solemn engagement with him, by publishing a certificate obtained from him, under a promise that it should be communicated to no one but the President—that this certificate was given at the most earnest solicitation of General Wilkinson, and to enable him to satisfy the mind of the President; that the publication of it, at a time when General Wilkinson knew that he (Power) was summoned as a witness in Burr's trial, was calculated to injure the reputation of him (Power) by holding him up as a person who had certified one thing, and was ready to testify another; that for the justification of his conduct, and the support of his character, he was determined to publish the whole affair, with documents in his possession to support his statement, if he could procure the permission of the Marquis de Cassa Yrujo; and that he was going to Philadelphia for the purpose of obtaining such permission. Having conceived a very ill opinion of General Wilkinson's public and political integrity, from the facts and circumstances which had then become public, I took some pains to obtain from Power all the information that I could, respecting these transactions between General Wilkinson and the Spaniards; but he would state nothing more particular than is above related.—I some time afterwards learned, not from Mr. Clark, but from a gentleman with whom we are both intimate, that Power had not been able to obtain the desired permission from the late Spanish Minister; but had left his papers, with a narrative, in writing, of the whole transaction, in the possession of Mr. Clark, with permission to use them as he might think proper. I never spoke to Mr. Clark respecting those documents and narrative; but I told the gentleman who communicated the matter to me, that as Mr. Clark was now a representative of the people, and General Wilkinson in a situation where treachery and corruption might prove in the highest degree detrimental to the public interest, I thought it Mr. Clark's duty to make the matter known to Congress, so that an enquiry might be instituted into General Wilkinson's conduct. I did not then know the particular nature of the documents, nor that Mr. Clark had himself any knowledge of General Wilkinson's pecuniary transactions with the Spanish government. This gentleman, however, then informed me, that Mr. Clark had much knowledge of this kind, but did not state the particulars.—I added, that, if Mr. Clark thought it best, he might make the communication through Mr. Randolph; but that it was my decided opinion, that it was his duty to make it in some way or other; and I authorised and requested the gentleman to state this to Mr. Clark as my opinion and advice. This the gentleman afterwards informed me that he had done immediately after his return to Washington, where Mr. Clark then was. I heard nothing more of the matter until I received from Mr. Lloyd, of this state, a copy of Mr. Clark's first communication; nor did I ever see the documents until they appeared in print.—I believe that Mr. Clark delivered the documents to Mr Randolph, and that he did so in consequence of my advice and persuasion. Soon after he made the communication, I learned from him, that after his return from New Orleans in the summer of 1807, he had received there intelligence, which convinced him of General Wilkinson's having received the ten thousand dollars in 1804; and that it was paid by the Marquis de Cassa Calvo, which circumstance prevented the payment from appearing in the book of ordinary expenditures for that year; and that this discovery had given him an entirely different impression of General Wilkinson's character and conduct, and rendered him more willing than he should otherwise have been to communicate to Congress what he knew concerning General Wilkinson's former connections with the Spanish government. I recollect nothing more on this subject."

10th. To the tenth he answers—" I have frequently heard Mr. Clark, in speaking of Colonel Burr's enterprize, after it became known, and of the " Mexican association," say, that he considered all individual or unauthorised attempts on Mexico as not only unlawful, and therefore improper, but as visionary, impracticable and foolish. But that he believed that an army of twenty thousand men, well appointed and commanded, and acting under the authority of the American or British governments, might effect a revolution in the Mexican provinces, and erect an independent government there."

11th. To the eleventh he answers—" I never did hear Mr. Clark mention such a project, except as a criminal and visionary scheme, attributed, and perhaps justly, to Col. Burr, and a few of his associates."

Being asked by General Wilkinson who the gentleman was, that is alluded to in his answer to the ninth interrogatory, he answers—" It was Richard Reynoll Keen, Esquire, formerly of New-Orleans, and now in Cuba. I received from him the information of Mr. Clark's knowledge, and possession of the documents in question, and it was through him that I communicated the advice to Mr. Clark, as stated in my answer to the ninth cross interrogatory."

   (Signed)   ROBERT G. HARPER.

The foregoing answers to the direct interrogatory, and to the cross interrogatories of General Wilkinson, hereto annexed, were reduced to writing, and subscribed by the witness, in my presence, read over by him, in the hearing of General Wilkinson, and then sworn to by the said witness, before me.

(Signed)   SAMUEL CHASE.

NOTE No. 55.

DANIEL W. COXE'S TESTIMONY.

I AGREE that the deposition of Dan. W. Coxe, Esq. shall be taken, and read in evidence, on behalf of General Wilkinson, before the Court of Enquiry, whereof Colonel Burbeck is president.

            W. JONES, junior,
          Officiating as Judge Advocate.

Washington, June 2d, 1808.

INTERROGATORIES,

To be exhibited to Daniel W. Coxe, Esquire, on the part of Brigadier General Wilkinson.

Inter. 1st. Have you ever held conversations with Daniel Clark, Esq. respecting the political situation of the territory of Orleans, and the sentiments of its inhabitants towards the United States? If so, relate the tenor of his conversations, particularly at the period Col. Burr was engaged in the prosecution of his plans.

Ans. 1st. I have frequently conversed with Mr. Daniel Clark on the political situation of Louisiana, and well recollect that he considered the inhabitants as attached to the United States at the period of the cession, and that it depended entirely on the General Government to cement the bonds of union, by pursuing a sound and judicious policy. Mr. Clark himself being a strong American in principle (even prior to the cession of that province) and having on various occasions exerted his influence in favour of this country, at the hazard of his liberty and fortune (as is well known to the present and former administrations) it consequently follows, that the people of Louisiana, who derived their opinions principally from him, passed under the American government with the strongest impressions in favour of its wisdom and justice. Mr. Clark, however, considered the policy adopted by the administration (after taking possession of Orleans) as neither wise nor conciliatory, and but ill calculated to inspire the inhabitants of that country with confidence in the liberality of its views and disposition towards them. At the period of Burr's conspiracy, and since, Mr. Clark believed the

Creole inhabitants loyal, disinclined to revolution, and averse from turbulence and those political schisms, which appeared to disturb the newcomers among them.

Inter. 2d. Do you remember any conversation respecting a plan of separation of that territory from the United States, the manner of its accomplishment, the period when it would take place, or the character of and the individuals concerned in the same?

Ans. 2d. I remember no mention, by Mr. Clark, of any plan for the separation of Louisiana from the United States, except the old Western conspiracy for dismembering the Union, and General Wilkinson's agency in that affair, which, after the developement of Burr's plot, I know he believed to be the source of those enterprizes, in which he considered Burr and Wilkinson as united.

Inter. 3d. Have you ever heard Daniel Clark, Esquire, mention that Col. Burr was to be at the head of such a combination, and that he was to be president, with a salary of fifty thousand dollars per annum?

Ans. 3d. After the explosion of Burr's conspiracy, I have heard Mr. Clark express his opinion that Wilkinson and Burr had been acting in concert, but I have no recollection that he ever mentioned to me that Burr was to be president, with a salary of fifty thousand dollars per annum.

Inter. 4th. Do you know, or have you any reason to believe, any correspondence took place between Daniel Clark, Esq. and Aaron Burr, during the years 1806 and 1807? If so, relate your knowledge of the same, and how obtained.

Ans. 4th. I know of no correspondence between Burr and Daniel Clark, except a letter that Mr. Charles Biddle informed me Burr had left with him, to be delivered to Mr. Clark on his arrival from New Orleans, and which I supposed to relate to Burr's baggage, part of which he told me was left in New Orleans, and called with Mr. Biddle at my counting-house, to enquire if I had received it by any of my vessels. I accompanied Mr. Clark, after his arrival, to Mr. Biddle's, to receive the above mentioned letter, and perfectly recollect his saying, rather peevishly, that Burr and Wilkinson made him of much importance, and would pester him with letters, but that he had declined corresponding with Burr. No baggage or letters were, however, received by me from Col. Burr, for Mr. Clark, or any other person. In further answer to this query, which appears to insinuate a connexion between Mr. Clark and Col. Burr, I beg leave to state, that having myself been always strongly impressed with a belief that Burr was a dangerous and unprincipled man, and the Marquis de Cassa de Yrujo having jestingly observed to me, that he understood Mr. Clark was going to Vera Cruz, and was intimate with Burr when at New Orleans, I immediately wrote Mr. Clark (which was about the end of the year 1805) respecting the Marquis's observations, and advised him to have nothing to say to Burr in any way. The following is an extract from Mr. Clark's answer to me on the subject, the entire original of which is annexed hereto, with post-mark thereon.

" *New Orleans, 6th Feb.* 1806.

" MY DEAR FRIEND,

" I received this day your favour of 20th December, by post, and thank you for the information contained in the private enclosure. Be pleased to assure the respectable person, who informed you I was closely connected with Colonel Burr, that he has been much imposed on in this particular, that I never was acquainted with him until he came last summer to New Orleans, and that I neither was, nor could be, mad enough to attach myself to a man of desperate fortunes, whose stay among us did not exceed a fortnight. If he, or any of his friends, have said any thing that could induce people to believe I had any connexion whatever with him, I disclaim it, and time will prove the truth of mine or their assertions; and I shall be glad to learn that an eye were kept to my proceedings. What, in God's name, have I to expect or could hope from Colonel Burr? And is it probable I should commit my fortune, and perhaps reputation, at my period of life, to commit follies for him? No, the thing is too improbable to think seriously of, and I solemnly assure you there never has, nor ever shall be, any connexion between him and me. I lent him, when on the point of departure, a pair of horses, to take him to Natchez, with a servant to bring them back, and bought his bill for 300 dollars on Philadelphia, which I remitted to you; and this is all the politeness or intercourse I had with him, except once inviting him with a party to dinner, and less I could not do, in consequence of the letters of which he was the bearer to me.* I have entered into this long explanation, to set you at rest on this subject; and I beg you will return many thanks to the person from whom you received your information, for giving me an opportunity of being on my guard against the attempts that might be made to eatrap me into any thing, which could appear like a connexion or intimacy with Mr. Burr, should he ever return to this quarter.

" Benjamin Morgan has a vessel called the Patty, belonging to John Craig, of Philadelphia, consigned to him, and this vessel has one of the permissions mentioned in a former letter. Morgan has agreed with the Captain, that he and I shall avail ourselves of this

---

* *These letters were from General Wilkinson himself.*

permission, and shall ship a cargoe in the vessel; and the Marquis de Cassa Calvo will give us the necessary certificates. We propose that the cargo shall amount to forty thousand dollars, to be consigned to me; and a friend, whom I shall name another time, shall have one third interest.

" We pay for vessel and permission at the rate of two dollars per bbl. freight, for the quantity we ship, and I count on our gaining one cent. per cent. on the amount of the adventure. We shall have 15,000 dollars insured here; and Price and you, when you hear further from Morgan, and Chew and Relf, can have the rest covered at home for the voyage out. As for the returns back, I must trust to circumstances to be able to advise you. We have on hand almost all the goods we shall ship, and shall consequently have little or no advances to make, which could interfere with any advances intended for you, and even in the event of capture, the amount insured will be a remittance to you; this is but a hint to you for the present—to-morrow, when things are more matured, I shall write to you.

" I expect to sail on the 9th, in the William Wright, as advised some time since. The Caroline dropt down the river a day or two ago.

" Your's affectionately,
(Signed) " DANIEL CLARK.

Inter. 5*th.* Have you considered General Wilkinson and Daniel Clark, Esq. at any time on a friendly footing? Do you know whether any change took place in Daniel Clark's opinions, and when, of General Wilkinson?

Ans. 5*th.* I never considered Mr. Daniel Clark and General James Wilkinson as being friends beyond mere appearances. Mr. Clark always thought ill of the General on account of his Spanish connexions, and never to me (even in confidence) uttered an opinion in his favour. I know that he was impressed for a long while with the idea that Wilkinson had relinquished his pension from Spain, and finding him still patronized by the administration (though it was acquainted with his former agency in the old western conspiracy) he continued to maintain an intercourse with him, which both his own public situation, as consul for the United States at New Orleans, and Wilkinson's, as military commander in the south western country, rendered necessary. A great change to the General's further disadvantage, however, took place in Mr. Clark's opinion, from a variety of circumstances, among which may be noticed the following:—1st. The period and manner of Wilkinson's communication to the President, accompanying his deposition of the contents of Burr's cyphered letter to him. 2d. His proceedings, denunciations and arrests in New Orleans, which Mr. Clark conceived to be outrageous and improper. 3d. His affidavit before the grand jury at Richmond, who, on the simple facts before them at the time, had nearly found a bill for treason or misprision of treason, against Wilkinson, as a coadjutor of Burr, and Mr. Clark declared to me on his arrival in this city, last October, that he considered the perfidy of Wilkinson, in his capacity of commander of the American army, as without a parallel, and was fully convinced of his being the author of the conspiracy which he claimed the merit of frustrating. I am thus particular, as I have been so pointedly interrogated as to the causes of Mr. C.'s alienation from the General, after an intimacy of many years, and I deeply regret the necessity of using terms and epithets, which alone are adequate to convey my knowledge of Mr. Clark's opinion of General Wilkinson.

I will further state, that though Mr. Clark was convinced at one time, that the General did not receive, in 1804, the ten thousand dollars from the Spanish government, of which so much mention has been made, he, however, changed his opinion on subsequent information, and was convinced that Wilkinson did receive the money, in violation of his promise to him to drop his Spanish connexions, though it did not appear charged on the Spanish treasury books, on account of its being part of a larger sum of secret service money, placed at the disposal of the military Governor of Louisiana, and not of the fiscal and and accounting officer. Mr. Clark also believed, that the General, by way of screening himself from the suspicion of being connected with Burr, and of increasing executive confidence in his fidelity, had denounced many innocent persons (and his name among them) in a letter to the President, which has never been published. The foregoing circumstances furnished additional reasons for the ultimate and entire estrangement of Mr. Clark from General Wilkinson, and completed his disgust at and abhorrence of his conduct.

Inter. 6*th.* Do you recollect D. Clark's opinions, and when, of General Wilkinson's conduct at New Orleans in 1806 and 1807, whether he confided in his loyalty to the United States, or suspected him? Relate any knowledge you may have, and whether, from Daniel Clark's opipion of the General, or your own knowledge, you have ever proffered your assistance, mercantilely or otherwise, in advancing his interests?

Ans. 6*th.* The first part having been already answered, I will merely add, that I am unacquainted with any offer of mercantile or other aid having been made by Mr. Clark or myself to advance General Wilkinson's interests; though as to what Mr. C. may have done, I cannot speak with certainty beyond my own knowledge.

Inter. 7*th.* Have you, since the charges exhibited in the House of Representatives of the United States in Congress by John Randolph and Daniel Clark, Esquires, gone to Lancaster? Was the motive of the visit to see or communicate with Andrew Ellicott? Did you see or communicate with Andrew Ellicott, and what respecting? Were you induced by the desire of any other person to take that visit?

Ans. 7th. I did visit Lancaster last Jan. and for the express purpose of seeing Mr. Andrew Ellicott, and inducing him to attend the Court of Enquiry, as an evidence, which however he declined doing, unless the bill, giving Courts Martial power to coerce the attendance of witnesses, was passed, in which case he said he should go to Washington, although he considered the Court of Enquiry as incompetent to the proper investigation of Gen. Wilkinson's conduct. My journey to Lancaster was my own free act, and without the knowledge or instigation of any person. It arose from a conversation I had a few days previous with Captain John Dunlap in this city, who informed me that he had conversed with Mr. Ellicott on his return through Lancaster, who corroborated Mr. Clark's statement, as laid before the House of Representatives, and declared Wilkinson to be a pensioner of Spain. On entering Mr. Ellicott's house, the evening of my arrival at Lancaster, I found him engaged in explaining to a number of gentlemen of the Legislature the affair of the old western conspiracy, and Wilkinson's participation therein, which Mr. E. was elucidating by references to his printed journal when commissioner on the part of the United States for running the southern boundary. He confirmed the correctness of Mr. Clark's statement, and mentioned his own agency in detecting Willkinson's connexion with the Spaniards, by means of intercepted letters, &c. the circumstances of which he said he had communicated in cypher to our government at the time, and the following is a memorandum I made on returning to my lodgings, of some other important circumstances mentioned to me by Mr. Ellicott:—" Jan. 30. Andrew Ellicott informed me this evening, that in the month of June, 1801, (as well as I recollect) he communicated, personally, to Mr. Jefferson, the exact sum of money that had beeen sent by Don Thomas Portel to General Wilkinson; that this money was not on account of any mercantile transactions, but of the pension allowed the General by the Spanish government; that General W. was not a man to be trusted; and if continued in employ, would one day or other disgrace and involve the government in his schemes."

Inter. 8th. Do you know any other matter or thing that may be of use in the enquiry respecting the conduct of Brigadier General Wilkinson, which the military Court of Enquiry is now prosecuting at Washington?

Ans. 8th. I declare, that, under the authority of Mr. Clark to receive and open in his absence all letters addressed to him, I have lately received per mail the one hereunto annexed, addressed to him by Mr. Thomas Gemmel, and dated Pinkneyville, 22d March, 1808, and which I conceive it my duty to lay before the Court of Enquiry.

Pinkneyville, March 22d, 1808.

" DEAR SIR,

" From a short and imperfect acquaintance, I have taken the liberty of writing to you. I have been informed by a gentleman of undoubted veracity attached to the United States army, now stationed at the camp near this place, that General Wilkinson has written to two officers of the army, to wit, Colonel Kingsbury and Captain Boyer, both stationed at said camp, requesting each of them to give testimony relative to the interview you had with General Wilkinson at fort Adams, at the time mentioned in your communication to Congress. You may perhaps have heard and know better the relative situation or standing of those deponents with the General than I, and what influence he may have with them. The first, I am credibly informed, has been promised a furlough; the second flattered with a prospect of promotion to a majority. Each of them have received a letter from the General, holding forth fair promises at the commencement, and concluding with an earnest request that they be punctual in sending on their depositions, the purport of which is intended to invalidate that part of your testimony, which relates to the interview with the General at Fort Adams; and each of those gentlemen have been heard to say that you were with the General but a few hours at that time.

" The General has also requested that those depositions be written by Major Stoddard, who was immediately sent for to the upper country of this territory for that purpose. He has arrived, and they are now at work.

" Having heard Captain Sterrett, of New Orleans, speak of your visit to the General, and knowing that his statement will correspond with yours, as to time and duration of stay, I have written to him, requesting that his deposition might be taken in legal form, and forwarded to you as soon as possible. Mr. Evans, of Fort Adams, I think can testify the same. There are several gentlemen in this neighbourhood, whose testimony would go in corroboration, who will not come forward voluntarily. Mr. Evans, I presume, will. If so, I will have his deposition taken, and enclose it to you. The unusual anxiety and interest the friends of General W. express on this occasion, altho' they endeavour to conduct the business as secretly as possible, has induced me to take the part I have. Conscious that it can do you no injury, I shall feel happy, if I have had it in my power to render you a service.

Your Friend, &c.

(Signed) THOS. GEMMEL.

DANIEL CLARK, ESQ."

Post-mark outside as follows:
" Pinkneyville, M. T. Ma. 24th.
" Washington, May 18."

Having a personal acquaintance with the Baron de Carondelet, Thos. Power, and the late Governor Gayoso, and Philip Nolan, and previously seen the documents laid by Messrs. Randolph and Clark on the table of the House of Representatives, I do aver and declare, from my own knowledge of the hand writing of those four persons, that the statement of Daniel Clark, in regard to the genuine writing or signatures of them, is true and correct. I have examined them, with a view of proving the same, if ever called upon for that purpose.

I also declare that I have lately perused the official copy of a public dispatch, in the Spanish language, from the Marquis de Casa Yrujo to Don Pedro Cevallos, Secretary for Foreign Affairs in Spain, dated Philadelphia, 18th December, 1806, which communicates the entire conviction of the Marquis that General Wilkinson (well known and designated in the correspondence of state under the name or appellation of No. 13,) was united with Burr in a plan to sever the western country from the Union, and that there was nothing to fear from their views, which were not directed against the Spanish possessions, but against their own country.

I further declare, that on the arrival of Mr. Thomas Power in this city from Richmond last October, I had many conversations with him, and he appeared much incensed against General Wilkinson, for having (as he said) faithlessly published a certificate which he had given him the preceding spring at New Orleans, at his particular request, under a solemn promise that it was intended merely for Mr. Jefferson's private inspection, to quiet his suspicions, and should never be made public. Mr. Power likewise related to me an interview he had with General Wilkinson, on arriving at Richmond from New Orleans, as follows : After being conducted (I think by night) to the General's chamber, or the General to his, Wilkinson locked the door, and with emotions of agony and despair, raising his head and hands towards heaven, exclaimed——What, Power—are you come here to do?—and what evidence do you intend giving before the Court?—Can't you go out of the way?——To which Power replied—I shall answer nothing which can implicate my own government.——" If so," said the general, " I

" am safe; give me your hand, and do you promise this?" Power answered, that was his intention.

I further declare, that I have obtained information, which I believe may be fully relied on, that William Lewis, Esq. of this city, Counsel for Colonel Burr, possesses facts, statements and documents, which will prove that there existed between Burr and Wilkinson an agreement and mutual understanding in relation to the conquests which they projected making in the West, and that they were to co-operate in the accomplishment of that object.

PENNSYLVANIA, ss.

Before me, Thomas Smith, Esq. one of the Judges of the Supreme Court, personally came D. W. Coxe, of the city of Philadelphia, merchant, and being duly sworn, declareth and saith, that the foregoing Answers to the foregoing Interrogatories contain the truth, the whole truth, and nothing but the truth, in the subject matter, according to the manner therein stated.

  (Signed)   D. W. COXE.

Sworn, and duly subscribed, before me,
 this 13th of June, 1808.
  (Signed)   THOMAS SMITH.

NOTE No. 56.

EL Baron de Carondelet, Cavallero de la Religion de San Juan, Brigadier de los Reales Exercitos, Gobernador, Vice Patrono de las Provincias de la Louisiana, Florida Occidental, é Inspector de sus Tropas, &c.

Certifico que el bergantin Americano el Gran Sachem, su Capitan Ebenezer Baldwin, y propió de Jonathan Arnold, llego aqui procedente del puerto de Baltimore en el mes de Diciémbre del ano pasado, consiguente al permiso de la real orden de 9 de Junio del mismo, consignado a Don Daniel Clark; y que salio de aqui dicho barco en el mes de Julio del presente, cargado con propiedad Americana. Certifico ademas que qualquiera otros efectos que se embarcaran a bordo de dicho buque pertenecen a mercaderes Americanos; y venian dirigidas a esta plaza en virtu de dicho real permiso; y para que obre los efectos, que convenga doy la presente firmada de mi mano, sellada con el sello de mis armas, y refrendada por el enfrascrito Secretario por S. M. de este Gobierno, en la Neuva Orleans, a 15 de Noviembre de 1794.

[L. S]   EL BARON DE CARONDELET.
ANDRES LOPEZ ARMESTO.

TRANSLATION OF NOTE No. 56.

THE Baron de Carondelet, Knight of the Order of St. John, Brigadier of the Royal Armies, Governor, Vice Patron of the Provinces of Louisiana and West Florida, and Inspector of their Troops, &c.

I certify that the American brigantine, the Grand Sachem, Captain Ebenezer Baldwin, belonging to Jonathan Arnold, arrived here from the port of Baltimore in the month of December of the last year, agreeable to the royal order of the 9th June of said year, consigned to Daniel Clark; that she sailed from hence in the month of July of the present year, loaded with American property. I further certify that any other effects loaded on board said vessel belong to American merchants, and came consigned to this city in virtue of said royal order; and that it may produce the necessary effect, I grant the present, signed with my hand, and sealed with the seal of my arms, and countersigned by the under written Secretary for his Majesty in this government. New Orleans, 15th November, 1794.

             EL BARON DE CARONDELET.
ANDRES LOPEZ ARMESTO.

NOTE No. 57.

DON Francisco Renden, Intendente de Exercito y Real Hacienda de las Provincias de la Louisiana, Florida Occidental, Superentendente Subdelegado y juez de Arribadas de ellas en los negocios mercantiles de su trafico y commercio, &c.

Certifico que el bergantin nombrado el Charleston, su Capitan Don Ebenezer Baldwin, de la pertenencia de William y James Thayer, llego a esta con cargamento por cuenta de sus armadores, y que pase al puerto de Charleston, con registro de la administracion de rentas de esta plaza, consequente a la cedula de commercio de esta provincia, expedida en 9 de Junio del ano pasado, de 1793; y para que conste, doy la presente, firmada de mi mano, sallada con el sello de mis armas, y refrendada por el Secretario de esta Intendencia, en la Neuva Orleans, a 28 de Noviembre, de 1794.

[L. S.]   FRANCISCO RENDEN.
CAYNO. VALDES.

TRANSLATION OF NOTE No. 57.

DON Francisco Renden, Intendant of the Army and Treasury of the Provinces of Louisiana and West Florida, Superintendant Subdelegate and Judge of the Admiralty of them, in the mercantile affairs of their commerce and traffic, &c.

I certify that the brigantine called the Charleston, Ebenezer Baldwin, Captain, the property of William and James Thayer, arrived at this port, loaded for account of her owners, and on the same account sails for the port of Charleston, with a clearance from the royal customhouse of this place, conformable to the cedula of commerce of this province, granted the 9th of June of last year, 1793; and that it may appear, I grant the present, signed with my hand, sealed with my arms, and countersigned by the Secretary of this Intendancy, in New Orleans, the 28th November, 1794.

[L. S]   FRANCISCO RENDEN.
CAYNO. VALDES.

NOTE No. 58.

EL Baron de Carondelet, Caballero de la Religion de San Juan, Brigadier de las Reales Exercitos, Gobernador, Vice Patrono de los Provincias de la Louisiana, Florida Occidental, é Inspector de sus Tropas, &c.

Concedo libre y seguro pasaporte a Don Ebenezer Baldwin, Capitan del bergantin Americano el Charleston, para que pueda pasar de esta puerto al de Charleston, cargado con frutos de esta provincia, con registro que ha sacado de esta administracion de reales rentas y la tripulacion que consta del rol, que me ha presentado, con la expresa condicion de no recibir a su bordo persona alguna de las prohibidas, ni las que no lo son, sin licencia mia.

Por tanto mando a los Capitanes y Patrones de las embarcaciones sujetos a este gobierno, ruego y encargo a los Senores Commandantes de las esquadras y baxales de S. M. y demas potencias, no le pongan embarazo alguno en su viage, antes bien le daran los auxilios que hubiere menester.

Dado el presente firmado de mi mano, sellado con el sello de mis armas, y refrendado por el infrasrito Secretario por S. M. de este gobierno, en la Nueva Orleans, a 28 de Noviembre, de 1794.

[L. S.]   EL BARON DE CARONDEDET.
ANDRES LOPEZ ARMESTO.

TRANSLATION OF NOTE No. 58.

The Baron de Carondelet, Knight of the Order of St. John, Brigadier of the Royal Armies, Governor, Vice Patron of the Provinces of Louisiana and West Florida, and Inspector of their Troops, &c.

I grant a free and safe passport to Mr. Ebenezer Baldwin, Captain of the American brigantine the Charleston, to go from this port to that of Charleston, loaded with the produce of this province, with a clearance which he has taken from the Royal Custom-house, and the crew which appears on ship's articles which he has presented to me, with the express condition of not receiving on board his vessel any prohibited persons, or any otherwise, without my permission.

Therefore I order the Captains and Patrons of vessels subject to this government, and request and intreat the Commanders of His Majesty's squadron and ships, and those of other powers, to put no impediment to his voyage, but rather to give him such assistance as he may need.

Given under my hand, and sealed with the seal of my arms, and countersigned by the undermentioned Secretary for His Majesty in this government, in New Orleans, 28th November, 1794.

[L. S.]   El BARON DE CARONDELET.
ANDRES LOPEZ ARMESTO.

NOTE No. 59.

UNITED STATES OF AMERICA,
STATE OF NEW-YORK, SS.

BY this public Instrument, be it known to all whom the same doth or may concern, That I, George D. Cooper, a Public Notary in and for the State of New-York, by letters patent under the great seal of the said state, duly commissioned and sworn; and in and by the said letters patent invested " with full power and **authority to** attest deeds, wills, testaments, codicils, agreements, and other instruments in writing, and to administer any oath or oaths to any person or persons;" do hereby certify, that on the day of the date hereof, before me personally came and appeared John Blagge, of the city of New-York, merchant, who being by me duly sworn deposeth and saith, that in the year one thousand seven hundred and ninety-one he, this deponent, together with John Jackson and Leffert Lefferts, both of the said city of New-York, were the owners of the brig Grand Sachem, and that Thomas Wooster, who sailed in the said brig Grand Sachem in the year last aforesaid, from New-York to New-Orleans, had not at that time, nor has he at any subsequent period had, any transfer or conveyance of the said brig Grand Sachem from this deponent and the said John Jackson and Leffert Lefferts, nor had he, the said Thomas Wooster, any interest or concern whatsoever in the said brig, at that or any subsequent time, prior to the sale of the said brig to Jonathan Arnold; he further saith, that he, this deponent, together with the said John Jackson and Leffert Lefferts, sold the said brig Grand Sachem, and conveyed her, after her return from New-Orleans in the year one thousand seven hundred and ninety-two, to Jonathan Arnold, of the said city of New-York, and that this deponent and the said John Jackson and Leffert Lefferts made no other transfer or conveyance of the said brig Grand Sachem than the one to the said J. Arnold.

J. BLAGGE.

Whereof an attestation being required, I have granted this under my Notarial Firm and Seal.

Done at the city of New-York, in the state of New-York, the twentieth day of April, in the year one thousand eight hundred and eight.

IN PROEMISSOREM FIDEM.

GEO. D. COOPER, Not. Pub.

NOTE No. 60.

DON Andres Lopez de Armesto, Secretario que fue del Gobierno de la provincia de la Louisiana, de la Comision de Limites de ella por Su Majestad, Commisario Honorario de Guérra, y actualmente destinado para la Revista de Milicias de la plaza de la Havana.

Certifico que habiendo llégado à la provincia de la Louisiana, en fines de Mayo de 1772, y sido nombrado Secretario de aquel Gobierno en 1779, tube la satisfaccion de tratar, y reciber particulares favores de Don Daniel Clark, defunto, Coronel de las milicias de los Estados Unidos, en Natchez, con quíen seguí la mas estrecha amistad, y union. Por esta causa, desde los primeros dias del arrivo de Don Daniel Clark, el joven, su sobrino, en Diciembre, de 1786, tuvo principio mi natural, y amistosa connexion con este, que ha continuado sin alteracion hasta mi forzosa salida de Neuva Orleans, en principios de Marzo, de 1806. Durante la residencia de tio y sobrino en Neuva Orleans, observé, con singular placer, que el generoso, amable caracter del anciano Clark, y su vírtuosa consorte, era distinguido amado, y celebrado general, y particularmente por los Senores Gobernadores, Oficiales, y empleados del gobierno Espanol, cuyas calidades ha conservado sin interrupcion, el sobrino Daniel Clark con particular aceptacion, en los gobiernos de los Senores Don Estevan Miro, Barón de Carondelet, Don Manuel Gayoso de Lemos, y Marqués de Cassa Calvo. Certifico iqualmente que el joven Don Daniel Clark no ha hecho el juramento de fidelidad à Espana; aunque en diferentes ocasiones se le haya propuesta; y que lograba en el gobierno Espanol la singular indulgencia de continuar gozando los privilegios concedidos en favor del comercio y agricultura, de la Luisiana, como habitante de la provincia, sin la menor inquietud, ni incommodidad y para que conste, y obre los necessarios effectos, que convenga, a pedimento del mencionado joven, doy con singular satisfaccion, la presente, en la Havana, a 25 de Junio, de 1808.

ANDRES LOPEZ ARMESTO.

TRANSLATION OF NOTE No. 60.

I, DON Andres Lopez de Armesto, formerly Secretary to the government of the province of Louisiana, one of his Majesty's commissioners of limits, honorary commissary of war, and at present authorised to review the militia of the Havanna, do hereby certify, that having arrived in the province of Louisiana about the latter end of May, 1772, and been appointed secretary of that government in 1779, I had the satisfaction to communicate with and receive particular favours from Mr. Daniel Clark, deceased, colonel of the militia of the United States, at Natchez, with whom I maintained the strictest union and friendship. Hence originated, from the first day of the arrival of Mr. Daniel Clark, jun. his nephew, in December, 1786, my close and friendly connexion with him, which continued without intermission until I was forced to leave New Orleans, about the beginning of March, 1806. During the residence of both the uncle and nephew in New Orleans, I observed, with singular pleasure, that the generous and amiable character of old Mr. Clark, and his virtuous consort, were universally acknowledged, and particularly by the governors, officers, and others in the employ of the Spanish government; and that his nephew, Daniel Clark, has invariably maintained the same reputation, and with more particular distinction during the administration of Don Stephen Miro, the Baron de Carondelet, Don Manuel Gayoso de Lemos, and the Marquis de Cassa Calvo. I also certify that Daniel Clark never took the oath of allegiance to Spain, although he was solicited so to do on different occasions, and that he was allowed by the Spanish government the special indulgence of continuing to enjoy the same commercial and agricultural privileges, in Louisiana, as an inhabitant of the province, without the slightest interruption or molestation; and in order that it may be known to whom it may concern, and serve the necessary purposes, I hereby, at the request of the above mentioned gentleman, grant this certificate, with particular satisfaction. Havanna, 25th June, 1808.

(Signed)   ANDRES LOPEZ ARMESTO.

NOTE No. 61.

No. 5. Five.

IN pursuance of an act of the Congress of the United States of America, entitled " An Act concerning the registering and recording of " ships or vessels,' Jonathan Arnold, of the city, county, and state of New-York, Merchant, having taken or subscribed the affirmation required by the said act, and having affirmed that he is the only owner of the ship or vessel called the Grand Sachem, of New-York, whereof Ebenezer Baldwin is at present master, and is a citizen of the United States, and that the said ship or vessel was rebuilt in the state aforesaid in the year seventeen hundred and eighty-nine, as appears by certificate of registry, No. 92, granted at this port on the 28th day of December, 1791, and now given up to be cancelled, on account of transfer of property; and John Lasher, Surveyor of this district, having certified that the said ship or vessel has one deck and two masts, and that her length is seventy feet five inches, her breadth twenty feet, her depth ten feet ten inches, and that she measures one hundred thirty-three tons; that she is a square sterned brig, has a round tuck, quarter badges, and man head; and the said Jonathan Arnold having agreed to the description and admeasurement above specified, and sufficient security having been given, according to the said act, the said brig has been duly registered at the port of New-York.

GIVEN under our hands and seals, at the port of New-York, this tenth day of January, in the year one thousand seven hundred and ninety-three.

(L. S.) JOSEPH NOURSE, Register.
(L. S.) CHARLES TILLINGHAST, Dep. Col.
(L. S.) BEN. WALKER, N. Off.

DISTRICT OF NEW-YORK, PORT OF NEW-YORK.

WE certify the within to be a true copy of the original certificate of registry of the brig Grand Sachem, taken from the record on file in this office.

GIVEN under our hands and seals of office, at the Custom-house of this port, this twentieth day of April, one thousand eight hundred and eight.

(L. S.) D. GELSTON, Collector.
(L. S.) S. OSGOOD, N. Officer.

NOTE No. 62.

AFFIDAVIT OF WILLIAM PORTER.

WILLIAM PORTER, of the city of Baltimore, being solemnly sworn on the Holy Evangelists of Almighty God, deposeth and saith, that he lived in the family of Mr. Daniel Clark, of New Orleans, in the years 1793 and 1794, and that he was in the employment of Mr. Clark from the year 1793 to 1799, during which time he had constant access to his books and papers; that the brig Grand Sachem, with Mr. Jonathan Arnold, her owner, on board, arrived from Baltimore at New Orleans in the year 1793, and proceeded for the Havanna in the beginning of 1794, with the Governor's lady, daughter, and suite on board; that when she sailed from the city of New Orleans she had American colours flying, and was known to the Governor, and other officers of the government, to be American property; that to satisfy the Governor of this vessel's being really American property, he understood, and believes, that Mr. Clark shewed to the Governor the American register and papers of said brig, which induced him to send his family in her, for their security, as Spain was then at war with France; that, to the best of his knowledge and belief, Mr. Jonathan Arnold was the sole owner of said vessel; that Mr. Clark, as will appear from his books, had nothing more to do with the Grand Sachem, than merely to receive a commission for transacting her business; that this deponent kept, himself, the accounts of said vessel, and furnished them to Mr. Arnold, as her owner; and that during her continuance in New Orleans he never saw her wear Spanish colours, but, on the contrary, when celebrating the fourth of July, 1794, she wore American colours during the day in the harbour, and notoriously belonged solely to Mr. Arnold, and was American property.

WM. PORTER.

Sworn and subscribed before
    GEO. GOULD. PRESBURY.
April 28th, 1808.

NOTE No. 63.

New Orleans, 7th September, 1805.

DEAR SIR,

MANY absurd and wild reports are circulated here, and have reached the ears of the officers of the late Spanish government, respecting our ex Vice-President. You are spoken of as his right hand man, and even I am now supposed to be of consequence enough to combine with Generals and Vice-Presidents. At any other time but the present, I should amuse myself vastly at the folly and fears of those who are affected with these idle tales; but being on the point of setting off for Vera Cruz, on a large mercantile speculation, I feel cursedly hurt at the rumours, and might, in consequence of Spanish jealousy, get into a hobble I could not easily get out of. Entre nous, I believe that Minor, of Natchez, has a great part in this business, to make himself of importance. He is in the pay of Spain, and wishes to convince them he is much their friend. This is, however, matter of suspicion on my part, but the channel through which the information reached me makes me suppose it. Power, whose head is always stuffed with plots, projects, conspiracies, &c. &c. &c. and who sees objects through a mill-stone, is going to Natchez, next week, to unravel the whole of this extraordinary business, and then God have mercy on the culprits, for Spanish ire and indignation will be levelled at them. What in the name of heaven could give rise to these extravagancies? Were I sufficiently intimate with Mr. Burr, and knew where to direct a line to him, I should take the liberty of writing to him. Perhaps, finding Minor in his way, he was endeavouring to extract something from him. He has amused himself at the blockhead's expence, and then Minor has retailed the news to his employers. Enquire of Mr. Burr about this, and let me know at my return, which will be in three or six months. The tale is a horrid one, if well told. Kentucky, Tennessee, the state of Ohio, with part of Georgia and Carolina, are to be bribed, with the plunder of the Spanish countries west of us, to separate from the Union. This is but a part of the business. Heavens, what wonderful doings there will be in those days. But how the devil I have been lugged into the conspiracy, or what assistance I can be of to it, is to me incomprehensible. Vous qui savez tout can best explain this riddle. Amuse Mr. Burr with an account of it, but let not these great and important objects, these almost imperial doings, prevent you from attending to my land business. Recollect that you ——, then, if you intend to become Kings and Emperors, must have a little more consideration for vassals ; and if we have nothing to clothe ourselves with, for we can be clothed with the produce of our lands only, and if Congress take the lands for want of formalities, we shall then have no produce, we shall make a very shabby figure at your courts. Think of this, and practice those formalities that are necessary, that I may have from my Illinois lands wherewith to buy a decent court dress, when presented at your levee. I hope you will not have Kentucky men for your masters of ceremonies.

I remain, dear sir, very sincerely,
Your humble servant and friend,
(Signed)   DAN. CLARK.

Brigadier General WILKINSON.

The preceding is a true copy, and the young man who writes for me having absented himself, unexpectedly, has caused the delay of your receiving it.

Truly thine,
(Signed)   JA. WILKINSON.

Hon. D. C.

NOTE No. 64.
St. Louis, March 8th, 1806.

DEAR SIR,

NOT knowing whether you have returned from Mexico or not, I have forborne to address you since the receipt of your land claims, and the tale of a tub of Burr, &c. &c. But by the bearer, Mr. Wilkinson, I think proper to advise you, that your claims have been all registered. Though they have not been acted upon by the Commissioners, yet I have collected from two of the Board, that one only of them is indisputable, I think for five thousand acres, and granted in your own name—the rest stand in need of explanations and testimony. I do not comprehend as yet the particulars, but you may rest assured of my attentions, and that nothing shall be left undone to support your rights. By the next conveyance you shall be more particularly informed, as I mean to bring forward those claims in a few days, in order to ascertain the sentiments of the Board. As I do not know whether this will find you in New Orleans or not, I must not enlarge, but will refer you to my nephew for the news of this territory, should he find you at home.

What think you of the purchase of the Floridas by the U. S.? Entre nous, I verily believe it is done——something of *great importance* has been done in conclave, and that something is to pepetuate our peace with Spain——again entre nous. I write in haste, and am, with much friendship, Your's,

JA. WILKINSON.

D. CLARK, ESQ.

NOTE No. 65.

AFFIDAVIT OF M. DE LA CROIX.

ON this day, the eighth of March, in the year of our Lord one thousand eight hundred and nine, and the thirty-third of our Independence, before Alexis Cesar Bonamy, one of the Justices of the Peace in the city and for the parish of Orleans, appeared Francis Du Suan de la Croix, a Member of the Legislature of the territory of Orleans, an inhabitant of this parish, who, being duly sworn on the Holy Evangelists of Almighty God, did depose and say, that about the middle of the month of October, in the year 1806, he was spoken to by Mr. Daniel Clark respecting the projects imputed to Colonel Burr, which were then the general themes of conversation in the city, and was invited by the said Daniel Clark to be present at a meeting of a number of his friends, which took place immediately afterwards, among whom he recollects Mr. Dominique Bouligny, now of the House of Representatives of this territory, Mr. Joseph Deville Degoutin Bellechasse, then Colonel of the city militia, and member of the Legislative Council, and Mr. Peter Derbigny, then and still Secretary of the Legislative Council, when Mr.

D. Clark, after stating what he understood to be the views imputed to Colonel Burr, as well in the newspapers as by report, entreated all present in the most urgent manner to forget any personal animosity towards the Governor, and to rally round the government, and die, if necessary, in its defence. That the said D. Clark further stated his regret at being about to depart for Congress at so critical a moment, and mentioned his fears of the Governor's incapacity to head the well disposed inhabitants, whom he advised us to encourage to join and support him; and lastly he entreated us, by all we hold sacred, in case of any hostile project on the part of Colonel Burr against the peace of this country, which might be followed by a momentary success, not to attend any meeting of the Legislature, or suffer any other member to attend it, whom we could influence, as we might be forced to give sanction to measures, which would for ever ruin ourselves and country, which he then and always assured us could only prosper by its utmost attachment and adherence to the government of the United States.

DU SUAN DE LA CROIX.

Signed and sworn before me,
AIS. BONAMY, Justice of the Peace.

NOTE No. 66.

AFFIDAVIT OF D. BOULIGNY.

PAR devant moi soussigné l'un des Juges de Paix de la ville de la Nouvelle Orleans, est comparu en personne Mr. Dominique Bouligny, habitant de cette paroisse, Membre de la Chambre des Representants de ce territoire, lequel apris avoir été duement assermenté suivant la loi, a dit et declaré, que dans le mois d'Octobre, 1806, les projets du Col. Burr et de ses adherens etant alors le sujet general des conversations dans cette ville, le deposent eut occasion de s'en entretenir avec Mr. Daniel Clark, lors Delegué de ce territoire au Congrès, qui l'invita a assister à une conference qu'il devoit avoir à ce sujet avec plusieurs de ces amis; que le deposant, s'y etant rendu, y trouva plussieurs personnes parmi lesquelles il se rappelle du Coronel Bellechassé, de Mr. De la Croix, et de Mr. Derbigny; que Mr. Clark leur exposa ses craintes sur le sort de ce territoire, et les exhorta à oublier toute recrimination personnelle envers le Governeur, et a se rallier autour de lui pour la defense de leur pays; qu'il leur exprima ses regrets d'être forcé de partir pour Washington dans de parcilles circonstances, et leur temoigna ses inquietudes sur l'incapacité du Gouverneur de Commander les bons citoyens; qu'il les conjura, au nom de tout ce qu'il y avoit de sacré, pour eux de ne point assister à l'assembleé de la Legislature, dans le cas ou le Col. Burr, venant à reussir dans son entreprise, chercheroit à s'étayer des authorités constituées pour consolider son usurpation ; qu', enfin, il leur representa que les projets du Colonel Burr ne tendoient qu' à la ruine entire de ce pays cy ; que s'il avoit quelques succés, ils ne pouvaient étre que momentanés, et entraineraient des consequences encore plus facheuses ; que les bons citoyens n'avoient d'autre salut a esperer, qu'en defendant leur gouvernement au prix même de leur sang. A la Neuvélle Orleans, ce 8 Mars, 1809.

D. BOULIGNY.

Juré et affirmé,
 DUTILLET, Juge de Paix.

TRANSLATION OF NOTE No. 66.

BEFORE me, the undersigned, one of the Justices of the Peace for the city of New Orleans, personally appeared Mr. Dominick Bouligny, an inhabitant of this parish, and Member of the House of Representatives of this territory, who, being duly sworn according to law, did depose and say, that in the month of October, 1806, the projects of Colonel Burr and his adherents being then the general subject of conversation in this city, the deponent had occasion to converse about them with Mr. Daniel Clark, then Delegate from this territory to Congress, who invited him to a conference which was to take place between several of his friends respecting this business ; that the deponent, having attended, found several several persons, among whom he remembers Colonel Bellechasse, Mr. De la Croix, and Mr. Derbigny; that Mr. Clark stated his fears respecting the situation of this territory, and exhorted them to forget any personal pique against the Governor, and to rally round him for the defence of their country ; that he mentioned his regret at his departure for Washington under such circumstances, and signified his uneasiness at the incapacity of the Governor to command the well disposed citizens; that he conjured them, in the name of whatever they held sacred, not to assist at any meeting of the Legislature, in case Colonel Burr, succeeding in his enterprize, should endeavour to avail himself of the constituted authorities to consolidate his usurpation ; that, in fine, he represented to them that the projects of Colonel Burr could tend only to the entire ruin of the country ; that if he had any success, it could be only momentary, and would be attended by the worst of consequences, and that the good citizens had no other safety to

hope for, but in defending the government, at the expence of their lives,
New Orleans, 8th May, 1809.
(Signed) D. BOULIGNY.
Sworn and signed before me,
(Signed) DUTILLET, Justice of the Peace.

NOTE No. 67.

AFFIRMATION OF S. B. DAVIS.

PERSONALLY appeared before me, the undersigned, one of the Justices of the Peace for the parish of New Orleans, S. B. Davis, Harbour-Master of this city, who, being duly sworn on the Holy Evangelists of Almighty God, did depose and say, that about the time that information of Colonel Burr's expedition first arrived, he, the deponent, met with Dr. Wm. Flood, of this city, at the Coffee house, who informed him that the said Burr was expected to be on his way, or was about to descend the river, with intentions hostile to the government of the U. S. and added, that it was the duty of every good citizen to oppose him, at the risk of his life; upon which this deponent hastened to communicate what he had heard to Mr. Daniel Clark, then about to depart as Delegate from this country to Congress, and after conversing with Mr. Clark on the subject, he was advised by him to serve and support the government of the U. S. by all means in his power, and to make use of Mr. Clark's name with all his friends, and any whom it might influence to act in the same manner; and the deponent further declares and says, that he was afterwards informed by Colonel Bellechasse, that Mr. Clark had used all his influence to rally his friends in defence of the country; and further this deponent saith not.

S. B. DAVIS.

Sworn and subscribed before me, this eleventh day of March, 1809.
AIS. BONAMY, Justice of the Peace.

NOTE No 68.

AFFIDAVIT OF COLONEL BELLECHASSE.

PAR devant moi, F. Dutillet, l'un des Juges de Paix pour la ville et paroisse de la Neuve le Orleans, est comparu le Sieur Deville Degoutin

Bellechasse, President du Conseil Legislatif de ce territoire, le quel apris avoir été duement assermenté, a dit et declaré, que vers le mois de Novembre, 1803, au moment où la Louisiane alloit être transfereé par l'Espagne au gouvernement François, il fut solicité par le Prefet François, M. Laussat, d'accepter le commandement des milices de cette province ; mais que ne conaissant pas les intentions et les vûes du Prefet, qui lui ferait cet offre, il crut ne pas devoir y consenter, et qu'il fit part de ce refus a M. Clark, alors Consul des Etats Unis dans cette ville, qui le blama de n'avoir pas accepté le rang qui lui etait offert, lui observant en même tems, qu'el serait advantageux pour la conservation de la tranquilité publique, qu' une place aussi importante fut acceptée par un homme qui possedait la confiance de ses concitoyens, qu'en l'acceptant il rendrait un service dont les Etats Unis lui tiendrait compte, et qu'il lui conseillait, s'il en était encore tems de faire connoitre au Prefet ses intentions d'accepter le commandement des milices, en consequence de cette conversation le declarant annonça à M. Laussat son intention de profiter de son offre; et des que la Louisiane ent été rendue a la France, il fut revetû du commandement des milices de la province ; et le declarant dit et declare, qu' aprés l'arrivé des Commissaires Americains, et aussitot que la colonie leur ent eté remise, le commandement de milices lui fut de nouveau offert, et qu'il l'auroit refusé, sans les avis de M. Clark, qui lui representait sans cesse qu'il devait ses services a son pays ; et depuis cette epoque jusqu' au moment oû le declarant a resigné sa place, il declare que toutes les fois que les desagremens qu'il eprouvait dans le service le portaient a vouloir l'abandonner, M. Clark, pour l'en empecher lui représentait que sa patrie avait droit a ses services, et qu'il devait faire de grand sacrafices, plutot que d'encourager les autres a resigner leur commission par son example ; et le declarant dit, que dans le commencement de l'anneé, 1806, lorsqu' il lui fut proposé d'entrer dans la Société Mexicaine, il demanda si les vues de cette société etoient connus à M. Clark, et ayant appris qu'il n'en était pas membre, il refusa de s'y faire recevoir, et communiqua immediament a M. Clark les proposition qui lui avaient été faites, M. Clark blama beaucoup le declarant d'avoir écouté des semblables propositions, vu la place importante qu'il occupait, et lui conseilla d'en faire part aux autorités, ce qu'il fit ; et le declarant dit aussi, que dans le mois d'Octobre de la suidite annee, et peu de tems avent son depart pour se rendre au Congres des Etats Unis, M. Clark ressembla plussiers de ses amis (et le declarant était de nombre) et leur fit part des vues et des intentions que l'on imputait au Col. Burr, dont les projets etaient alors le sujet exclusif des toutes les conversations, et qui commençaient deja, d'apris les bruits que repandaient les personnes arrivant du Kentucky, a exciter beaucoup de crainte, M.

Clark conseilla à tout ses amis de faire usage de leur influance pris des habitants de ce territoire pour les engager à defendre le gouvernement des Etats Unis, et se rallier outour du Gouverneur, quoisqu' il avança en même tems qu'il il le croyait peu propre a rendre des servies d'utilité dans la partie des armes, il les assura qu'en se conduisant ainsi s'il etait vrai qu'il fut menacé d'une attaque ils sauveraint leur pays, et pruveraint leur attachement au gouvernement des Etats Unis, ainsi bien que la fausseté de bruits qu'on avait fait circuler contre eux; et le declarant dit, que M. Clark recommenda fortement aux Membres de la Legislature qui se trouvaient present, de ne pas assister a aucune des seances qui pouvaient avoir lieu dans le cas qui le Col. Burr renssirait a obtenir possesion de cette ville, que les personnes qui auraient l'imprudence de se preter a ses vues s'exposeraint á des punitions aussi graves qu' elles seraient merités, puisque leur mesures auraient occasionnée la ruine de la province ; et le declarent dit et declare de plus, que ce qu'il vient de déferer, il l'a partisipé au Gouveneur, en presence du Major Notte, qui lui seroit d'interprete aupris de son Excellence, et que vers du commencement de Décembre, 1806, époque de l'arrivé du General Wilkinson dans cette ville, le declarant lui communiqua les proposition qui lui avaient été faites au sujet de l'Association Mexicaine, ainsi que des conseils que lui avoit donné M. Clark, d'eviter de se lier avec cette societé et de particiiper a ces measures.

Neuvelle Orleans, 20 Mars, 1809.

J. D. DEGOUTIN BELLECHASSE.

Jure et affirme devan nous,
F. DUTILLET, Juge de Paix.

TRANSLATION OF NOTE No. 68.

PERSONALLY appeared before me, Francis Dutillet, a Justice of the Peace of the parish of New Orleans, Mons. Joseph Deville Degoutin Bellechasse, President of the Legislative Council of this territory, who, being duly sworn, did depose and say, that on the ninth of November of the year 1803, he was solicited by the French Colonial Prefect, Mons. Laussat, to accept the command of the militia of the province of Louisiana, then about to be delivered to him by Spain, and that not knowing with what view the Prefect was actuated, he resisted his offer, which circumstance he communicated to Mr. Daniel Clark, then Consul for the U. S. in this city, who disapproved of his refusal, and earnestly recommended that, if it was not too late, he should accept the proffered command, giving as a reason, that he believed the tranquility of the country would be insured by so important a trust being confided to a man attached to good order, and who possessed the confidence of his fellow-citizens, and he was persuaded such conduct would be agreeable to the government of the U. S. in consequence of which, this deponent informed the Prefect he would take the command of the militia, which was given him as soon as Spain surrendered the country; and further this deponent declares, that on the arrival of the American Commissioners, and possession of the city being given to them, the command of the militia was again offered him, which he would have declined, had it not been for the advice of Mr. Clark, who constantly represented to him the obligation he thought he was under of serving his country; and from that period, until within these few days, when this deponent resigned the command of the first regiment of the city militia, whenever he experienced any disgust in the service, and was about to throw up his commission, he was constantly prevented by Mr. Clark, who never failed to suggest that the deponent had a duty to fulfil, and ought to make great sacrifices, rather than encourage others by his example to withdraw from the service; and the deponent further declares, that at an early period of the year 1806 he was applied to to join what was then called the Mexican Society, when he asked if their views were known to Mr. Clark? and on being informed that he was not a member, he also refused to join it, and immediately gave Mr. Clark notice of the proposal, who blamed the deponent for having listened to it, as he was an officer with a high command, and recommended him to give information of the proposal to the magistracy, which he did; and the deponent further declares, that in the month of October of the aforesaid year, a very few days before Mr. Clark left this city to go to Congress, he called together a number of his friends, amongst whom this deponent was one, and informed them of the views and intentions imputed to Colonel Burr, which were then almost the sole topic of conversation, and which, from the reports daily arriving from Kentucky, had caused a serious alarm, and he advised them all to exert their influence with the inhabitants of the country to support the government of the U. S. and to rally round the Governor, although he thought him incapable of rendering much service as a military man, assuring them that such conduct only would save the country, if any hostile projects were entertained against it, and that this would be the best method of convincing the government of the U. S. of the attachment of the inhabitants of Louisiana, and of the falsity of all the reports circulated to their prejudice; and Mr. Clark strongly recommended to such members of the Legislature as were then present, not to attend any call or meeting of either House, in case Colonel Burr should gain possession of the city, stating that such a measure would deservedly expose every individual concerned to punishment, and would occasion the ruin of the country; and this deponent further declares, that what he has last deposed he gave information of to the Governor, in the presence of Major Nott, who served him as an interpreter with his Excellency, and that on the arrival of General Wilkinson in this city, on or about the middle of December 1806, he informed him of the proposal made to him to join the Mexican Association, and of the advice given him, the deponent, by Mr. Clark, to avoid all connexion or participation in it; and further this deponent saith not.

New Orleans, 20th March, 1807.
  (Signed) J. D. DEGOUTIN BELLECHASSE.
Sworn and subscribed before me,
  (Signed) F. DUTILLET, Justice of the Peace.

NOTE No. 69.

AFFIDAVIT OF MR. DERBIGNY.

TERRITORY OF ORLEANS.
CITY OF NEW ORLEANS, SS.

BEFORE me, the undersigned, one of the Justices of the Peace in and for the said city, personally appeared Peter Derbigny, Esq. Counsellor at Law, who, being duly sworn on the Holy Evangelists, did depose and say, that some time in the fall of 1806, a few days before the departure of the Hon. Daniel Clark, their Delegate from this territory to Congress, for the city of Washington, this deponent was invited by said Clark to his house, to be present at a meeting of some of his friends, with whom he wished to converse on important matters; that there this deponent met Messrs Deville Bellechasse and Dominique Bouligny, both members of the Legislature, and Mr. Francis De la Croix, now a member of the House of Representatives; that Mr. Clark shewed to all present much anxiety for the fate of this territory, in consequence of the projects of Colonel Burr and his confederates, which were then the general topic of conversation in this country; that Mr. Clark manifested some fears, lest, in a case of emergency, the Governor of the territory should not be capable of heading the faithful and well disposed citizens; that he entreated all present, nevertheless, to use their endeavours to persuade their fellow-citizens to rally round him, and support the government; that he advised them particularly, in case Colonel Burr should come and overwhelm the government, to prevent, if possible, any of the inhabitants of this country from co-operating in his measures, and above all not to suffer the Legislature, if called by him, to meet; that Mr. Clark expressed his regret of being bound by his duty to absent himself at so critical a conjuncture, and finally recommended them to call forth all their firmness and courage in defence of their government, and to spare not even their lives, to save their country from ruin; and further this deponent saith not.

P. DERBIGNY.

Sworn before me, at New Orleans, the
   28th day of February, 1809.
AIS. BONAMY, Justice of the Peace.

NOTE No. 70.

New Orleans, December 10th, 1806.

MY DEAR SIR,

I REFER you to the bearer, Mr. Donaldson, for the interesting scenes which agitate our darling city and poor devoted Louisiana. I am here to defend her against revolution and pillage by a hand I have loved. Suspicion is afloat, and numbers are implicated. Thank God, your advice to Bellechasse, if your character was not a sufficient guarantee, would vindicate you against any foul imputation. By the last advice Burr expected to reach Natchez with 2000 men the 20th inst. If he brings no more, he will not dare approach this place, where I shall to-morrow have 1000 regular troops; and your creoles will turn out with great vivacity. I am pushing an armed flotilla high up the river, to drive the revolutionists on shore, and save your plantations and prevent the insurrection of your negroes. Farewell, my dear sir, and believe me, ever yours,

      (Signed) J. WILKINSON.

HON. D. CLARK.

NOTE No. 71.

Letter without a date, but bearing the post-mark of the 8th January, 1808, from New Orleans. It is from Wilkinson, intended for me, and was addressed to Mr. Daniel W. Coxe, of Philadelphia, who, having read it, forwarded it to me, knowing that it must be meant for me, and stating it to be in Wilkinson's hand, which he knew.

IT is a fact that our fool has written to his contemptible fabricator, that you had declared, if you had children, you would teach them to curse the U. States as soon as they were able to lisp, and he gave the Mayor and Gurly for authors. Cet Bete is at present up to the chin in folly and vanity. He cannot be supported much longer; for, Burr or no Burr, we shall have a revolt, if he is not removed speedily. The moment Bonaparte compromises with G. Britain will be the signal for a general rising of French and Spaniards, and if the Americans do not join, they will not oppose. Take care! suspicion is abroad; but you have a friend worth having. You will see Livingston's philippic to W********; it is replete with falsehood, and is laughed at here by every body. So much for the establishment of an improved character. Your's,

R. R.

Workman and Kerr have been discovered in an intrigue to corrupt the army, and to plunder the bank. It is said Lieut. G. A. Murray has detected them.

D. C. Esq.

NOTE No. 72.

Written by Wilkinson, though unsigned.

[Confidential.]

New Orleans, March 20th, 1807.

THE animosities which have been excited in this city by Burr's friends and well-wishers and his enemies and opposers are deep, rancorous, and deadly. It would seem that the former, composed almost exclusively of our own countrymen and foreigners, embrace the mass of talents and enterprize; but the latter comprize almost the whole of the ancient inhabitants, and the great mass of established character and fortune. Pour example, in the first party you find Livingston, Workman, Kerr, Watkins, P. Jones, Daneyark, Bradford the printer, and the Bar in general; in the other, P. Lanuse, Garrick, Poidrass, B. Morgan, Bellechasse, Fortier, the Urquharts, both Pollocks, Dubourg, Gurley, Duncan, Flood, &c. It has been hinted, that much pains have been employed to induce you to believe that General Wilkinson is hostile to you, and even reported you. This is a stale device to augment the numbers of a desperate party, for the suggestion is without a shadow of foundation; and though Mr. Burr and his accredited agents have made, or endeavour to make, much use of Mr. Clark's name, General W. has never mentioned it. Burr, Bollman, and their agents, have made use of the house of Chew & Relf to cover their correspondence. Mr. R. has delivered to the General one letter of importance from Burr to Bollman. He offered another, which he said was for Bollman, tho' it was *not addressed*. " For your own sake," said the General to him, " take that " letter away, destroy, and say nothing of it ;" because it appeared extraordinary, indeed, that he should know for whom the letter * was *intended*. Yet this thick sculled beast has taken it into his head that he has been very ill used by the General, and joins in his abuse. The concord and confidence of the community is, I fear, destroyed for a long period, property is falling, and misfortunes will overtake many—yet the seeds of discontent are deeply sown, and will germinate on the first favourable occasion. In the mean time, the Chiefs of Mexico are ready to declare for independence, on the slightest encouragement of the U. S. to whom they look for alliance and support. I write *facts*, which I have enterprized and hazarded much to *ascertain* since November last. The opportunity appears to be a golden one, and I hope it may suit the policy of our country to adopt it. The poor devils on the side of Texas have all retired, and Nacogdoches is left with its usual guard. They will never attempt another campaign in that quarter. W. C. C. C. leaves this the first of May, and Graham sends in his resignation. Livingston, and my quondam friend, I. B. I understand, are praying for and promising the arrival of Monroe. I have written you twice, and have no answer.

Your ancient and principled friend,

D. C. Esq.

* *The General would not read it.*

NOTE No. 73.

Balize, 24th May, 1807, at night.

MY DEAR SIR,

I REGRET deeply that I did not see you before my leave of New Orleans. I remained at my quarters until the day was advanced, and the order for sailing being at twelve, I felt it proper to embark. Let me repeat, that your noble, manly interposition in my behalf, as reported by my friend General Smith, at the seat of government, was not necessary to secure to you a friendship, founded on almost twenty years acquaintance, but makes it my peculiar duty, pending the highly important developements which are at issue, to watch over and defend your fame, should it be implicated in the discussion. I did earnestly desire a conciliation between yourself and the Governor of the territory, because I considered such coalition in the present moment might insure a happy tone to the great substantial and important interests of the American nation, which believe me has escaped a hellish scourge, to be ascribed to that decisive conduct for which I have been stigmatized, but will ultimately be thanked. I have never attempted to justify the infractions of the law which were forced on me in New Orleans by an impending great calamity, and I shall hold myself ready to go even to the stake, should our country require it, to do away the dangerous tendency of the precedent; yet I can never repent what I have done, and would repeat it a thousand times—for if a destructive evil to a national community can be arrested by the ruin of an individul, should he pause? I think not, and under this impression I have acted.

Guard against the blandishments of faction—be on the watch of the needy, greedy, unprincipled adventurers, who are sucking the best blood of your ancient fellow-citizens—analize their characters, and views, and motives, and their seductive arts, and acknowledged talents, will prove unavailing. Cling to the plain, simple, well-meaning natives of your country, and such solid industrious citizens as Donaldson, Urquhart, Lane and Morgan, and you will contribute to the happiness and prosperity of Louisiana. I write you in haste, and more from the heart than head. You will know how to estimate this licence, and must believe me, most truly, dear sir,

Your friend and servant,

(Signed) JA. WILKINSON.

The Hon. D. CLARK, ESQ.

NOTE No. 74.

[Confidential.]

Richmond, October 5th, 1807.

DEAR SIR,

HITHERTO your name has not been mentioned, as I understand, in Burr's trial. I have received several letters from New Orleans lately, which have occasioned me some surprize. They impart, that you were coming round with Capt. Power, to do me all the injury you were able, and that, to induce Power to come, you had accommodated him with the means, and had agreed to support his family.

This I could give no credit to, after the justice you had repeatedly rendered me, not only by your long statement to Mr. Perkins respecting my first voyage to New Orleans, and the consequences, given at a late period, of which I have the copy you furnished me, but also by the declarations you made to General Smith last winter, and your recent assurances made Captain M'Clelan in New Orleans, of which I have certificates. What may be Mr. Power's object I cannot divine, since he voluntarily, in May last, tendered me, in his own hand, a declaration of my innocence, against the charges which were fulminated by Bradford, and of my ignorance of his mission to Kentucky from the Baron Carondelet, as far as comes within his knowledge, to which he offers to make oath.

Cenas writes me, that you desired him to inform me you were bound to Philadelphia, but would not come here, unless compelled by an attachment. This is utterly unintelligible; but no doubt, if Burr calculates on you, by ripping up our correspondence, to throw a slur on my character, he will send forward such an attachment. I have laboured assiduously to avoid the violation of private correspondence, whilst Mr. Burr, in the true character of a depraved villain, had adverted to a letter said to be received from me, in terms calculated to excite suspicions injurious to me, yet to my reiterated demand refuses either to bring forward that letter, or to give me leave to bring forward his private letters which I received at St. Louis, one of which relates to your communication received from New-Orleans, in which you mention Power and Minor, and the report of a meditated Mexican expedition, and the revolt of the Western States, &c. &c. I had mislaid this letter when I wrote you from Washington, but have since found it. You will recollect you desired me to write Burr on the subject, which I did; and also gave his brother-in-law, Dr. Brown, an extract of your letter, to transmit him, the receipt of which he acknowledges. Much pains were taken by Bollman to induce me to believe you were concerned. Swartwout assured me Ogden had gone to New

Orleans, with dispatches for you from Burr, and that you were to furnish provisions, &c. Many other names were mentioned to me, which I have not exposed, nor will I ever expose them, unless compelled by self defence, because I believe much fraud, artifice and falsehood, were imposed on me, as well as others, to cheat, deceive, impose, and, in case of discovery, to implicate. Among other documents handed me in New Orleans is a bill on you from G. W. Ogden, in favour of P. V. Ogden, whom I sent round, drawn, as he says, on account of the land purchase. This I have never uttered. Things of this nature, and our correspondence of twenty years torn up before a court of justice, in this hour of distrust and suspicion, may effect irreparable injuries to the innocent. Burr has said in Court, that he expected testimony from New Orleans, to prove that " himself and the country had both been " sold." I shall be happy to hear from you, and am, with respect and esteem,   Dear Sir,
      Your's,
       JA. WILKINSON.

DANIEL CLARK, ESQ.

NOTE No. 75.

DEAR SIR,

HEARING of your movement from New Orleans, I addressed the enclosed to you in Philadelphia, where I expect lieut. Murray waits for you. I wrote him since your arrival, and he will be here in three or four days. I am desirous to see you, but the reports in circulation make it matter of great delicacy. With respect and esteem,
    I am, Dear Sir,
      Your obedient Servant,
  (Signed)   JA. WILKINSON.
Richmond, October 12th, 1807.
THE HONORABLE DANIEL CLARK.

NOTE No. 76.

New Orleans, 27th September, 1806.

DEAR SIR,

I HAVE been favoured with your letter from the Heights, and had you previously informed me when you might be expected there, I should have been on the spot at the time of your arrival. Removed as you now are to a distance of one hundred and fifty leagues from Orleans, it will be morally impossible for me to undertake a journey to see you, as the near approach of winter renders my departure for the Atlantic States indispensable within a fortnight, and I shall not be here till some time after Congress breaks up. Neither myself nor any other of your friends will ever doubt that you will act with the Spaniards with as much prudence as your orders permit; and if hostilities should be the consequence, your superior must be responsible to the nation, and not you, for the conduct. The only thing I fear is, that you should not have force enough to defend the country in case of an attack, as Folch has at least 1200 to 1500 regulars in Pensacola; and if you strike on the side of Natchitoches, you ought to be prepared for a retaliation on his part against this quarter. On the militia of Lower Louisiana you must place no reliance. They never have been organized, they are unarmed, and I know there are in the stores but 2500 stand of spare arms, a great part of which I presume it would be necessary to keep for the troops, to supply them, in case of accident. Besides, you know that the planters and merchants will not easily leave their homes, to the utter ruin of their affairs, when there is no force to compel them.

I know I am entering into a THORNY PATH, and shall *expect a great deal of trouble. I* WOULD THANK *you for your advice, to direct me; and if you would give me a line to some of your friends in Congress, disposed to favour or serve Louisiana, you would, perhaps, afterwards find your account in it.* You may direct to me, to the care of Mr. Daniel Wm. Coxe, at Philadelphia, until the session commences.

I received the rejected grants of lands, and would be obliged to you to give me what information you are possessed of respecting the proceedings of the board of Commissioners, what the people in the upper country expect, and what it would be proper to attempt for them, with any hope of success.

You will oblige me much by giving me, from time to time, advices of what is passing on the frontiers, and point out in what way you think I may be of service to you.

I remain, with esteem,

Dear Sir,

Your most obedient servant,

(Signed) DANIEL CLARK.

Brigadier General WILKINSON.

NOTE No. 77.

Houmas, 2d October, 1806.

DEAR SIR,

I HEARD by Captain Turner that you had got to the Rapids of Red River, and were to proceed next morning for Natchitoches. I long to learn your arrival there, and the result of your communications with Herrara, which I presume must be unsatisfactory, as he cannot in honour recede, after what has already passed, even were his orders discretionary. I therefore suppose hostilities must take place, and were the preparations and means in your power equal to the object, I should have no doubt but you would bring matters to an honourable issue for yourself and your country. I flatter myself, however, that if your force is small, you will not expose your reputation, unless circumstances should be so favourable as to promise you victory.

Captain Turner informed me that you expected I would see you at Natchitoches. On reflecting, you must perceive the impossibility of realizing such an idea, as I have not time sufficient to undertake the journey, and return to Orleans previous to the time requisite for embarking for the seat of government; and however strong the desire of seeing you is, on my part, I must defer the pleasure till my return in the spring, or beginning of summer. Of this I had already advised you, previous to leaving town, and for fear of accident now mention it a second time, that you may not be disappointed by waiting to take any measures till you saw me.

Peace between England and France was confidently expected, messengers were daily passing between them, the English funds had raised, and concurring advices from other quarters give every reason to expect that this great event may take place. It may have a great effect on our politics, and I wish we may not be exposed to the vengeance of the three great maritime powers of Europe, by our conduct to each of them. You are, however, better able to calculate the effects to be feared or expected than myself, and I shall refrain from further observations. I shall write to you from New Orleans, previous to my departure, and will advise you from thence of any thing in my absence. I sincerely wish you success, and that the means of insuring it depended upon yourself alone.

I remain, Dear Sir,
Your's sincerely,
(Signed)   DANIEL CLARK.

Brigadier General WILKINSON.

NOTE No. 78.

MY DEAR SIR,

I DID not answer your letter by Taylor, but I did better; I procured him a pension of twenty dollars per month. I was to have introduced my friend Burr to you, but in this I failed by accident. He understands your merits, and *reckons* on you. Prepare to visit me, and I will tell you all. We must have a peep at the unknown world beyond me. I shall want a pair of strong carriage horses, at about 120 dollars each, young and sound, substantial, but not flashy. I am in health, and, in spite of the neglect of friends, and the shameful omissions of attornies, have this day given sir —— a damper. Perdition overtake the Jew scoundrel; he had nearly destroyed me by a decree, of which I have had no intimation, although it is almost seven years old. Enough for the present. Thine ever,

JA. WILKINSON.

Rapids of Ohio, May 28*th,* 1805,
  11 *o'clock, A. M.*
I sail in an hour.
Gen. ADAIR.   Write me.
  Private.

NOTE No. 79.

Copy of a letter from General Dayton to General Wilkinson, written in cypher, except those parts printed in Italics. This cypher was designed by General Dayton, and founded on the hieroglyphics known to General Wilkinson and Colonel Burr.

July 24*th,* 1806.

X Λ ! .) O ⌣ I ⊤ ⌢ " V ⌢ — O- IV"
  [ ]

It is now well ascertained that you are to be displaced in next session. Jefferson will affect to yield reluctantly to the public sentiment, but yield he will; prepare yourself therefore for it: you know the rest. You are not a man to despair, or even despond, especially when such prospects offer in another quarter. Are you ready? Are your numerous associates ready? Wealth and Glory, Louisiana and Mexico. *I shall have time to receive a letter from you before I set out for Ohio*——

O H I O. *Address one to me here, and another to me in* Cincinnati. *Receive and treat my* nephew *affectionately, as you would receive your friend.*

DAYTON.

[.]

NOTE No. 80.

July 16*th*, 1807.

MY DEAR FRIEND,

As you are said to have removed your head-quarters down the river, and there is a report that the Spaniards intercept our mails which pass necessarily through the territory occupied by them, in order to reach you, I think proper to address you in cypher, that the contents may be concealed from the Dons, if they make so free as to open the letter. Take the following for the catch word or check word (and you may very readily decypher the figures.) Viz. in your own hieroglyphic [.]; but in your own alphabet thus—

[Hieroglyphics.]

V ⌒ — o -- *I* ∧

Every thing, and even Heaven itself, appears to have conspired to prepare the train for a grand explosion ;—are you also ready? For I know you flinch not when a great object is in view. Your present is more favourable than your late position, and as you can retain it without suspicion or alarm, you ought by no means to retire from it until your friends join you in December, somewhere on the river Missisippi. Under the auspices of Burr and Wilkinson I shall be happy to engage, and when the time arrives you will find me near you.

Write, and inform me by first mail what may be expected from you and your associates. In an enterprize of such moment, considerations even stronger than those of affection impel me to desire your cordial co-operation and active support.

DAYTON.

Wealth and honor. ⎫
Adieu. ⎬ Burr and Wilkinson.
Courage and union. ⎭

Let me hear from you by mail, as well as by the first good private conveyance, and believe me, with the best wishes for your prosperity and happiness, most truly,

Your friend and servant,
JONA: DAYTON.

If you write in cypher ⎫ [Hieroglyphics.]
use the same word, viz. ⎭ V ⌒ — o -- *I* ∧

NOTE No. 81.

WILKINSON'S SECOND AFFIDAVIT.

I, JAMES WILKINSON, brigadier general and commander in chief of the army of the United States, to warrant the arrest of Samuel Swartwout, James Alexander, Esq. and Peter V. Ogden, on a charge of treason, misprision of *treason*, or such other offence against the government and laws of the United States, as the following facts may legally charge them with, on the honour of a soldier, and on the Holy Evangelists of Almighty God, do declare and swear, that in the beginning of the month of October last, when in command at Natchitoches, a stranger was introduced to me by Colonel Cushing, by the name of Swartwout, who, a few minutes after the Colonel retired from the room, *slipt* into my hand a letter of formal introduction from Col. Burr, of which the following is a correct copy:

" *Philadelphia*, 25th *July*, 1806.

" DEAR SIR,

" Mr. Swartwout, the brother of Colonel S. of New-York, being on his way down the Missisippi, and presuming that he may pass you at some post on the river, has requested of me a letter of introduction, which I give with pleasure, as he is a most amiable young man, and highly respected from his character and connexions. I pray you to afford him any friendly offices which his situation may require, and beg you to pardon the trouble which this may give you.

" With entire respect,
" Your friend and obedient servant,
(Signed) " A. BURR.

His Excellency General WILKINSON."

Together with a packet, which he informed me he was charged by the same person to deliver me *in private*. This packet contained a letter in cypher from Colonel Burr, of which the following is *substantially* as fair an interpretation as *I have heretofore* been able to make, the original of which I hold in my possession:

" I, Aaron Burr, have obtained funds, and have actually commenced the enterprize. Detachments from different points, and under different pretences, will rendezvous on the Ohio, 1st November. Every thing internal and external favours views: protection of England is secured —
T—— is *going* to Jamaica, to arrange with the Admiral on that station; it will meet on the Missisippi——England——Navy of the United States are ready to join, and final orders are given to my friends

and followers: it will be an host of choice spirits. Wilkinson shall be second to *Burr* only: Wilkinson shall dictate the rank and promotion of his officers. *Burr* will proceed westward 1st August, never to return; with him go his daughter; the husband will follow in October, with a corps of *worthies*.

" Send forthwith an intelligent and confidential friend, with whom Burr may confer; he shall return immediately, with further interesting details: this is essential to concert and harmony of movement: send a list of all persons known to *Wilkinson*, west of the mountains, who may be useful, with a note delineating their characters. By your messenger send me four or five of the commissions of your officers, which you can borrow under any pretence you please; they shall be returned faithfully. Already are orders to the contractor given to forward six months' provisions to points Wilkinson may name: this shall not be used until the last moment, and then under proper injunctions: the project is brought to the point so long desired. Burr guarantees the result with his life and honour, with the lives, the honour and fortunes of hundreds, the best blood of our country. Burr's plan of operations is, to move down rapidly from the Falls on the 15th November, with the first 500 or 1000 men, in light boats now constructing for that purpose, to be at Natchez between the 5th and 15th of December; there to meet Wilkinson; there to determine whether it will be expedient in the first instance to seize on or pass by Baton Rouge: on receipt of this, send an answer; draw on Burr for all expences, &c. The people of the country to which we are going are prepared to receive us: their agents now with Burr say, that if we will protect their religion, and will not subject them to a foreign power, that in three weeks all will be settled. The Gods invite to glory and fortune: it remains to be seen whether we deserve the boon: the bearer of this goes express to you; he will hand a formal letter of introduction to you from Burr; he is a man of inviolable honour and perfect discretion; formed to execute rather than to project; capable of relating facts with fidelity, and incapable of relating them otherwise: he is thoroughly informed of the plans and intentions of   , and will disclose to you as far as you enquire, and no further: he has imbibed a reverence for your character, and may be embarrassed in your presence: put him at ease, and he will satisfy you.

" 29*th July.*"

I instantly resolved to avail myself of the reference made to the bearer, and in the course of some days, drew from him (the said Swartwout) the following disclosure: " That he had been dispatched by Colonel

Burr from Philadelphia, had passed through the states of Ohio and Kentucky, and proceeded from Louisville for St. Louis, where he expected to find me, but discovering at Kaskaskias that I had descended the river, he procured a skiff, hired hands, and followed me down the Missisippi to Fort Adams, and from thence set out for Natchitoches, in company with Captains Sparks and Hooke, under the pretence of a disposition to take part in the campaign against the Spaniards, then depending. That Colonel Burr, with the support of a powerful associatiation, extending from New-York to New Orleans, was levying an armed body of 7000 men, from the state of New-York and the western states and territories, with a view to carry an expedition against the Mexican provinces, and that 500 men, under Colonel Swartwout and a Colonel or Major Tyler, were to descend the Alleghany, for whose accommodation light boats had been built, and were ready." I enquired what would be their course? He said, " this territory would be revolutionized, where the people were ready to join them, and that there would be some seizing, he supposed, at New-Orleans; that they expected to be ready to embark about the first of February, and intended to land at Vera Cruz, and to march from thence to Mexico." I observed that there were several millions of dollars in the Bank of this place; to which he replied, " We know it full well ;" and on remarking that they certainly did not mean to violate private property, he said they " merely meant to borrow, and would return it ; that they must equip themselves in New Orleans; that they expected naval protection from Great Britain ; that the Captain ———— and the officers of our navy were so disgusted with the government that they were ready to join ; that similar disgusts prevailed throughout the western country, where the people were zealous in favour of the enterprize, and that pilot boat built schooners were contracted for along our southern coast for their service; that he had been accompanied from the Falls of Ohio to Kaskaskias, and from thence to Fort Adams, by a Mr. Ogden, who had proceeded on to New Orleans with letters from Colonel Burr to his friends there." Swartwout asked me whether I had heard from Doctor Bollman; and on my answering in the negative, he expressed great surprize, and observed, " That the Doctor and a Mr. Alexander had left Philadelphia before him, with dispatches for me, and that they were to proceed by sea to New Orleans, where he said they must have arrived."

Though determined to deceive him, if possible, I could not refrain telling Mr. Swartwout it was impossible that I could ever dishonour my commission ; and I believe I duped him by my admiration of the plan, and by observing, " That although I could not join in the expedition, the engagements which the Spaniards had prepared for me, in my front, might prevent my opposing it:" Yet I did, the moment I had decyphered the letter, put it into the hands of Colonel Cushing, my adjutant and inspector, making the declaration that I should oppose the lawless enterprize with my utmost force. Mr. Swartwout informed me he was under engagements to meet Colonel Burr at Nashville the 20th of November, and requested of me to write him, which I declined; and on his leaving Natchitoches about the 18th of October, I immediately employed Lieutenant T. A. Smith to convey the information, in substance, to the President, without the commitment of names; for, from the extraordinary nature of the project, and the more extraordinary appeal to me, I could not but doubt its reality, notwithstanding the testimony before me, and I did not attach solid belief to Mr. Swartwout's reports respecting their intentions on this territory and city, until I received confirmatory advice from St. Louis.

After my return from the Sabine, I crossed the country to Natchez, and on my descent of the Missisippi from that place, I found Swartwout and Peter V. Ogden at Fort Adams: with the latter I held no communication, but was informed by Swartwout, that he (Ogden) had returned so far from New Orleans, on his route to Tennessee, but had been so much alarmed by certain reports in circulation, that he was afraid to proceed. I enquired whether he bore letters with him from New Orleans, and was informed by Swartwout that he did not, but that a Mr. Spence had been sent from New Orleans through the country to Nashville, with letters for Colonel Burr.

I reached this city the 25th ultimo, and on the next morning James Alexander, Esq. visited me; he enquired of me aside whether I had seen Doctor Bollman, and on my answering in the negative, he asked me whether I would suffer him to conduct Bollman to me, which I refused. He appeared desirous to communicate something, but I felt no inclination to inculpate this young man, and he left me. A few days after he paid me a second visit, and seemed desirous to communicate, which I avoided until he had risen to take leave; I then raised my finger, and observed, " Take care, you are playing a dangerous game." He answered, " It will succeed." I again observed, " Take care;" and he replied, with a strong affirmation, " Burr will be here by the beginning of next month." In addition to these corroborating circumstances against Alexander, I beg leave to refer to the accompanying documents, A. B. From all which I feel no hesitation in declaring, under the solemn obligation of an oath, that I do believe the said Swartwout, Alexander, and Ogden, have been parties to, and have been concerned in the insurrection formed or forming in the states and territories on the Ohio and Mississippi rivers, against the laws and constitution of the United States.

              (Signed)   JAMES WILKINSON.

Sworn to and subscribed, before me, this 26th day of December, in the year of our Lord 1806.

              (Signed)   GEORGE POLLOCK,

        Justice of the Peace for the county of Orleans.

NOTE No. 82.

MR. BOTTS called for the key to the cyphered letters of Col. Burr. Gen. Wilkinson handed him a small pocket dictionary, and a paper containing certain hieroglyphics. Mr. Botts—In the duplicate received by Dr. Bollman there is an erasure. Will you be so good as to explain the cause of it?

Gen. Wilkinson—That erasure was made by myself, and the words afterwards introduced by me. I have a deposition which will be more satisfactory than my own explanation. Mr. Botts—Whose deposition? *A.* Mr. Duncan's. [Mr. Wirt read the deposition of Mr. Duncan, for which see note H.] Mr. Botts—When was the erasure made? *A.* During the sitting of the Legislature in New Orleans. *Q.* When were the words restored? *A.* I cannot now state with certainty. *Q.* Was the letter exhibited to the Legislature? *A.* It was introduced, but I confined myself to oral communications. *Q.* What was the occasion of the erasure? *A.* To put it out of the power of a certain faction in the Legislature, to whom, at that time, I intended to submit the paper; to conceal it from that faction who were opposed to my measures, and who, I believed, were inimical to the true interests of their country, and were labouring to excite suspicions that I was connected with Col. Burr, in order to destroy the public confidence in me, and thus to defeat my measures. At the head of this faction I considered John Watkins, Esq. the Speaker. Having determined not so submit the letter, I restored the words. *Q.* Did you prepare any translation to submit to the Legislature? *A.* No. I only made notes. *Q.* Did you make a translation for any other purpose? *A.* Only a partial and imperfect one. *Q.* For what purpose? *A.* To understand it. *Q.* Was there any other occasion for which a translation was made? *A.* No. *Q.* Did you make any translation for the Executive? *A.* No. *Q.* Were those words, " your's post-marked 13th of May is received," erased? *A.* Yes. *Q.*

Where is the copy of your letter, covering a copy of that of Col. Burr, and your deposition to the President of the United States? *A.* It is among my papers. Mr. Hay—Do I understand you correctly, when I suppose you say, that the translation intended for the Legislature of New Orleans was sent to the President? *A.* No. [Mr. Hay immediately observed, that, on recollecting dates, he perceived that he had misunderstood General Wilkinson; that the letter was sent to the President before the session of the Legislature of New Orleans.] Mr. Botts—Do I understand you to say that this was *your* translation of the letter which was intended for the Legislature of New Orleans? *A.* No. It was Mr. Duncan's. Mr. Botts—Have you ever sworn that this was a true translation? *A.* No. Only substantially so. [General *Wilkinson*—May I be permitted to offer a few words of explanation? When Dr. *Bollman* was arrested, I will confess to you that I was so little acquainted with judicial proceedings, that I did not know it was necessary to do more than accompany him with a letter of advice. I was about to send him off in this way, when Mr. *Duncan* suggested to me the propriety of sending forward a deposition, to justify his commitment. I put the letter into the hands of Mr. *Duncan*, with the key; and he made out the interpretation. When Mr. *Duncan* presented the translation to me, I stated my objections to the omissions. He urged me to sign the deposition. The time was urgent; the express waiting; and I confess that I feared a rescue. This did not give me much time to consult my understanding. If I had, it is probable that I should have resisted the signing of the deposition, with those omissions, notwithstanding my confidence in the judgment and integrity of my counsel. I was, also, at the time, oppressed by domestic afflictions; and my mind was hurried and agitated by the painful and interesting scenes which surrounded me.

Mr. *Botts*—Were there variations between this original letter in cypher, and that sent on to the President? *A.* Yes. Mr. Botts—Were they noticed by you, or by Mr. Duncan in your presence? *A.* I suppose so; because I objected generally to the omissions.

Mr. *Wickham*—Have you ever accurately decyphered the letter sent to the President? *A.* No. I have said before that the only interpretation I ever made was hastily done at Natchitoches. Mr. *Wickham*—Then you are not able now to point out the difference between Mr. Duncan's translation and the original letter? *A.* Specifically I cannot; *substantially* I can. Such parts were left out as were calculated to inculpate me, for the reasons already stated.

NOTE No. 83.

AFFIDAVIT OF MR. A. L. DUNCAN.

DURING the commotions excited in New Orleans last winter by what was termed Colonel Burr's conspiracy, and his associates and accomplices in that place, I was called upon in my professional capacity by General Wilkinson, for counsel and advice in some measures which he was about to adopt. The temper and disposition which I had discovered in New Orleans, and the reports which daily reached that city from above, induced the belief that half measures were not suited to the times, and that the public safety required the exertion of extraordinary energies. I therefore urged the General repeatedly to the seizure of suspected persons, and the declaration of martial law. When Bollman was seized, I suggested to the General the expediency of transmitting with him a statement of facts, on oath, to justify the step, and to warrant his commitment. He then put the letters which he said were written to him by Colonel Burr, and which he also said were transmitted to him by Swartwout and Bollman, into my hands, on which, together with some further information and knowledge of their views which the General possessed, *I framed the deposition which accompanied Bollman, intentionally omitting every thing which was calculated to inculpate the General, or which might, by exciting suspicions, have a tendency to weaken his testimony.* Having prepared the deposition, I presented it to General Wilkinson, to be deposed to, who strongly and repeatedly objected to the omission I had made, and urged warmly that the whole should be introduced. He also desired that a declaration of Bollman, with which he frequently interlarded his conversations, should be entered, viz. " That he had come to New Orleans with views to the settlement of lands on the Ouachita, and was a mere spectator." And it was only after a full exposition of the sole objects of the document, that I could prevail on him to depose to it. It is idle and absurd to impute any sinister intention to the omission, because, on any trial which might ensue, it was known the original documents must be introduced, as they have been. I recollect, during the winter, Gen. Wilkinson was called before the Legislature of the territory to give an account of the state of public affairs, and he informed me he had intended to submit to their inspection Col. Burr's duplicate, *he having erased such parts as had been intended to implicate him*, as he knew several of the Members, and particularly the Speaker, to be interested in opposition to his measures, and for the promotion of such a state of things as was best calculated to favour Colonel Burr's enterprize. I understand that the erasure made on this duplicate was but partial, the General having determined to give oral information to the Legislature, which employed him two successive days; and that he considered the duplicate unimportant, (whilst the original has been preserved untouched) excepting the short paragraph relative to Bollman, which is preserved in its original state, and the only words erased, " your letter post-marked 13th " May is received," have been re-inserted in the General's own hand. On or about the 15th of August, since my arrival in this city, general Wilkinson put into my hands and those of J. L. Donaldson, Esq. four or five letters, observing to us, " I submit to you those letters, which I have " not examined since I left St. Louis; they are from Col. Burr. I do " not recollect their particular contents, but *having received them in con-* " *fidence, and knowing they blend personalities with politics, I have not permit-* " *ted myself to re-examine them, because I feel an insuperable repugnance to* " *violate the trust of any man.* I give them to you, here is the cypher, " decypher them, consider their contents well, and then inform me " whether their promulgation may be necessary to my honour." We did so, and we gave the General our opinion, that the promulgation might be necessary and proper. From an examination of those letters, and the *General's evident surprize, and prompt declaration of his ignorance, when we communicated certain passages of these letters, it was my own and Mr. Donaldson's opinion that he had but partially decyphered them.*

In answer to interrogatories on the part of Col. Burr, I recollect to have solicited the command of a party to Natchez, for the purpose of arresting Col. Burr, and discovered from the instructions which the General possessed, together with the state of things at that period, that the measure was warrantable; and having seen several communications from the government to General Wilkinson, and particularly that in reply to his letter of the 21st of October, I had no doubt of the sanction of government to any measures which were calculated to defeat the views of Col. Burr. I have seen communications of a confidential nature from the President to General Wilkinson, and I believe in reply to the General's letter of the 21st of October.

    (Signed   A. L. DUNCAN.

CITY OF RICHMOND, SCT.
Sworn to and subscribed, before me, this
  5th day of September, 1807.
   (Signed)   HENRY S. SHORE.

A true copy,   Teste,
  (Signed)   WILLIAM MARSHALL, Clerk.

NOTE No. 84.

MESSAGE from the President of the United States, communicating documents and information touching the official conduct of Brigadier-General James Wilkinson, in pursuance of a resolution of the House of Representatives of the 13th instant.—Read (January 20, 1808) and referred to Messrs. J. Montgomery, Nicholas, Upham, Smilie, Taylor, G. W. Campbell, and J. K. Smith.

TO THE HOUSE OF REPRESENTATIVES OF THE UNITED STATES.

SOME days previous to your resolutions of the 13th instant, a court of enquiry had been instituted, at the request of General Wilkinson, charged to make enquiry into his conduct, which the first resolution desires, and had commenced their proceedings. To the Judge Advocate of that court the papers and information on that subject, transmitted to me by the House of Representatives, have been delivered, to be used according to the rules and powers of that court.

The request of a communication of any information which may have been received at any time since the establishment of the present government, touching combinations with foreign agents for dismemberment of the Union, or the corrupt receipt of money by any officer of the United States from the agents of foreign governments, can be complied with but in a partial degree.

It is well understood, that in the first or second year of the presidency of General Washington, information was given to him relating to certain combinations with the agents of a foreign government, for the dismemberment of the Union; which combinations had taken place before the establishment of the present federal government. This information, however, is believed never to have been deposited in any public office, or left in that of the President's Secretary; these having been duly examined; but to have been considered as personally confidential, and therefore retained among his private papers. A communication from the Governor of Virginia to President Washington is found in the office of the President's Secretary, which, although not strictly within the terms of the request of the House of Representatives, is communicated, inasmuch as it may throw some light on the subjects of the correspondence of that time, between certain foreign agents and citizens of the United States.

In the first or second year of the administration of President Adams, Andrew Ellicott, then employed in designating, in conjunction with the Spanish authorities, the boundaries between the territories of the United States and of Spain, under the treaty with that nation, communicated to the Executive of the United States, papers and information respecting the subjects of the present enquiry, which were deposited in the office of State. Copies of these are now transmitted to the House of Representatives, except of a single letter and a reference from the said Andrew Ellicott, which, being expresly desired to be kept secret, is therefore not communicated; but its contents can be obtained from himself in a more legal form; and directions have been given to summon him to appear as a witness before the court of enquiry.

A paper, " on the commerce of Louisiana," bearing date the 18th of April, one thousand seven hundred and ninety-eight, is found in the office of state, supposed to have been communicated by Mr. Daniel Clark, of New Orleans, then a subject of Spain, and now of the House of Representatives of the United States, stating certain commercial transactions of General Wilkinson in New Orleans: an extract from this is now communicated, because it contains facts which may have some bearing on the question relating to him.

The destruction of the war office by fire, in the close of 1800, involved all information it contained at that date.

The papers already described, therefore, constitute the whole of the information on these subjects, deposited in the public offices, during the preceding administrations, as far as has yet been found; but it cannot be affirmed that there may be no other, because the papers of the offices being filed, for the most part, alphabetically, unless aided by the suggestion of any particular name which may have given such information, nothing short of a careful examination of the papers in the offices generally could authorise such an affirmation.

About a twelvemonth after I came to the administration of the government, Mr. Clark gave some verbal information to myself, as well as to the Secretary of State, relating to the same combinations for the dismemberment of the Union. He was listened to freely; and he then delivered the letter of Governor Gayoso, addressed to himself, of which a copy is now communicated. After his return to New Orleans he forwarded to the Secretary of State other papers, with a request that after perusal they should be burnt. This, however, was not done; and he was so informed by the Secretary of State, and that they should be held subject to his orders. These papers have not yet been found in the office. A letter therefore has been addressed to the former chief clerk, who may perhaps give information respecting them. As far as our memories enable us to say, they related only to the combinations before spoken of, and not at all to the corrupt receipt of money by any officer of the United States; consequently they respected what was considered as a dead matter, known to the preceding administrations, and, offering nothing new to call for investigations, which those nearest the dates of the transactions had not thought proper to institute.

In the course of the communications made to me on the subject of the conspiracy of Aaron Burr, I sometimes received letters, some of them anonymous, some under names true or false, expressing suspicions and insinuations against General Wilkinson. *But one only of them, and that anonymous, specified any particular fact*, and that fact was one of those which had been already communicated to a former administration.

No other information, within the purview of the request of the house, is known to have been received, by any department of the government, from the establishment of the present federal government. That which has been recently communicated to the House of Representatives, and by them to me, is the first direct testimony ever made known to me, charging General Wilkinson with a corrupt receipt of money; and the House of Representatives may be assured that the duties which this information devolves on me shall be exercised with vigorous impartiality. Should any want of power in the court to compel the rendering of testimony obstruct that full and impartial enquiry, which alone can establish guilt or innocence, and satisfy justice, the legislative authority only will be competent to the remedy.

TH: JEFFERSON.

January 20, 1808.

NOTE No. 85.

FRANCISCO DE RIANO'S AFFIDAVIT.

[TRANSLATION.]

I, the undersigned, do certify and declare, that about the end of the year 1797, the majority of the Cabildo of this city, of which I myself was a member, being desirous of electing for the office of Procurator Syndic (who is the person particularly charged with the interests of the people) a man whose character for firmness and integrity was well known, and who would not refuse to do his duty on account of the danger he might thereby incur, commissioned me to propose to Mr. Daniel Clark to accept this office, assuring him that he would have nine votes of the twelve of which the Cabildo was composed. In consequence of this resolution I made the proposal to Mr. Clark, stating to him at the same time, that the principal service which was expected of him was, that he should oblige Don Manuel Gayoso, then Governor, to account for the public monies which he had got into his possession. Mr. Clark requested me to return thanks to those who had requested me to make him this proposal, and to assure them, in his name, that he would accept the commission with the greatest pleasure, if they would dispense with his taking the oath of allegiance to the government, of which he was not looked on as a subject, although until then he had, through particular considerations, enjoyed its favour and protection. Having communicated his answer to the members, and perceived with sorrow that his objection was insurmountable, we made choice of another person to carry our views into execution.

New Orleans, 15 March, 1809.

(Signed)   FRANCISCO DE RIANO.

NOTE No. 86.

ANTONIO DE ARGOTE'S AFFIDAVIT.

[TRANSLATION.]

I, the undersigned, a resident since the year 1780 in the city of New Orleans, do certify and declare, that in the month of February, 1798, in consequence of some personal disagreement which took place between the Seignor Don Manuel Gayoso, then Governor of Louisiana, and Mr. Daniel Clark, jun. he (the Governor) compelled Daniel Clark, sen. the uncle of the said Clark, jun. to take from him his general power of attorney which he had given him to transact his business, stating that, as D. C. jun. was not a subject of Spain, he could not make use of that power in any affair before the tribunals of that nation, and that the uncle refused; and having set out for his plantation in the district of Natchez, the aforesaid Governor had him stopped by two armed dragoons, at some leagues from this city, and brought back to it, where he put him under arrest, until he agreed to the revocation of the aforesaid power of attorney, which was then given to me by the aforesaid Daniel Clark, sen. in the office of Don Carlos Xemenes, Notary Public, dated the 10th February, of the said year 1798, which I attest in due form, to answer the necessary purposes.

New Orleans, 7th April, 1809.

(Signed)   ANTONIO DE ARGOTE.

NOTE No. 87.

THOMAS JEFFERSON, PRESIDENT OF THE UNITED STATES OF AMERICA,

To all who shall see these presents, Greeting:

KNOW YE, That reposing special trust and confidence in the abilities and integrity of Daniel Clark, a citizen of the United States, resident at New Orleans, I have nominated, and by and with the advice and consent of the Senate, do appoint him Consul of the United States of America, for the port of New Orleans, and such other ports as shall be nearer thereto than to the residence of any other Consul or Vice-Consul of the United States within the same allegiance; and do authorise and empower him to HAVE and to HOLD the said office, and to exercise and enjoy all the rights, pre-eminences, privileges and authorities, to the same of right appertaining, during the pleasure of the President of the United States for the time being: He demanding and receiving no fees or perquisites of office whatever, which shall not be expressly established by some law of the said United States. And I do hereby enjoin all Captains, Masters and Commanders of ships and other vessels, armed or unarmed, sailing under the flag of the said States, as well as all other of their citizens, to acknowledge and consider him the said Daniel Clark accordingly. And I do hereby pray and request His Catholic Majesty, his Governors and Officers, to permit the said Daniel Clark fully and peaceably to enjoy and exercise the said office, without giving, or suffering to be given unto him, any molestation or trouble; but on the contrary to afford him all proper countenance and assistance; I offering to do the same for all those who shall in like manner be recommended to me by his said Catholic Majesty.

IN TESTIMONY WHEREOF, I have caused these letters to be made Patent, and the Seal of the United States to be hereunto affixed.

[L.S.] GIVEN under my Hand, at the City of Washington, the twenty-sixth day of January, in the year of our Lord one thousand eight hundred and two; and of the Independence of the United States of America the twenty-sixth.

TH: JEFFERSON.

BY THE PRESIDENT,
JAMES MADISON,
Secretary of State.

NOTE No. 88.

Extract of a letter from Daniel Clark, to the Secretary of State, dated New-Orleans, March 8, 1803.

AS a proof that expectations of assistance from ourselves against our own government have been always relied on by the Spaniards, and that they have constantly looked to a divulsion of our western states from the general government, I now forward you an order to receive from Washington Morton, Esq. of New-York, a sealed packet which I left in his possession when I set out for Europe, and which I then mentioned I would shew you at my return, not thinking at that time that circumstances would occur so soon as to render the disclosure a measure of immediate necessity. Among other papers of less importance in this packet is a small part of the correspondence of the Baron de Carondelet with the officer commanding fort St. Ferdinand, at the Chickasaw Bluffs, in which he suffers his plans and views to be clearly perceived, and which were solely aimed at our destruction ; the remainder are, as well as I recollect, copies of talks and letters to and from the Chickasaw Indians ; and, by the Baron de Carondelet's letter to the officer, you will perceive that the fact I advised you of, respecting the annual pension of five hundred dollars to Uguluycabe cannot be disputed.

Should you think these documents of sufficient importance to require my presence in Washington, to elucidate any part of them, I shall immediately sacrifice all private business of my own, and hasten there ; and, in the mean time, will endeavour to collect from undoubted sources such other information relative to this subject as may be acceptable.

Although for four or five years past I had a perfect conviction that the intrigues of the Spaniards with the western country were not for the time dangerous, on account of the incapacity of the Governors of of this province, and their want of pecuniary means ; yet, fearful of what might happen in future, should more enlightened and ambitious chiefs preside over it, I could not last year resist the temptation of hinting my suspicions of what had been *formerly* done in this way to the President, at an interview with which he honoured me, and I even went so far as to assert that a person, supposed to be an agent from the state of Kentucky, had been here in the end of 1795 and beginning of 1796, to negociate on the part of that state, independent of the general government, for the navigation of the Missisippi, before the result of the treaty of St. Lorenzo was known, wishing that this hint might induce the President to cause enquiry to be made into the circumstance, which he could easily find the means of investigating ; but, as he made no other enquiry of me respecting it than merely in what year the thing happened, it then struck me that he must have had other information on the subject, and that he thought it needless to hear any thing more about it. By great accident I have lately learned something which induces me to suppose that any information he may have received respecting the measure alluded to has been incorrect, and given with the view of misleading him, and I request you will mention the subject anew to him, that you may know how far I am right in my suspicions. The information I possessed on the subject, could not, from the way in which it was obtained, be accompanied with what would be proof to convict the person concerned, or I should have openly accused him in the face of the world; but to me it amounts to a moral certainty of his guilt, and my conduct to him shewed, on all occasions, how much I detested his object and his person. The same want of proof positive, sufficient to convict him, prevents me at present from naming him; but if enquiry is diligently made about the influential character from Kentucky, who at that period was so long in Natchez, and afterwards here, what his business was, and what was the idea entertained of him, enough will doubtless be discovered to put our government on its guard against him and others of his stamp, and against all foreign machinations in that quarter in future.

NOTE No 89.

New Orleans, 24th January, 1804.

SIR,

SINCE the arrival of our Commissioners in this city, when my functions as Consul ceased, by possession of the province being given to them, I have forborne to write to you, persuaded there would be no further need of any communications from me, as they could be more satisfactorily made by them. But in justification of my conduct, and in proof of what I have constantly asserted were the views of the French government and of the Prefect, with respect to the U. S. had they once got firmly established here, I think it necessary to intrude once more on you, and mention that, at an entertainment given to our Commissioners by Monsieur Laussat, he unreservedly informed Governor Claiborne that Bonaparte, previous to the departure of General Victor from Paris, had told him, that he might count on a war with Great-Britain, in less than twelve months after his arrival in Louisiana, and that he must, immediately after a knowledge of that event, take possession of Canada. When asked by the Governor how he was to get there? the reply was, through your country: our plan was, to take post on the Lakes, and with this view we should have cantoned the major part of our forces in Upper Louisiana, to have them always in readiness. He added, that England had a right to half the waters of these Lakes, and there was no way of drawing a line on the water, to separate the two nations; and as she had a right to the navigation, she of necessity must be entitled to make use of the shores for her safety; and therefore France had a right to occupy them, and would have done so, to dispossess the English, without its being possible for the U. S. to prevent them. He alluded to a conversation he held with Gen. Dayton, who had represented to him the impossibility of our living on friendly terms with France, if she possessed Louisiana, as she would attempt the dismemberment of our country, and said he could not deny but such would be her policy; that it was not however their fault, but that of the *mountains*, which were the natural boundary of the U. S. He further confessed having mentioned his utter disbelief of the success of Mr. Munroe's mission, till officially advised by his own government; and said, that had it not been for the situation of affairs in Europe, Mr. Munroe would not have *dared* to propose the cession of Louisiana to the U. S. even after his arrival in Paris. He boasted of the facility, with which he could have defended this country against all the force of the U. S. had he only 7000 French troops; and ridiculed the idea of our attempt to dispossess him, as he said we were unacquainted with grand movements, and unable to defray the expences they would occasion, with many other remarks of a similar nature. I was surprised at these communications, as I knew no good purpose they could possibly answer, and for the truth of them refer you to the Governor himself, who could not easily get over the impression they made on him. He came to this country much prejudiced in favour of the Prefect, but I believe he is by this time very desirous of getting fairly rid of him, and convinced that the differences formerly subsisting between Laussat and myself did not proceed from any fault of mine, but from the violence and impetuosity of his temper, which led him very frequently to speak of our country and its government in a manner so disrespectful, as could not be borne by a person holding a commission under it. As his language and conduct changed, so did mine; with respect to him, and his dispatches to Mr. Pichon, as well as in his communications to our Commissioners and the public here, he has given ample testimony of the satisfaction he experienced in my co-operation, and the assistance I afforded him; and I may even flatter myself that it contributed more than all his own measures to preserve good order and tranquility during his short administration. To our own Commissioners I have given every possible aid and assistance, whenever it could be useful, and shall continue to do so while my services can avail them. They have many difficulties to encounter, and some of those which I have long foreseen now present themselves.

On these subjects, however, as they do not regard me, I shall be silent; but I take the liberty to suggest to you the necessity of making some immediate regulations with respect to the shipping owned by the citizens of the country, and having the revenue system put in force here in the same manner as in the U. S. as the payment of duties on our exports (especially to the U. S.) causes universal dissatisfaction, and the people complain that in this respect they are placed in a worse situation than when subjects of Spain, for under her government imports from thence and exports to the mother country paid no duty whatever, and to her colonies but two per cent. and imports from them nothing. They have an idea, that the government of the U S. having put itself in the place of Spain, imports from and exports to them should be free of duty; that it was so contemplated by our government, but misunderstood by the Collector; and on these subjects a petition has been forwarded, through the Governor, to Congress, which, if attended to, will produce a great effect, and the sums to be returned will be trifling. The Collector has mentioned to me his intention of representing to the Secretary of the Treasury the propriety of complying with the wishes of the people in this particular, and with your assistance, I presume there would be no difficulty in accomplishing it. The shipping belonging to the port, formerly entitled to Spanish registers, are deprived of these documents, and, not being hitherto furnished with American papers, are laid up, to the prejudice of their owners, who, had they been inclined to emigrate to other Spanish colonies, instead of remaining citizens of the U. S. would have their vessels employed, and every favour and indulgence shewn them by the officers of the Spanish government; and it is to be hoped this conduct will not be productive of injury to them.

I remain, &c.

The Hon. JAMES MADISON.

NOTE No. 90.

Washington, February 10th, 1804.

DEAR SIR,

THE inclosed letter was sent to me by Mrs. Clark, with a request that it might be forwarded to you.

I take this occasion of congratulating you on the successful termination of the measures for placing Louisiana in our hands, and of repeating my acknowledgments for the active and useful services which you have rendered on the occasion. The bill providing a government for this acquisition has not yet passed through Congress. The novelty of the circumstances, added to the nature of the subject, has given rise to an unusual diversity of opinions and length of discussion.

The papers which you were so good as to transfer into my hands from those of Mr. Morton, of New-York, remain subject to your orders. Shall I forward them to you, and how? or is there any other disposition of them that would be preferred by you. I remain, Sir, with much esteem, Your obedient servant,

JAMES MADISON.

NOTE No. 91.

Bayou Sarah, M. T. 15th March, 1804.

SIR,

I HAVE been favoured this day with your letter of the 10th ult. and am thankful for your kindness in forwarding its enclosure.

I feel myself obliged by your mention of my services. They were due, and were willingly rendered; for I flattered myself that the inhabitants of Louisiana would be rendered happy by the change. If they have become discontented, and feel uneasy in their present situation, after being enthusiasts in favour of our government, you will probably ere this have learned the cause, through other channels.

The papers you mention to have received from Mr. Morton were perhaps imprudently intruded on you; but I wished you, from them, to have a proof of what was formerly transacting. As things have so fortunately terminated, and they can be of no further use, I take the liberty of requesting you to burn the whole, in order that you may be put to no further inconvenience by them. I have the honour to remain, very respectfully, Sir,

Your most obedient servant,

JAMES MADISON, ESQ.

NOTE No. 92.

SIR,

IF I had as much confidence in the attachments of your friends towards you, as they make claim to, I should not address you this letter. But I have not; and the subject is too important to be pretermitted.

The dangers I fear may be trivial or distant, but as on the other hand they may be near and momentous, and in such case your being early apprised of them highly important, it is a duty I owe you, as the chief of my government, to give you timely hints, whereby you may forestal the dangers, and bring the traitors to punishment in due season.

Spanish intrigues have been carried on among our people. We have traitors among us.

A separation of the Union in favour of Spain is the object *finally*. I know not what are the means.

I am told, that Mr. Ellicot, in his journal, communicated to the office of state the names of the Americans concerned.

If this be true, you are long since guarded; but I suspect either that it is not, or has escaped you; or you have considered the affair dead; BECAUSE YOU HAVE APPOINTED GENERAL WILKINSON AS GOVERNOR OF ST. LOUIS, WHO, I AM CONVINCED, HAS BEEN FOR YEARS, AND NOW IS, A PENSIONER OF SPAIN. SHOULD YOU ASK ME TO PROVE IT, I MUST RESORT TO AN EXTENSIVE CHAIN OF CIRCUMSTANCES, WHICH, SEPARATELY, SEEM SMALL AND INCONCLUSIVE; and to informations I have received from various persons and sources, which, perhaps, I have not a right to refer to; nor is it necessary. An hint is all you want; and due enquiry will ascertain and develope the whole matter and partners.

A very exalted magistrate of this country has lately drawn on Spain for his pension: of this I have the most unquestionable testimony. Before this was told to me, I was laid under an injunction of secrecy; but I abhor such confidence, and told my informant (who is a man of integrity) that I would let you know of it, though I would not, unless it would become necessary, make known the name of the magistrate. If you find it necessary, and command me, it shall be instantly communicated, and my name given up. But you will scarce think it right to spring the mine, before you have laid your train.

This plot is laid wider than you imagine. Mention the subject to no man from the Western Country, however high in office he may be. Some of them are deeply tainted with this treason. I hate duplicity of expression; but on this subject I am not authorised to be explicit; nor is it necessary. You will dispatch some fit person into the Orleans country, to enquire, having with him letters from the suspected gentlemen, and he can fully and easily develope the whole business. It is enough that I put you on your guard.

If you desire it, I will enclose you a schedule of the names of the suspected persons.

Do not think this a slight advertisement. If you do, and launch into a Spanish war, you may most heartily wish you had treated it more seriously. May be, the out come of this matter may explain the pertinacity and forwardness of the Spaniards in going to war with us.

In case of such a war, let neither the first nor second in command be appointed out of the western country.

No one existing knows of this letter or its contents, and I design it to be strictly secret with you. If, however, you, in your discretion, should wish it to be seen by Mr. Madison and Mr. Gallatin, I give you leave to show it, under unexceptionable injunctions of silence; and I confide that you will not use it otherwise than I direct, though you do not assent to my restrictions. Depend on it you have traitors around you, to give the alarm in time to their friends. If I am alarmed at trivial dangers, I must make it up some time hence, by being unmoved when the danger is real.

It would be gratifying to me to know that this letter was received, and how far the discretionary power of communication had been or would be exercised. I am, Sir, very respectfully,

Your most obedient servant,

JOSEPH HAMILTON DAVEISS.

Cornland (near the Yellow Banks) 10th Jan. 1806.
His Excel. TH. JEFFFRSON,
President of the United States.

NOTE No. 93.

Washington, Feb. 15, 1806.

SIR,

YOUR *letter of January* 10 *came safely to hand a week ago.* According to your permission it has been communicated to Mr. Madison and Mr. Gallatin. I have also communicated it to General Dearborne, because one of the persons named by you is particularly under his observation; so far it was necessary, and not further. I will be responsible for its secrecy. The information is so important, that it is my duty to request a full communication of every thing known or heard by you relating to it, and particularly of the names of all persons, whether engaged in the combination, or witnesses to any part of it, at the same time I pledge myself to you that it shall be known no further than it now is, until it shall become necessary to place them in the hands of the law; and that even then no unnecessary communication shall be made of the channel through which we receive our information.

You will be sensible that the names are peculiarly important to prevent a misplacing of our confidence, either in the investigation of this subject particularly, or in the general trust of public affairs. In hopes of hearing from you without delay, I pray you to accept my salutations and assurances of great respect.

Tн: JEFFERSON.

Mr. Daveiss.

NOTE No. 94.

Sir,

THE post has arrived, but brings no letter from you. Can it be possible that my two letters, of the 10th of January, and 10th of February, have miscarried? If either has failed, every further attempt of mine will be abortive. I pray you inform me only of this point, by a letter to me at the Yellow Banks' post office, without delay; for I am now determined to raise money upon my own credit, and pursue my enquiries into this matter—confident, that if my government will give me no aid, it will throw no obstacles in my way. If you deem my information too trival to be noticed by the chief of a great nation, you will surely, nevertheless, be just enough to me, to keep it inviolably secret, till I return from my present pursuit. Every day gives me new causes to confide in the justness of my impressions and opinions on this matter; and to make it more probable, that to this source is to be traced the eagerness of the Spaniards for war.

This day I have seen the very man, through whom Wilkinson, for a long time, carried on his correspondence with the Spanish government, clandestinely. And he knows of Philip Nolan, the great horse trader, bringing several kegs of dollars to fort Washington, for that gentleman.

But this gentleman, my informant, will not suffer his name to be mentioned; so the information cannot assume the shape of legal evidence although it may serve to satisfy your mind.

The man I knew for many years. His integrity is wholly unquestionable.

JOSEPH HAMILTON DAVEISS.

Now at Frankfort, 5th of March, 1806.
His Excellency Tн: Jefferson.

NOTE No. 95.

Extract of a letter from J. H. Daveiss to Mr. Jefferson, dated March 28th, 1806.

" AT date of my last I had learned much new matter on this subject: I now know more; and as you desire a full and free communication, I shall proceed without the least apprehension of a disclosure, giving you full permission whenever you find it needful to give up my name, warning me at the same time thereof. *The man alluded to in my last, through whom Wilkinson carried on his correspondence with the Spanish government, would not let me give up his name: he is a man of as high standing for integrity, as any other in the world. The correspondence was addressed to the Secretary, whose plain name, stripped of all titles, is Gilbert Leonard, the son of a shoemaker, who by his great talents raised himself to so high a function.*

" *The plot began between Wilkinson and Governor Miro. Owings, who was killed coming up the river, had six thousand dollars of Wilkinson's money, and seven thousand dollars were shipped to the port of Philadelphia. Nolan the the great horse trader brought several kegs of dollars to Fort Wasington for him; and in the hearing of one of my informants, who he was then very fond of, he used to say that Governor Miro and him had agreed to lay up a few thousand dollars for a time of need, and this was the first of that money, alluding to the kegs.—As to the two first sums he told another gentleman that he was thought by Wayne and his party to be very poor, but he was not, for he had thirteen thousand dollars. This was before the shipment of it from Orleans.*

" I find that in the Convention of 1788, at Danville, he *(Wilkinson)* rose and proposed a separation and Union with Spain to that body, (this was the convention who proposed a separation) and   the senator rose, and in a short speech supported Wilkinson, saying, " that " he had it from the highest authority, that if we would join Spain, " we might have any thing we pleased, and any kind of trade we want- " ed." Wilkinson then read almost a quire of paper, which he called a letter, written by him to the Governor at Orleans; and read the Governor's answer, to corroborate what he and   had said; but it was so badly received, that it was dropped, and its being spoken of since is much resented by its friends, as an imputation on them.

         is my informant, and I am going to get the journals of that body, to copy off the names of the members, to be used when necessary.   was the first mover of this business here, and wrote many letters to the influential men here, to draw them into the measure. When he offered for Congress winter before last, I published this, and offered that my fortune should stand responsible, if it was slander, and offered to prove his treasonable correspondence with Gardoqui for this purpose. One of the members opposed to   came to me, to know if he might give up my name—I gave him leave, and he went all over town and told it—but, dont be startled—   did not lose one vote by it; nor was I ever called on.

"This was very astonishing, and filled me with the utmost concern. How wonderfully numerous the friends or neutrals of this infernal scheme!!!

"You will see what a hurricane they will blow up round my ears when I come back.

"Judge Sebastian, of our Court of Appeals, is the man who drew lately on Spain for his pension. Mr.   saw the draft, and knows his hand well. It was in favour of John A Seitz, of Lexington, and payable to him. Seitz died there, and this paper was in his pocket-book, and is still there, and   will by draft order its delivery to me when I get there.   and   are pensioned without doubt.

"I fully expect some are the friends of these traitors, who are not pensioned, and several such persons are named to you heretofore.

"Alas! that men so highly raised by their country in trust and honour should thus betray her.

"If I am suspected, the chances of my getting back are very slender.

"I observe that the Marquis Cassa Calvo and all the Spanish officers are prohibited from crossing the lines. It might be well, if reasons of state would permit, to relax this, so as to allow that gentleman to come to Natchez. I would much rather see him there, than go into the Spanish government to do it;—and at Orleans   would give him warning of me immediately.

"I wish to see one   below Orleans. He commanded the boat which was searched by Secretary Steele, at Natchez, some years ago. He says, had Steele looked into a bucket on the top of the boat, containing old tobacco, he would have found papers enough to hang Wilkinson and himself.

"I feel greatly strengthened by having the support of government, and freely apologize for any expressions of despondency or doubt on that subject in my last letter.

"I am, Sir, very respectfully,

"JOSEPH H. DAVEISS."

NOTE No. 96.

Extract of a letter from J. H. Daveiss, to Mr. Jefferson, dated March 29th, 1806.

" Perhaps you are surprized at my speaking, in the other letter, so highly of the integrity of him, through whom General Wilkinson so long carried on his correspondence with Spain. I asked him to explain it. He said he thought the thing at that time a mere *fetch* of Wilkinson's, to get money, and had no idea of any serious result from it; and besides, he himself had no sort of participation in it, but only afforded conveyance for the letters.

" It was a bad excuse; but might be deemed by many an honest man a good one.

" Some years ago, H. the son of ———, (of Baltimore) came to an intimate friend and relation of his, and told him that he (H.) had been offered 2000 dollars for his trouble in circulating 6000 dollars; and asked ——— if he would take a part of it. ——— enquired what was the object in circulating the 6000 dollars, and was told it was to make friends to the king of Spain, who should mark the public tone and report it. ——— told him to have nothing at all to do with it.

" I said, in May last, that many knew of these treasonable doings who had no pensions. It may turn out that ——— and ——— are of these. I have no doubt the first knew of all Wilkinson's doings, and I have heard, but dare not enquire now, that ——— sent the murderers of Owings to Wilkinson, at fort Washington. The second, I am confident, knew well of the treason at first, I don't know how it is lately. He knew all about the 100,000 dollars."

NOTE No. 97.

Extract of a letter from J. H. Daveiss, to Mr. Jefferson, dated Cornland, near the Yellow Banks, 21st April, 1806.

" If you chance to hear any thing about a Captain Collins (of Florida) attend to it. This man has been a very active agent for Wilkinson. He carried the 7000 dollars to Philadelphia for Wilkinson; and is the man whom he sent as a spy round by Canada; and a long story was told about his being captured by the Indians, and the many hardships he suffered. I think it likely you'll find some report of Wilkinson's on this subject in the war office, unless it was burned. But from the information I have received from a gentleman, who I know does not go on light conjectures, I fully believe that this man was sent to Col. England, of Detroit, on a very friendly mission; being at that time in the pay of Great-Britain. If Newman is living in the southward, *as is said,* I have no doubt it may be proved that Wilkinson is the man who *sent him to the Indians, to warn them of the approach of Wayne's army."*

NOTE No 98.

Monticello, September 12, 1806.

SIR,

YOUR letter of Aug. 14 has been just received. The first, of Jan. 10, was acknowledged in mine of Feb. 15. After that, those of Feb. 10, March 5, April 5, and 21, came in due time. As their matter did not require answer, their acknowledgment was postponed, to avoid the suspicions of which you seemed to be aware, as well as to await your return from the journey you had undertaken. The acknowledgments of their receipts is now therefore made, to relieve you from any anxiety respecting their safety; and you may rely on the most inviolable secrecy as to the past and any future communications you may think proper to make. Your letters are not filed in the offices; but will be kept among my private papers.

Accept my salutations, and assurances of respect,

TH: JEFFERSON.

J. H. DAVEISS, Esq.

NOTE No. 99.

Lancaster, January 31st, 1808.

DEAR SIR,

LAST night a paper printed by Mr. Binns, of Philadelphia, was handed to me, in which I observed a number of my communications to the Department of State. These communications are perfectly nugatory, not being accompanied by the documents referred to. Why those documents have been withheld I cannot conceive. Mr. Eppes's resolution, so far as I had any agency in the business, appeared to remove the injunction of secrecy. Under this impression I forwarded a letter to General Wilkinson, a copy of which you will find enclosed, and which you have my permission to communicate confidentially to Mr. Randolph.

I am, Sir,

Your sincere friend, and

Humble servant,

(Signed)   ANDREW ELLICOTT.

HON. DANIEL CLARK, ESQ.

Postscript.

SINCE the preceding pages were sent to the press, some documents have been received, which are calculated to strengthen some of the charges. The first is a letter from Mr. Collins, stating the sum which he received for general Wilkinson, and the precise period at which it was paid to him. [Note A.]

The next is a letter lately received, from Mr. Beverly Chew, at Amsterdam, stating, that a Spanish officer of high rank, a near connexion of governor Miro's, had asserted the fact of Wilkinson's actually holding a *commission in the Spanish army*, at a public table in Paris, and asserted it as coming within his own knowledge. [Note B.]—Americans! your disgrace has become the table talk of Europe—your Commander in Chief not only a pensioner, but holding a commission, *subject to the orders* of a foreign power!——How long is this to be endured?

My next supplementary document is drawn from the cabinet of an intelligent foreign minister. It may be supposed, that, during the preparations of colonel Burr, Mr. Yrujo was not a disinterested spectator. He was busily employed in collecting intelligence for his court; and on the 18th December, 1806, wrote a dispatch, of which an extract is contained in [Note C.] This proves the former connexion of W. with Spain, since he was " *well known as No.* 13"—it proves the idea that was entertained of his connexion with Burr— and contains some shrewd conjectures as to the nature and tendency of his movements. I also add a letter, which, tho' no testimony in itself, will direct the researches of government to the person from whom it may be obtained. [Note D.]

[E.] is a letter from Laussat, the French Prefect, written soon after we had taken possession of Louisiana. It shews what he thought of the subject of the present discussion, and that, as a husband is sometimes the last to hear of his own dishonour, so no one but the President of the United States was ignorant of the infamy of the commander of his armies. I have not the original of this letter. It was, however, seen by governor Claiborne, and the translation can be proved to be true.

I will not close this publication, without doing an act of justice to the characters of two gentlemen, whose names are mentioned in some of my documents. Mr. H. Innes and Mr. G. Nicholas were applied to, in order to engage them in the Spanish interest. A copy of their answer is annexed, [Note F.] and shews the manner in which this proposition was received.

I have already shewn, that while Wilkinson was flattering governor Claiborne and Mr. Jefferson, he spoke of the one as a *fool,* and the other as his " *con-* " *temptible fabricator.* The two letters [G. and H.] will give those gentlemen his real opinion of them ;—and if they do not please quite as much as the incense he now offers, they will at least put them on their guard against adulations, which may endanger the safety of a nation.

I omitted also a reference to the declaration of Mr. Newman, which he published some time since in the Berkley Intelligencer. [Note I.] It strongly corroborates Mr. Power's testimony, throws great light on the whole transaction, and adds one more to the list of witnesses, upon whom the government may call, whenever they choose to lay open this maze of iniquity.

New Orleans, May 1*st,* 1809.

NOTES,

REFERRED TO IN THE POSTSCRIPT.

[A.]

Paskagoula, 10th *of March*, 1809.

DEAR SIR,

I RETURNED yesterday from Mobile and Pensacola, and found your letter of the 19th of February last, requesting me to send you the date I received the money from Don Gilberto Leonard, in New Orleans; therefore have had recourse to my journal round the Florida Point. I find that we left Bayou St. John on the 22d of August, 1794, and must have received the 6334 dollars about the 19th or 20th of August the same month. I am,

Your very humble servant,
JOSEPH COLLINS.

Mr. DANIEL CLARK.

[B.]

Extract of a letter from Mr. Beverly Chew, of New Orleans, dated Amsterdam, 4th October, 1808, to his partner, Richard Relf.

" I have read, with the deep interest you can readily imagine, the publication of our respected friend, D. Clark, Esq. in the National Intelligencer of April, in his own defence, against the pompous, vain and false assertions of Wilkinson. I feel perfectly easy under the conviction that he will produce such a cloud of evidence in support of his own testimony, that incredulity itself cannot doubt of the criminality of Wilkinson. It may be useful to mention, that while at Paris I was informed that General Pontalba * had, at a dinner where there was a

---

* *General Pontalba married the niece of Governor Miro, who was the person by whose means Wilkinson entered into his arrangements with the Spanish government. Pontalba was a Colonel in the Spanish service in the time of Carondelet, and in his confidence. Every thing was known to him.*

large company, stated, that he had seen, and held in his hands, a commission of Wilkinson as a Spanish officer. Mr. Skipwith, who goes home in the Hope, was present, and can testify to the above effect, if required. M. Reynes told me that it was generally understood among the Spaniards at New Orleans, that Wilkinson was a Spanish pensioner, and that he had, on a particular occasion, insinuated the same to Wilkinson, who, far from being hurt, only laughed at it."

[C.]

Extract of a dispatch from M. Yrujo to Don Pedro Cevallos, dated December 18th, 1806.—Translated and certified by Peter S. Duponceau, Esq.

" IN order to put Congress more completely under the impossibility of taking such measures, Wilkinson, who undoubtedly acts in concert with Burr, has, under the pretence of danger on the frontier of Texas, endeavoured to draw all the disposable force of the U. S. to that distant point; and in order that orders should not be given to weaken his little army, he is clearly inventing incidents to keep it together. We were informed some time ago that he had dismissed all the militia which had been sent to him from the Missisippi Territory, from New Orleans, *Atacapas*, and Opelousas, in consequence of a convention that he had made with the Spanish commandant, that the latter should withdraw to the westward of the Sabine, that the American troops should withdraw in the same manner to Natchitoches, and that the territory in controversy should be completely evacuated by both parties, until its fate should be decided on by negociation. By the last news from that country we are informed that General Wilkinson, well known by the number 13, instead of acting as by the said convention it was to have been expected, and affecting great zeal for the rights of the United States, was going to advance with his little army as far as the river Sabine, on the eastern bank of which he intended to erect a fort. This movement must have produced fresh embarrassments, at least in appearance. The Spanish commandant, it was said, was going to oppose himself to Wilkinson's resolution, and in this manner a kind of crisis has been produced, by means of which the federal government will not dare to diminish his force, by drawing them to other points. From all this it results, that the small effective force of the United States will in fact be of no use to them, to prevent or to counteract the movements of Burr, and that he will have free scope for all his operations at the outset, flattering himself, no doubt, that he will be able, by the influence of the commander in chief, and by the offers which he may make to the troops of double rations, grants of lands, and other temptations of the same nature, to bring them over to his party. In this situation of things, the United States have no resource left but the militia; that of the adjoining states, except a part of that of Kentucky, will be directed by Burr, instead of acting against him; and that of the Atlantic states will not be willing to go in the depth of winter to so great a distance, to fight against their fellow-citizens, who, according to the principles laid down in the declaration of the independence of this country, have the same right to separate themselves, which these colonies had to sever the political bands which united them to England. By this means we may perceive the motives which may have induced Burr to levy a considerable armed force, to purchase provisions, and, in one word, we find a key to all the apparently inconsistent movements of General Wilkinson."

[D.]

New Orleans, January 13th, 1809

DANIEL CLARK, Esq.
    SIR,

ON my way to Kentucky, some time in August, 1807, I called on Captain John Chiles, of Jessamine county, Kentucky, and while in his company, he, the said Chiles, informed me that he had been at a public dinner at Travellers' Hall, in Lexington, some time in July. At dinner, the late Colonel Pain, of Scott county, espoused the cause of General James Wilkinson, and said different things in favour of said Wilkinson. To which Captain Chiles observed—Colonel Pain, if you knew as much of General Wilkinson as I do, you would think differently.——Aye, said Colonel P. what do you know of General W.?—— To which Captain C. observed—About seventeen years past I was in Frankford, and being an old acquaintance of General W. he invited me to his house, and while in his company there he informed me that he had something of high importance to communicate to me, and that he wished me to engage in the plan, which was to sever the Union. He, the said W. offered me 2000 dollars, if I would take an active part in the plan; and further observed, that he was authorised so to do by the government of Spain. I then asked General W. if this would not be the cause of a great deal of bloodshed?—Oh! damn them, said he, what do we care, so we get our ends answered. To which I replied, that I would not be the cause of one innocent man's blood being spilt, for all the wealth of Peru. To which General W. replied, that General S. and Colonel C. had sanctioned the measures, and that the Eastern States had treated the Western States very improper with respect to the trade of Missisippi. I made my apology to General W. and mounted my horse and rode to General S. and informed him what General W. had said. He, General S. observed, that it was a damn'd lye; and if he heard of General W. taking those liberties with him again, that he would shoot him. I then went to Colonel C. whose reply was much the same. Finding that things were not in so alarming a situation as I had thought them, I returned home. Some time afterwards I saw General W. in Danville, and he observed to me, that he had found his plans would not answer, and requested me not to expose him, which I have not made known to any person for seventeen years. I am, Sir, with sentiments of respect,

Your obedient servant,
LEWIS CRAIG, JUNIOR.

[E.]

MR. LAUSSATT, in his letter to the Minister, says—" I ought, in taking my leave of Louisiana, to acquaint your Excellency with the state of the public mind, and of its general character. The President of the United States, pressed to take an hasty possession of this country, appointed two men, the nearest at hand, of note, as Commissioners— Mr. Claiborne, Governor of the Missisippi Territory, and General Wilkinson, Brigadier, and commander of the 3000 men, that composes the land forces of the United States. The first a man of very little means, and still less character. The latter, a man who passes three quarters of his time in wine, committing many weak (étourderies) and inconsistent actions, and generally known to have been subsidized by Baron Carondelet, when he wished to disturb the United States in the early settlement of their western country. The inhabitants, who were at first bore away by the flattering hopes of an imaginary liberty, have now discovered the illusive charms, and the more they become acquainted with their new masters, the more they dislike them, and all their affections are returning towards the mother country. The Governor shews a childish preference for his native countrymen; hence discontent, jealousies and disgust—which was first manifested at the public ball, (attended by the first society.) The dispute originated about a country dance, whether they should have the English country dance so much liked by the Americans; the Creoles prefered the French country dance. Violins broken, the ladies frightened and run away, some leaping from the windows, disputes, threats and challenges followed. At length a number of American seamen, disguised in the Kentucky dress, were brought in, headed by a fire brand (fier bras) who formerly served in our revolutionary war at St. Domingo, and now Captain of the port, assaulted the young men with fists and clubs. Let your Excellency now behold our national character; a few young Frenchmen, joined by a handful of young Creoles, repulsed these bravadoes, and held their ground when the ball closed, and all this passing in the presence of the American Commissioners.

The American Commissioners now endeavour to cast the odium of these transactions, or what they term *passe volants*, on the French lately arrived from our colonies. They have written to me again and again, complaining of this conduct. I have investigated the whole affair with care, and am well convinced of the falsehood of their charges; and in my answer to them have fully and victoriously removed this their only resource to reflect on our countrymen. As to myself, I keep quite retired, and a silent spectator, and know every thing, and am dumb.

The Creoles and French established in the country all unite in favour of France, nor can you persuade them that the convention for the cession of this country is but a political trick, and that at peace it will again return under the dominion of France. Neither the American ; with all their means and sarcasms, nor their hired politicians to satyrize the French government, alter in the least their belief. *Oh! let Bonaparte go on, every thing will come right at peace, reply the Creoles.* At one time there is a report that Canada is revolted, at another that 50,000 men are landed in Ireland, and then that the descent on England has actually taken place, and now say they we shall soon behold the tricolour flag floating on the banks of the Missisippi. Although these are but the fanciful dreams of the imagination, I think it my duty to impart them to your Excellency, that the government may learn, from its proper agent on the spot, the true dispositions and character of the people they have so lately lost. As for myself, I can say that I am free from prejudice, being about to quit the country, never again to revisit it. I can say, with truth, that I have received the most flattering marks of friendship from all classes, both for my person and for our common country.

The Americans here are of the character and manners of the Chinese, extremely jealous of their new acquisition. The most trifling circumstance is sufficient to create in them the greatest alarm.

The Spanish Commissioners take advantage of the three months allowed them by treaty to evacuate the country, but a part of their troops have been sent away. The American Commissioners have written to me, in the most pressing manner, to cause the complete evacuation of the French and Spanish forces—It is thus they speak in their communications, applicable to I know not what. I have transmitted their demand to the Spanish Commissioners, who promise to hasten the departure of their troops as soon as possible. The time already consumed is much longer than I could wish. My own presence has become the cause of great uneasiness and ill humour to these gentlemen. They have become very importunate to gain possession of the arsenal and public stores, still retained by the Spaniards. They have behaved most basely towards the brig Express, bringing the last evacuation of our military hospital at Cape St. Nicholas Mole. They could discover nothing but a fresh cause of alarm at the arrival of about fifty of these unfortunate convalescents, about to make a descent. Rumours were industriously circulated, that they were infected with the yellow fever, plague, &c.

The brig was not permitted to come up to town, but to drop anchor at the bottom of the river, without conveniences or refreshments, in the most unhealthy situation, amongst the marshes, along while without tents, or even a hut to shelter them from the inclemency of the weather; and notwithstanding all my exertions to procure a remedy, I was only answered by some fine dissertations on the rights of humanity and laws of nations.

The Americans have given fifteen millions of dollars for Louisiana; they would have given sixty millions of dollars rather than not have possessed it. They will receive one million of dollars from their customs the present year, which is much more than the interest of their money at six per cent. without taking into consideration the value of the very great quantity of vacant lands.

As for the twelve years accorded to our vessels on the national footing, it will only appear but an illusive prospect, considering war, and of the impossibility of our being able to enter into competition with their merchantmen. Besides, all will in a short time turn to the advantage of the English manufactories, by the great means this place will exclusively enjoy, by its local advantages, to supply the Spanish colonies as far as the Equator. In a few years the country, as far as the *Rio Bravo*, will be in a state of cultivation, principally for sugar. At that period New Orleans will have a population of 30 to 50,000 souls;

when this province will produce sugar enough to supply all North America and a part of Europe. Let us not dissimulate. In a few years the existing prejudices will be worn away; the inhabitants will become gradually American, by the introduction of native Americans and English, a system already begun. The present inhabitants, disgusted, will leave the country. Those who have large fortunes will retire to the mother country, a great proportion will retire to the Spanish settlements, and the remaining few will be lost in the crowd of new comers. Should not some fortunate political combination intervene, what a magnificent *Nouvelle France* we have lost.

[F.]

Kentucky, Lexington, September 14th, 1797.

SIR,

WE have seen the communication made by you to Mr. Sebastian. In answer thereto we declare, unequivocally, that we will not be concerned, either directly or indirectly, in any attempt that may be made to separate the western country from the United States.

That whatever part we may at any time be induced to take in the politics of our country, that her welfare will be our only inducement, and that we will never receive any pecuniary or other reward for any personal exertions made by us to promote that welfare.

The free navigation of the Mississippi must always be the favourite object with the inhabitants of the western country; they cannot be deprived of it longer than necessity shall compel them to submit to its being withheld from them.

We flatter ourselves that every thing respecting this important business will be set right by the governments of the two nations; but if this should not be the case, it appears to us that it must be the policy of Spain to encourage, by every possible means, the freest intercourse with the inhabitants of the western country, as this will be the most effectual means to conciliate their good-will, and to obtain without hazard, and at reduced prices, those supplies, which are indispensibly necessary to the Spanish government and its subjects.

We are, Sir, your obedient servants,
HARRY INNES,
G. NICHOLAS.

Mr. THOMAS POWER.

[G.]

DEAR SIR,

YOUR sudden departure disappointed me, and your continued absence induces the belief that you have *prudently* proceeded to the city, to take care of your property—a precaution which should not be a moment unnecessarily suspended; for I fear your honest, manlike zeal has carried you beyond the limits of strict discretion, and that some humane friend may by loose whispers put your interests in danger. I speak not of personal considerations, because I know you despise them. I send you under cover, and in most sacred confidence, a literal extract from a letter written March 6th, by a gentleman* whom you found, at his own table, giving lessons to certain members of a great assembly. The puerility and weakness of this extract is perhaps unequalled but by the spirit which dictated it. Those who do not know how to preserve peace, or to make war, surely are unfit for exalted stations or public confidence. Another courier has gone down, which the G———r calls highly important, and that we shall certainly know what we have to expect in twelve days. God of Heaven!—that our honour, interests and safety should be confided to such hands. Take care of yourself, for rest assured you will not be supported or protected by those who owe both to you.

Yours, in corde.

April 30th, 1803.
DANIEL CLARK, Esq.

* *Mr. Jefferson.*

[H.]

Fort Adams, June 9th, 1803.

DEAR SIR,

YOUR letters by Tone came expeditiously to hand, since which I have received those by mail, and have done every thing you desired. I was taken ill, the morning after Tone's arrival, with a sort of bilious cholic, which still harrasses me too severely for writing, or thinking. I have kept Tone two days, in hopes of some relief; but I am obliged to send him with this scrawl, and the assurance you shall hear from me fully before I march, which will be the moment I am able. I must, however, express my pleasure at the measures you have accomplished to favour the poor people of Tombigbee. C. C. C. was afraid you should do any thing to deserve the thanks of our government. He is a mass of duplicity, meanness, envy, ignorance and cowardice.—Yet you must not make any attack on him at present.

Your's, truly and sincerely,

J. WILKINSON.

D. Clark, Esq.

[I.]

Mr. Alburtis,

TO comply in full with the remarks preliminary to the publication in your paper of the secret instructions given to Mr. Power, who was the agent in common between the Spanish government and the conspirators in Kentucky and the territories on the waters of Missisippi, would require a developement of facts and circumstances too lengthy for a newspaper. Such developements are, however, now preparing, and will be published at length, as soon as they are completed, and other circumstances will admit. I shall at present, therefore, only observe—that Mr. Power did, pursuant to the instructions given, call on me at Natchez, and presented certain interrogatories, in the hand writing of Captain Campbell Smith, which were, from the circumstances of the case, calculated to implicate General Wayne, and to establish certain charges against him, which General Wilkinson had thought it prudent to make. This business of turning the tables seems to be habitual to this gentleman. For the establishment of these charges he relied principally on me; and to induce me to co-operate in such views, the most ample rewards were offered, mingled with threats, in case I should decline the co-operation. Those views were inimical to the United States.

In consequence of certain facts and circumstances, discovered through me in 1794 in the army and in Kentucky, General Wayne was convinced that he was surrounded by a conspiracy of a very formidable nature, and therefore took measures to discover its extent and object, and especially the principal actors. General Wayne had acted precipitately in the first instance, and had given advantages to his adversary, the confidence of General Wayne having been betrayed to General Wilkinson, so far as the betrayer had it in his power. Had General Wayne lived, and his confidence not have been betrayed, he would probably have succeeded. This piece of treachery disconcerted the views of General Wayne. Mr. Power's visit to me in Natchez, and afterwards that of Mr. Nolan, placed within my knowledge the principal actors, their object, and the plans the conspirators had and were then pursuing against General Wayne, to get him removed from the head of the army. General Wayne and Captain Lewis were peculiarly obnoxious to the conspirators, but neither of those gentlemen were capable of keeping pace with the intriguing and corrupting faculties of the conspirators; for, like certain fish, they so discoloured their way, as almost bid defiance to pursuit. However, General Wayne, fortunately for them, died; and as to myself, they had the advantage of me, and had nothing to do but to cry mad dog, and (from the peculiarity of my case) I could not then help myself. This their dirty agents done meanly and sneakingly in all cases (such as Charles Hyde and others) when it was deemed necessary to excite prejudices against me. Mr. Hyde is the man who so persecuted Mr. Stockdale; first by causing him to be thrown into confinement, and thereby meanly oppressing him, and endeavouring to induce him to disclose the purpose of his visit to me, at Louisville, by order of Gen. Wayne. A considerable sum of money was offered Mr. Stockdale to disclose, by General Wilkinson. The transactions were published in the " Western World."

That General Wilkinson was in treaty with the Spaniards in 1796 and 1797, respecting the dismemberment of the Union, was clearly and distinctly known to me. But General Wilkinson as clearly and distinctly denied it, and gave the whole of the transactions in the western country such a turn, that, even in spite of myself, I have been in part deceived, as would appear by several letters addressed to him and others. But General Wilkinson, in Richmond, admitted to me he had held a correspondence with the Spaniards on the subject, but declared most solemnly that he never seriously designed the dismemberment of the Union; and that his only object was to cheat the Spaniards of their money, and that he had cheated them out of half a million of dollars for himself and friends. It would not perhaps have been material, my knowing the object of the conspiracy in 1796 and 1797, had General Wayne lived. I was within the power of the Spaniards and the conspirators, and they could have shaped my testimony as they pleased. My being thus situated was in consequence of the confidence of General

Wayne being betrayed to General Wilkinson. If there were none others in the United States concerned in this affair but General Wilkinson, there would be but little danger of either the Spaniards or the United States being again cheated in the same way. But there are others. They are behind the curtain. What excellent materials to cheat a French Emperor——if he should happen to fall in their way.

R. NEWMAN.

Mill Creek, June 18th, 1808.

The First American Frontier
AN ARNO PRESS/NEW YORK TIMES COLLECTION

Agnew, Daniel.
A History of the Region of Pennsylvania North of the Allegheny River. 1887.

Alden, George H.
New Government West of the Alleghenies Before 1780. 1897.

Barrett, Jay Amos.
Evolution of the Ordinance of 1787. 1891.

Billon, Frederick.
Annals of St. Louis in its Early Days Under the French and Spanish Dominations. 1886.

Billon, Frederick.
Annals of St. Louis in its Territorial Days, 1804-1821. 1888.

Littel, William.
Political Transactions in and Concerning Kentucky. 1926.

Bowles, William Augustus.
Authentic Memoirs of William Augustus Bowles. 1916.

Bradley, A. G.
The Fight with France for North America. 1900.

Brannan, John, ed.
Official Letters of the Military and Naval Officers of the War, 1812-1815. 1823.

Brown, John P.
Old Frontiers. 1938.

Brown, Samuel R.
The Western Gazetteer. 1817.

Cist, Charles.
Cincinnati Miscellany of Antiquities of the West and Pioneer History. (2 volumes in one). 1845-6.

Claiborne, Nathaniel Herbert.
Notes on the War in the South with Biographical Sketches of the Lives of Montgomery, Jackson, Sevier, and Others. 1819.

Clark, Daniel.
Proofs of the Corruption of Gen. James Wilkinson. 1809.

Clark, George Rogers.
Colonel George Rogers Clark's Sketch of His Campaign in the Illinois in 1778-9. 1869.

Collins, Lewis.
Historical Sketches of Kentucky. 1847.

Cruikshank, Ernest, ed,
Documents Relating to Invasion of Canada and the Surrender of Detroit. 1912.

Cruikshank, Ernest, ed,
The Documentary History of the Campaign on the Niagara Frontier, 1812-1814. (4 volumes). 1896-1909.

Cutler, Jervis.
A Topographical Description of the State of Ohio, Indian Territory, and Louisiana. 1812.

Cutler, Julia P.
The Life and Times of Ephraim Cutler. 1890.

Darlington, Mary C.
History of Col. Henry Bouquet and the Western Frontiers of Pennsylvania. 1920.

Darlington, Mary C.
Fort Pitt and Letters From the Frontier. 1892.

De Schweinitz, Edmund.
The Life and Times of David Zeisberger. 1870.

Dillon, John B.
History of Indiana. 1859.

Eaton, John Henry.
Life of Andrew Jackson. 1824.

English, William Hayden.
Conquest of the Country Northwest of the Ohio. (2 volumes in one). 1896.

Flint, Timothy.
Indian Wars of the West. 1833.

Forbes, John.
Writings of General John Forbes Relating to His Service in North America. 1938.

Forman, Samuel S.
Narrative of a Journey Down the Ohio and Mississippi in 1789-90. 1888.

Haywood, John.
Civil and Political History of the State of Tennessee to 1796. 1823.

Heckewelder, John.
History, Manners and Customs of the Indian Nations. 1876.

Heckewelder, John.
Narrative of the Mission of the United Brethren. 1820.

Hildreth, Samuel P.
Pioneer History. 1848.

Houck, Louis.
The Boundaries of the Louisiana Purchase: A Historical Study. 1901.

Houck, Louis.
History of Missouri. (3 volumes in one). 1908.

Houck, Louis.
The Spanish Regime in Missouri. (2 volumes in one). 1909.

Jacob, John J.
A Biographical Sketch of the Life of the Late Capt. Michael Cresap. 1826.

Jones, David.
A Journal of Two Visits Made to Some Nations of Indians on the West Side of the River Ohio, in the Years 1772 and 1773. 1774.

Kenton, Edna.
Simon Kenton. 1930.

Loudon, Archibald.
Selection of Some of the Most Interesting Narratives of Outrages. (2 volumes in one). 1808-1811.

Monette, J. W.
History, Discovery and Settlement of the Mississippi Valley. (2 volumes in one). 1846.

Morse, Jedediah.
American Gazetteer. 1797.

Pickett, Albert James.
History of Alabama. (2 volumes in one). 1851.

Pope, John.
A Tour Through the Southern and Western Territories. 1792.

Putnam, Albigence Waldo.
History of Middle Tennessee. 1859.

Ramsey, James G. M.
Annals of Tennessee. 1853.

Ranck, George W.
Boonesborough. 1901.

Robertson, James Rood, ed.
Petitions of the Early Inhabitants of Kentucky to the Gen. Assembly of Virginia. 1914.

Royce, Charles.
Indian Land Cessions. 1899.

Rupp, I. Daniel.
History of Northampton, Lehigh, Monroe, Carbon and Schuykill Counties. 1845.

Safford, William H.
The Blennerhasset Papers. 1864.

St. Clair, Arthur.
A Narrative of the Manner in which the Campaign Against the Indians, in the Year 1791 was Conducted. 1812.

Sargent, Winthrop, ed.
A History of an Expedition Against Fort DuQuesne in 1755. 1855.

Severance, Frank H.
An Old Frontier of France. (2 volumes in one). 1917.

Sipe, C. Hale.
Fort Ligonier and Its Times. 1932.

Stevens, Henry N.
Lewis Evans: His Map of the Middle British Colonies in America. 1920.

Timberlake, Henry.
The Memoirs of Lieut. Henry Timberlake. 1927.

Tome, Philip.
Pioneer Life: Or Thirty Years a Hunter. 1854.

Trent, William.
Journal of Captain William Trent From Logstown to Pickawillany. 1871.

Walton, Joseph S.
Conrad Weiser and the Indian Policy of Colonial Pennsylvania. 1900.

Withers, Alexander Scott.
Chronicles of Border Warfare. 1895.